Pawa

MW01532184

TRANQUEBAR PRESS

BATTLEGROUND U.P.: POLITICS IN THE LAND OF RAM

Manish Tiwari: Manish has been associated with the electronic and print media for almost fifteen years in different places, capacities and institutions - from newspapers in small towns (1996 in Ajmer) to top brands in the electronic media (Research Head for Devil's Advocate with Karan Thapar, 2011). Manish has intermittently taught sociology, journalism and media & cultural studies at different colleges and universities since 2006. He has also been DFG-Post Doctoral Guest Lecturer in Political Communication at the Siegen University, Germany, in 2010. Manish has done his schooling, graduation and post-graduation from Ajmer, where he grew up, and M.Phil and Ph.D from Jawaharlal Nehru University, New Delhi. Manish has co-edited a book on participatory democracy with Prof Anand Kumar in 2009 and another on social aspects of water-management will be published later in 2013. Manish now works independently in fields of communications and social research and lives in New Delhi with his wife and daughter.

*

Rajan Pandey: Born in Maharashtra, brought up in his hometown in Mainpuri (UP), educated in Rajasthan and Delhi, and married to his classmate from Assam, Rajan is a Ph.D candidate at the Centre for Political Studies, JNU. Rajan has a diverse range of interests, from literature to strategic affairs, travelling, cooking and but of course, eating. A voracious reader, he goes through crime fiction and serious academic stuff with equal gusto. He is currently in Goettingen, Germany on a Doctoral Visiting Fellowship at the Centre for Modern Indian Studies. Associated with student politics for seven years, Rajan intends to take up politics after finishing his Ph.D. Alongside a political career, he wants to start a farmers' cooperative in his home state on the lines of AMUL, which could bring similar prosperity and opportunities to rural Uttar Pradesh.

BATTLEGROUND U.P.

Politics in the Land of Ram

Manish Tiwari
Rajan Pandey

TRANQUEBAR

TRANQUEBAR PRESS
An imprint of westland ltd
61, Silverline Building, Alapakkam Main Road, Maduravoyal, Chennai 600 095
No. 38/10 (New No.5), Raghava Nagar, New Timber Yard Layout, Bangalore 560 026
93, 1st Floor, Sham Lal Road, Daryaganj, New Delhi 110 002

First published in TRANQUEBAR PRESS by westland ltd, 2013

10 9 8 7 6 5 4 3 2 1

ISBN: 978-93-83260-10-2

Typeset in Adobe Garamond by SÜRYA, New Delhi
Printed at HT Media Ltd., Noida

Contents

Acknowledgements

WRITING THE ACKNOWLEDGEMENTS IS DEFINITELY A TOUGHER JOB than writing the book. The fear of missing out important names not just fills you with the guilt of being thankless, it is also very dangerous professionally as you turn admirers and friends into critics of the book who decide to tear it down the moment they finish reading the foreword. In a scenario like this, beginners like us are so terrified that they virtually write down each and every name they know, thus making the foreword look like a contact list, only without the numbers.

The other approach to writing it is to miss most of the names, and club them in broader categories like 'friends', 'family', 'teachers', 'experts', etc. Anyone complaining about the lack of acknowledgement could be cajoled by saying that since s/he was 'family' or 'friend' or the 'teacher', due acknowledgment of her/ his contribution has been made already. Since this is a safer approach, we would like to resort to this.

The first credit for this book goes to the people of the Land of Rama, Uttar Pradesh, who shared their views, opinions, aspirations and complaints with us without expecting anything in return. We have only tried to give voice to their concerns through this book, so that it could possibly reach the politicians and the policymakers who have lost touch with ground realities and folk-wisdom.

Numerous journalists, mostly rural and town based, shared

their insights with us in the course of writing this book. The accuracy of their information sometimes left us surprised. We believe that these numerous less-talked of soldiers of the 'fourth estate' possess an incomparable pool of information and knowledge, which could be of great significance in successful implementation and monitoring of governance and democratic functions.

We greatly appreciate the patience of our family members who peacefully endured our crazy pursuits when we decided to write the book and then spent month after month working on it, amidst the requirements of our respective professional careers. The lack of hostility shown by them in this regard would definitely qualify as 'support' and 'encouragement' and we sincerely thank them for not raising hell when we were working on it. Dear family members, here is the return for all your patience. You can now boast of being related to 'writers' and brag about intellectual stuff among your social circles.

We are extremely thankful to our teachers and to the ethos of JNU, which gave us an approach to understand the world and widened our perspective in dealing with it.

We also extend thanks to Writer's Side and its leader Kanishka Gupta for successful perusal of our case with the publishers. We extend our sincere thanks to the Westland-Tranquebar team for publishing the book.

We can't be grateful enough to those numerous, unmentioned people who helped us in innumerable ways during our journeys in the state of UP.

In the end, as is the custom, we accept that all shortcomings of the book are ours, and no one else needs to be blamed for the same.

New Delhi   MANISH TIWARI
March 2013   RAJAN PANDEY

PROLOGUE

THIS BOOK IS THE RESULT OF THREE EVENTFUL JOURNEYS THAT WE made across the state of Uttar Pradesh (UP) between 27 March 2011 and 3 March 2012. The first one was a bike ride from Delhi to Gorakhpur passing through a number of other places. The second was a train journey from Delhi to Lucknow and, finally, a non-stop two-month bike tour across the state. The first two trips occurred in 2011. In 2012, with the intention of focusing exclusively on the elections, we went from Delhi to Lucknow by train on 29 January. From there we went to Bahraich by bus, where we borrowed a motor-bike from a local contact to start the final phase of this exercise, which ended with the last round of voting on 3 March. In all, we travelled nearly 15,000 kilometres on the bike in one year, covering more than 350 constituencies in over sixty districts of Uttar Pradesh, including Mainpuri, Rajan's home district.

These journeys helped us understand a lot of things that we were unaware of. People gave us an insight into their conditions, thought processes, questions and concerns. These trips also helped us grasp regional differences—social, cultural, political and ecological—along with the historical legacies of the state. In the course of this exercise, we also changed—a little for the better, we would like to believe.

In the absence of a plan—what to do and how to do it—during the first trip, we took recourse to spontaneity, doing whatever struck us first when we reached a new place. To learn more and understand all perspectives, we made it a habit to talk to everyone possible, wherever possible . . . tea-shop owners, paanwallahs, dhabawallahs, journalists, farmers, political activists and leaders . . . we accosted them all with our volley of questions. We take pride in saying that we did not discriminate between the rich and the poor, the young and the old!

In the absence of any contacts in almost every place, we took to shamelessly using our gate-crashing abilities which had been developed during our hostel days and polished at Jawaharlal Nehru University (JNU), where we made it a routine to eat lunch and dinner at almost all the seminars held on campus— without attending a single session! Flaunting our JNU I-cards like the FBI or NYPD detectives in Hollywood movies, we tried hard to impress our audience. However, unlike those movies where the other party surrenders before the card-holder, our 'subjects' in UP were utterly indifferent. Some curious souls would take a look at the card, turn it around and return it without saying a single word, but most refused to be impressed and, as if following Gandhi's footsteps, took to being non-cooperative instead. It took a lot of pleading and flattery on our part before some gentle people agreed to share their valuable insights with us.

At some places, people suspected that we were sent by Rahul Gandhi to find out the real situation of the masses in UP. Such people showered huge favours upon us in the form of refreshments and sweets. Though we did try denying that we were a part of Mr Gandhi's team, it only further strengthened their suspicion and resulted in even greater favours! At other places, we were suspected of being a part of the Bharatiya Janata Party's (BJP) national president, Nitin Gadkari's survey to find suitable candidates. In such situations too, we received the same treatment.

However, life during the first two trips was not always easy. There were a lot of people who were too 'busy' to give time to 'useless fellows' like us. And since we had made it a point to go as deep as possible into the hinterland, many a time we found 'ourselves knocking for refuge on the doors of temples, ashrams or even sleeping villagers in rural areas, after realizing that there was no hotel or dharamshala at that place. At one point in Ramnagar, Barabanki, Rajan had to sleep alone in a big temple in the company of Hanumanji's idol and countless mosquitoes. On another occasion, when he could not find a place to stay in Auraiya, a kind-hearted gentleman, who had a very small one-room house, shared his broken cot with him.

During the elections, most of the hotels were occupied by government officials on election duty, forcing us to run from pillar to post, pleading with hotel managers to give us some space to sleep at night. In Pratapgarh, when Rajan could not find any place to stay, he wandered around until he discovered a sweetshop with 'lodge' written on it. His experience there was so fascinating that we would like to recount it in detail, in his own words.

> The shop was located on the city border, in a two-storey building that seemed to be a part of Pratapgarh's history, looking like it might collapse at any moment. The sweets in the dilapidated showcase also seemed to be there for display purposes only because during my stay there nobody came to buy them. A middle-aged man and his crazed servant managed the shop, their USP being tea and samosas. When I asked the owner about the lodge, he told me that this was the first ever hotel in Pratapgarh and all the political leaders of the district, from Raja Bhaiya to Pramod Tiwari, used to come there for tea. Now it was mainly the adda of low rank or chut-bhaiyya netas, as the high-ranking netas had better places to go to. Even as we talked, a few people in white kurta-pajamas wandered into the shop for a chat or tea after completing the day's campaign.
>
> The lodge was on the first floor and it could only be reached from within the shop by climbing an unlit, rickety old staircase. On the first floor, on each side, there were six unlocked rooms, each having two beds, mattresses and a fan. The corridor

between the rooms had no roof. I was told that the charge per night for one person was Rs 150 and that I would be the only guest in the hotel that night. The owner further said that, as he went back to his home at night, he would lock me inside the building with the semi-lunatic servant, who would sleep in the shop. Having no choice, I agreed to all the terms and conditions. But when the owner left and the night deepened and silence surrounded me, the feeling of being trapped in a haunted house grabbed hold of me. To distract myself, I started searching through the rooms only to discover used condoms, empty whisky bottles and copies of cheap Hindi erotic literature popularly called *Mastram*. Realization finally dawned on me about the sort of esteemed gentry that frequented the hotel nowadays. At last fatigue took over, allowing me to sleep in spite of the fear of being killed by ghosts, the crazed servant or by the building collapsing over my head.

Apart from such wonderful moments, these journeys also helped us discover things we had never thought about. For example, in the Lakhimpur Kheri and Pilibhit districts, we were shocked to stumble upon a mini-Punjab. Not only were there large numbers of Sikhs there, but their farming techniques, equipment, and even the greenness of their fields gave the impression of being somewhere in Punjab. We were amazed to see bright green fields with paddy in the month of May, only to be told later that this was a variety called saatha (sixty days) that could be reaped within two months, enabling the farmers to get two rice crops in one year from the same fields. These Sikh farmers had come here after Partition, when the new Uttar Pradesh government of Govind Ballabh Pant was trying to get settlements in this region of Terai.

Similarly, it is only through personal experience that we learnt how mystical and beautiful the Buddhist holy places and monuments of the eastern districts of Siddharthnagar and Balrampur look in the rains and fog of January and February. In contrast to the eastern districts that are densely populated, we saw that Bundelkhand was sparsely populated with as few as two assembly constituencies in some districts. In contrast, Azamgarh in Poorvanchal has as many as ten assembly constituencies. Moreover, western UP appears to be a totally different world, being inhabited by Braj- and Haryanvi-speaking people in many of the districts—dialects that are harsher to an outsider's ear than the Awadhi and Bhojpuri of Awadh and Poorvanchal.

Despite being popularly considered a backward state in terms of roads, UP has some of the finest local roads and highways. The East-West Corridor from Jhansi to Kushinagar, linking some of the main cities like Jhansi, Kanpur, Lucknow, Basti, Faizabad and Gorakhpur, is one. Similarly, the Golden Quadrilateral Corridor that links Mathura to Chandauli is an equally comfortable road and links cities like Varanasi, Allahabad, Kanpur, Etawah, Firozabad and Agra. The worst roads were in western UP, especially in the Baghpat-Saharanpur region. The roads leading to Uttarakhand via this route are completely broken and almost non-existent for kilometres at a number of places.

What was equally fascinating was an opportunity to dig deep into the oral and popular history and traditions of the state's people, learning new facts and fables about cities that we were totally unaware of. At Shahjahanpur, we were told that the district was home to three of the four revolutionary leaders of the Kakori Conspiracy of 1926. During this famous event of the Indian freedom movement, revolutionaries belonging to the Hindustan Republican Association had robbed government treasures at a station called Kakori near Lucknow. Ram Prasad Bismil, Ashfaqullah Khan and Thakur Roshan Singh, who were hanged by the British, were from Shahjahanpur. The fourth revolutionary to be awarded a death sentence, Rajendra Lahiri, belonged to Varanasi.

We were told in Bareilly that other than the Rohella chieftains, the 1857 Revolt and Wahabi sect that the district is known for, it is also famous for another historical object—the Khamba (pillar) press. Stories about the Khamba press have not been verified by any historical source (to our knowledge), but a number of people acquainted with Bareilly's history confirmed its existence. Oral tradition tells us that during the 1920s and 1930s, a person used to hang satirical verses on the city's pillars mocking the British and their lackeys. These verses were extremely popular among the common people. Such was the sharpness of his satire that he was nicknamed Iblis (Devil) by British sycophants.

Though we had to brave humiliation and the indifference of many people, Rajan was in for a bit of flattery and recognition as well, while in Bareilly. As he knew two journalists who worked at different dailies, the tables were turned and he was interviewed about his bike journey and book. Articles about him appeared in three main dailies, showering him with accolades!

However, things were not always this entertaining and going to different places was not always joyful. It was heart-breaking to visit the house of Lucknow CMO Dr B.P.Singh, who had been murdered by hired assassins in April 2011 in connection with the NRHM (National Rural Health Mission) scam. The family lived in deep insecurity. The two .303 rifle-wielding homeguards deployed for their protection were more interested in resting under a shady tree in the hot mid-April afternoon than in guarding the house's entrance.

Equally painful was the visit to the house, in Jehangarh (near Tappal), of Prashant Sharma—a fourteen-year-old boy who was killed in police firing during the Tappal farmers' agitation. We sometimes still feel sorry that we went to his home, reminding his mother of her tragic loss and causing her to cry for hours over her deceased son. But then we also think that it was necessary. It is important to create awareness among as many people as possible about Prashant and his family's story, along with the stories of thousands of such farmers who were treated like criminals in their own villages by a government that boasted of being the representative of the oppressed.

These are some of the innumerable moments of agony and joy that we went through while working on this book. We hope that our efforts to capture the political reality of Uttar Pradesh prove to be of some use to people who are interested in the inner workings of India's politically most significant state. In the pages to come, we will talk about the politics in UP in a manner that will, hopefully, both entertain and enlighten readers.

The book begins with the political rallies of the 2012 UP elections, their significance, regional peculiarities and the socio-political insights that can be gleaned from them. From there it will move towards the war rooms and election strategies of different parties, trying to figure out their tactics and the impact on the electorate. It will try to explain how the Samajwadi Party (SP) managed to take the lead in the political battle in the final moments of the election, leaving the much-hyped Congress and Bahujan Samaj Party (BSP) far behind.

The next chapter will focus exclusively on the BSP—exploring the reasons why the BSP nosedived in these elections and how, after leading a majority government in UP for five full years with more than 220 seats, it was reduced to a mere 80 seats in the 2012 elections. In this exercise, it will cover different issues, ranging from the limitations of political leadership to government policies and the broader discourse of the Dalit-Bahujan movement that led to BSP's emergence.

A special chapter about the electoral behaviour of castes and communities has been added to give a picture of 'who voted for whom' during these elections, underlining the strengths and weaknesses of different parties.

To give a more detailed view of the different traits, personalities and variants of political leadership in UP, a chapter has been devoted to UP politicians. It not only talks about the image of most of the netas in the state, but also tries to explain the variations among them through caricatures of some prominent political figures.

The Epilogue was written after the new SP government, led by Chief Minister Akhilesh Yadav, completed more than hundred days in power. It tries to revisit the themes, issues and people who made a difference in these elections, attempting to explore the change, promised and real, that the people of UP witnessed after the regime changed.

In the hope of writing a popular book on UP politics, we have consciously avoided the use of academic jargon, tables, charts and graphs, despite the risk of being branded 'non-serious' in certain circles.

We both hope that this book succeeds in its objective of engaging more and more people with Uttar Pradesh and its politics.

PART ONE

THE RALLY

THE WORLD OF HIGH THEORY AND THE HURLY-BURLY FIELD OF Uttar Pradesh realpolitik may appear distantly, if at all connected. If one were to go by the shrieking tenor of media analysis, there appears little more to the recently-concluded elections but a high drama of personages battling it out with smart one-liners, on giant television screens. However, if one were to tell the story of those months from the dusty small towns of Uttar Pradesh, from the myriad villages, from the big cities and small hamlets, we may find that there are small and big configurations of social issues of classes, castes, communities as well as micro-level specific details that lie buried and untold as we watch the big television screen of victors and losers. And the idea that politics is all about authoritative allocation of values (and resources), as claimed by eminent political scientist David Easton may not appear so remote. What did unfold from the everyday experience of touring every nook and corner of Uttar Pradesh is that this allocation has no hidden hand but real actors and real structures. The emergence of a stream of social and political currents and counter-currents, asserting their own method of distribution needs a capturing of many complex contexts within which many rituals are enacted. The ritual of rallies is a productive point of entry.

The clash of these socio-political currents takes different forms in everyday politics, from slander campaigns to civil (or guerilla) war, depending upon the political system and situation. However in democracies, elections are the most significant method of making one's desired method of allocation all powerful. And in run-ups to these all-important elections, rallies are the most significant method of physically depicting the strength of a particular socio-political current, corresponding to one method of allocation.

In Third World countries, where resources were scarce, population abundant, and the state the most important player in allocation of resources, political rallies have been historically considered a significant medium of flexing the might of a political idea or party. This bodily expression of power may have its roots in the anti-colonial movement, when mass deputations, rallies and barricading were the very stuff of struggle. Brought up in a political culture of mass participation of a large number of people in strikes, protests and huge gatherings around national leaders, it is not a surprise that post Independence Indian politics demonstrated two striking features—mass rallies on the one hand and charismatic leaders on the other.

Since the ballot was always secret in the Indian political system, rallies became the brute mode of showing the physical number of followers behind a party or leader, much before the counting. It not only expressed the political following behind 'the idea' which the party or leader represented, but also created a psychological impact on the adversaries, and on political commentators. Rallies in Indian politics became the meter of determining the strength and winnability of a party, and the popularity of a leader. They became the indicator of the gravity of an issue (e.g., the kisan rallies for higher returns during the 80s) or the advance signals for an imminent political change e.g., the Gandhi Maidan Rally of Jayaprakash Narayan, popularly known as JP, in 1975, which prophesied the defeat of Congress at the centre for the first time in Indian politics. Rallies represent the charisma of a leader, be it the Gandhi family, the south Indian demagogues, extremist, religious leaders like Bhindranwale or Left patriarchs like Jyoti Basu. Not only this, they also represent the shift of social bases, emergence of new players and the death of old powers in the political arena. In a multi-cultural country like India, identity politics is a natural part of political discourse, and rallies are one of the most powerful ways of asserting the strength of a particular identity or party, the symbol of its empowerment.

Rallies therefore are taken very seriously by all—be it political parties, leaders, media, analysts or the general electorate. The 'Chaupal Charcha of Janta-Janardan' i.e., informal discussions of layman political participants and experts, in numerous spaces, from tea-shops in cities, and kasbas (small towns) to the chabutras of temples in villages, still vets a political party or leader through the number of people present in its rallies. It is for this reason that no serious political player can take the risk of being associated with a sparsely-attended rally, during elections.

In earlier days, people would come on their own to the rallies, mostly by foot, to listen to their leaders and get a look of them. In the absence of an all-pervasive media, rallies were one of the few opportunities to do so. However with time, the grammar and aesthetics of rallies too changed drastically. Newer ways of attracting people to one's rallies were devised, ranging from arranging conveyance to distributing money. The arrangement of 'kiraye ki bheed' (hired crowds) became more and more common in political practice, and with it the usage of it in political discourse to discredit the rallies of opponents. Other than this, two unique instruments also became quite popular in pulling crowds, during the last fifteen or twenty years—Bollywood celebrities and 'the helicopter'.

For the majority of people in a backward state like Uttar Pradesh, watching a helicopter descend from the skies, a stone's throw away from where one stood, used to be a rare thrilling experience, something one could talk about for days. The political leaders made full use of this hype. A cursory look at the advertisement of the rally of any big leader in any newspaper during elections (in UP or in other north Indian states) will reveal the prominence of the key sentence, 'Helicopter Dwara Aagaman (arrival on a helicopter).' Even the loudspeaker campaign by rickshaws and jeeps makes it a point to mention the helicopter again and again as it helps in drawing crowds. However, its overuse has led to a decline in the crowd-pulling potential of the poor helicopter. We will return to this later in this chapter.

Cine stars and politics have not always gone as hand in hand in UP as in the south Indian states. In the south, many cinema personalities have reached the positions of chief ministers, party patriarchs and matriarchs. But in the north, Bollywood biggies have fared badly. Even a legendary actor like Amitabh Bachchan, who managed to win his Lok Sabha election against ex UP CM Hemvati Nandan Bahuguna from Allahabad in 1984, resigned after three years, never to return to politics. Other than some comparatively less-successful cases like Jayaprada and Raj Babbar (who are both Lok Sabha MPs only, along with seventy-eight more from UP), Bollywood stars in UP politics are limited to attracting crowds in rallies and road shows. The use of cine stars in rallies in UP though not uncommon earlier, gained exceptional proportion since the late 1990s, under the helmanship of Amar Singh of the Samajwadi Party. The tradition continues to this date, and in the 2012 elections, Bollywood stars like Sanjay Dutt, Raveena Tandon, Amisha Patel, Mahima Chowdhry, Celina Jaitley, Nagma, Vivek Oberoi, Hema Malini and Shatrughan Sinha dazzled UP's political scene, while the Bachchan family and Salman Khan were notable exceptions.

This time, one difference was remarkable. Congress brought in more cine stars than any other party, while SP, which traditionally topped the list, brought none. Still, there is one obvious limitation of celebrities in politics—they attract a large number of spectators, but can rarely translate them into voters, especially in case of a highly politicized state like UP.

In this political culture of mass rallies and charismatic leaders, a study of rallies would be imperative. In the following pages, we will try to present in a synoptic fashion the different brands of politics, target constituencies, strategies, and public response to various parties, through a detailed analysis of the rallies of different parties and leaders.

Bahujan Samaj Party (BSP) Rallies

When it comes to rallies, BSP is a hot favourite of the media and political pundits for various reasons. The party and its leader Mayawati command the trust of the most deprived and numerically largest constituency in UP, namely the scheduled castes or Dalits. The deprivation of this community, its loyalty towards the party and Mayawati, and its spontaneous mobilization to the call of the BSP is a spectacle worth witnessing. Blue flags in hand, thousands of men and women are seen marching to the rally grounds, on foot, bicycles and tractors. They listen to each and every word spoken by Mayawati with complete devotion.

The Bahujan Volunteer Force looks after the discipline and seating arrangements, leaving the policemen deployed for these jobs to act as mere spectators. The disciplined crowds present a contrast to the political scenario in UP where mayhem and indiscipline is commonplace. Pictures of Dalit icons like Dr B.R. Ambedkar, Jyotiba Phule, Kanshi Ram, and E.V. Ramaswamy Naickar 'Periyar' decorate the venue, along with blue flags. Ideological songs and speeches on Dalit empowerment resonate, rally after rally.

In December 1993, a joint SP-BSP rally was organized in Lucknow to celebrate the coronation of Mulayam Singh as chief minister, with BSP support. Eminent journalist Ajay Bose described the rally in following words:

The several hundred thousands who attended (the rally) came in two groups. One, supporting Mulayam Singh Yadav, was rowdy and full of swagger. The Samajwadi Party leader himself had to shriek at a particularly boisterous section and tell them to stop dancing and sit down when Kanshi Ram rose to speak. The second group, the BSP congregation, huddled together silently. Many were barefoot and not equipped for the Lucknow winter. For most of them it was their first trip to a big city like the state capital. Yet even if they were overawed by the occasion, their eyes glinted with the jubilation of a Dalit victory.

In the days to come, the BSP congregation would come to Lucknow on more and more occasions to be a part of more Dalit victory jubilations. The initial innocence and humility however, was lost forever.

As always, dramatics is an important part of BSP's politics. On the advice of the national secretary and Mayawati's trusted lieutenant, Satish Chandra Mishra, the BSP experimented with social engineering at a state level during the run-up to the 2007 assembly elections. The state of lawlessness under the SP regime was the rallying point, and BSP was trying to form an alliance with castes that were 'victims' of this lawlessness, like the Brahmins, Dalits, Baniyas and other smaller most backward castes (MBCs). People would not have forgotten that during the mega Brahmin Sammelan on 9 June 2005 in Lucknow (which marked the culmination of BSP's state-wide Brahmin Ekta Sammelans) Brahmins with traditional chotis or pigtails and red tilaks on their foreheads fell at Mayawati's feet, reciting 'Behenji, bachao (Behenji, save us)' to dramatically symbolize the SP government's Jungle Raj, and the aspiration of the people of the state to get rid of it via the BSP. Such spectacular scenes have always been an integral part of BSP rallies.

However, some things were missing this time around in the BSP rallies. The ambition of having a majority government in UP, with Behenji as the chief minister, had been fulfilled. The anti-establishment sentiment that had always characterized BSP was absent, for it was the BSP that represented the establishment now. The political instability, which was a regular feature of UP politics and which had always helped the BSP in increasing its vote banks, was missing for the first time in nineteen years. It also could not pass the responsibility of all wrongs on to others, be it 'unsupportive' partners like Bharatiya Janata Party (BJP), or political opponents like SP, as it had ruled on its own for full five years. Of course, the call for 'Phir sarkar banayenge (We will again form the government)' was present, but in comparison to the holier-than-thou approach and offensive tone that BSP was known for, this time it appeared to have lost some of its appeal.

Much before the notification for elections was announced, BSP organized massive rallies in Lucknow in April on Ambedkar Jayanti, and later in November and December. The massive turnout at these rallies puzzled political commentators, who read in this the absence of an anti-incumbency mood. The reality however was not such. The common man read it right: 'Satta paksh ki rally hamesha achchi hoti hai (the government in power always organizes good rallies)', many in Lucknow told us, 'But you must not read much into them, for they do not show the general mood of the people.' In the months to come, what they said proved to be correct.

*

The BSP announced its assembly constituency coordinators one year before the elections scheduled in 2012. These coordinators were going to be the election candidates, and in most of the cases, they were not changed by the party. Despite declaring their candidates ahead of others, unlike the last time, in the days to come it appeared that BSP's election preparations were inadequate. Mayawati, the star campaigner of the party, addressed rallies in only fifty-eight district headquarters out of the seventy-five districts in the state, in twenty-eight days. This was in sharp contrast to other big leaders like Mulayam Singh Yadav (91 meetings), Akhilesh Yadav (201 meetings), Uma Bharti (235 meetings) and Rahul Gandhi (211 meetings). Even Ajit Singh of the Rashtriya Lok Dal (RLD), whose party contested only forty-six seats in the state, addressed more meetings (eighty-five) than Mayawati. The stark absence of other faces that could pull in the crowds and youth leadership also marred the party—after Mayawati the two 'most popular' leaders who addressed the rallies were Satish Chandra Mishra and Naseemuddin Siddique.

As always, the BSP rallies presented the disciplined face of the well-oiled party machinery, unlike the routine hullabaloo that mars the rallies of other parties. In contrast to other leaders, Mayawati addressed only one or two rallies a day, with a maximum of three on very rare occasions.

The party arranged for these rallies at spacious grounds at the district headquarters, and all candidates of different assembly constituencies would be asked to come with at least a thousand supporters. Unlike old times, proper conveyance was arranged by the party machinery and candidates, and at most places chairs were placed to seat people. Some people alleged that the reason for having chairs in the rallies was to give an impression that the rally ground was full, even though a small number of people turn up, as chairs occupy more space. However, given the fact that Mayawati's rallies were as spectacular as ever, as far as attracting crowds was concerned, this explanation appears to hold little water.

When we asked a BSP activist about it, he replied, 'Hum humesha zamin pàr hi baithte aaye hain. Behenji ki sarkar ke chalte hi ab hum bhi charpai par baith pate hain. Yahi jatane ke liye rally main kursi ki vyavastha ki gayi hai (We Dalits have always sat on the ground. It was thanks to Behenji's government that now we can also sit on cots. Chairs have been placed in the rally to make this point).'

This statement by a Dalit party activist is indicative of the long history of oppression suffered by the Dalits; they were not even allowed to sit on cots in the presence of members of the upper castes till very recently.

For the 2012 campaign, Mayawati never held a rally at a place with less than three assembly constituencies. Generally, more than four assembly constituencies would be clubbed together, and a single Mayawati rally would be organized for them. In Gonda, for instance, a single rally was organized for the eleven assembly constituencies of the Gonda and Balrampur districts at a college ground. Such tactics helped in gathering bigger crowds, and in making the necessary impression on the opponents.

The rally venues were always painted blue decked with flags, and the administration would be on its toes, to avoid any problem. Party propaganda cassettes urging Dalits to vote and give Behenji a second chance played in the background. Bahujan Volunteer Force activists would efficiently and smoothly escort people to their seats; whenever any problem or disorder emerged, a call from the dais would be made to correct it, which would be immediately addressed.

All candidates and party leaders were given a chance to speak, and generally almost all the speakers finished speaking by the time of Behenji's arrival. In their speeches, the speakers would all talk about the welfare schemes of the BSP government, especially the Kanshi Ram Urban Poor Housing Scheme, which ensured small flats for the urban poor of all castes in all districts provided by the government. Keeping the demographic location of voters in mind, the candidates would highlight the exact balance of the caste-communal composition of the party candidates. For example, in upper-caste Muslim-dominated constituencies, speakers always emphasized how many Muslims or upper-caste candidates had been given a ticket by the party. This was done to highlight BSP's new logo: *Sarvajan Hitay* (welfare of all castes). Emotional speeches highlighting the sufferings of Dalit icons like Ambedkar were also made to inspire the vote base of the party.

The Mayawati cult was always clearly visible during the rallies, and party activists and leaders made a tremendous effort to have everything in perfect order before her arrival. Even the party slogans to be used would be rehearsed two or three times before her arrival. Though at most places the helicopter landing space and way to the dais were covered, people would try to steal a glimpse of Mayawati emerging from the helicopter by standing on their chairs, ignoring repeated appeals from the dais to be seated. The moment Mayawati stepped on to the stage and waved to the crowd, not one person remained seated; men and women barely controlling their smiles, waved back at her, as if she were a close relative or acquaintance. Almost all candidates would touch her feet, and it took a long time for people to settle down after her arrival.

The arrangement on the stage too worked towards reconfirming the Behenji cult status. There would be only one sofa, usually white, in the forefront for Mayawati. Other than some very rare exceptions, no one would sit on it beside Behenji. Other people would either stand around, or sit on simple chairs behind the sofa. Two daises would be arranged on the stage, and even people like Satish Mishra and Naseemuddin Siddique would speak from the smaller dais. Mayawati always addressed the crowd from the bigger dais. All party candidates would stand around her on the stage, mostly with their hands folded, while she continued to speak.

Political experts in UP recall the older days, when Mayawati spoke extempore in her trademark fiery style, establishing a direct contact with the listeners, stopping and engaging them in her rhetoric, encouraging them to respond with a 'Yes', 'No', or 'Wow'. In a rally in western UP about ten or twelve years ago, she addressed the crowd with the one-liner, 'Chamari hun, kunwari hun, tumhari hun (I am a Dalit, I am single, I am yours)', to establish a connection with the Dalit masses assembled there to listen to her amid heavy rains.

However, listening to her in recent times gave the impression of being in a headmaster's class rather than at a political rally (Mayawati is an ex-schoolteacher). Mayawati slowly read out a long, written speech, with thousands of people listening attentively. While speaking, she gesticulated with her hands, and looked up at the crowd from time to time. Women in the audience would often listen to her with folded hands and devotion reflected in their eyes. Who would not envy such a committed mass-base?

However, a few differences were evident this time around. Unlike the old times when nobody made a sound while Mayawati spoke, the crowd was quite unruly even during her speeches. In Gonda, a woman tried to reach out to her through the press gallery (which was directly in front of the stage), in the middle of her speech, with a newspaper cutting of her husband's death, demanding justice. This created a lot of chaos, as some youths started encouraging her to cross the security grill and reach out to Mayawati shouting, 'Let her go!' This led to more commotion, with people shouting and falling over each other, while the security men rushed to stop the woman from crossing over. In the melee, one could not hear a single word that Mayawati spoke. This situation continued for a long time, with the party leaders unable to control it. Mayawati seemed to be angry with this, but could not stop her speech in the middle. Similar distractions were also visible at other places, suggesting that

Mayawati's 'hypnotic hold' over the masses though not over, had weakened to some extent.

Not only did her speeches lack Mayawati's trademark fiery style, but the self-confidence that had radiated from her at the run-up to the 2007 elections was also absent. Instead of taking on the SP, its principal enemy, head-on, she spent not less than two-thirds of her speeches on the 'Congress and Central government's betrayal of the people'. When we asked why, political commentator Hari Narayan Shukla said, 'She is defensive this time. She is trying to save her voter base of Dalits from the Congress, which is poaching it. She knows she will not win so there is no point in antagonizing SP.'

Since political experts and analysts from all parties and institutions agree about the exactness and reach of the BSP organization, it seemed really far-fetched to believe that Mayawati was not aware that she was going to lose these elections. In this scenario, the above statement appears to be quite true. There was little in Mayawati's speeches this time to cheer about. Mayawati's dhaka hathi (covered elephants) did not prove to be worth sava lakh (one and a quarter lakh) as she declared in her speeches, 'Khula hathi lakh ka, dhaka sava lakh ka (An uncovered elephant is worth a lakh, but a covered one is worth one and a quarter lakh).'

Bharatiya Janata Party (BJP) Rallies

The Bharatiya Janata Party, or BJP, has been a significant player in UP politics since 1989, when the Ram Mandir card enabled it to win 57 out of the 275 seats that it had contested (in a house of 425), a feat which its erstwhile avatar, Jan Sangh, could never achieve. A fading Congress and a fragmented Janata Party led to the division of the Muslim vote. The only claimant to the Hindu vote was the BJP. Riding high on the Ram Janmabhoomi wave, in a short period of just two years, it increased its seats by about four times (221 seats) in the 1991 elections to the UP assembly. The party bombarded the people of UP with an aggressive variant of Hindutva with its fiery speeches, yatras and rallies. Since then, aggressive posturing, high-pitched rhetoric and oratory skills have become the BJP brand of politics.

BJP was and is a party of fine orators—from Atal Bihari Vajpayee, L.K. Advani, Sushma Swaraj, and Uma Bharti, to Kalyan Singh, Narendra Modi, Vasundhara Raje and Vinay Katiyar. Add to this mix, the VHP, RSS, and other groups who habitually jump onto the BJP bandwagon during elections, giving rise to figures like Sadhvi Ritambhara, Mahant Vedanti and many more.

As children we saw how grown-ups used to go to BJP rallies to listen to their leaders, or watch Vajpayee speak in the Lok Sabha on DD One, and then talk about it endlessly. Thus, expecting BJP leaders to resort to their oratory skills in the crucial UP polls was but natural. Especially when the fierce Uma Bharti was a star campaigner, as well as a state candidate.

Fireworks were expected with so many party leaders vying for space, visibility and the chief minister's position. In the pages to come, we will try to catch some of the varying moods of BJP's election rallies.

Scene 1: Mahasangram in Gorakhpur

The very first rally of the BJP that we witnessed was Nitin Gadkari's Mahasangram rally in Gorakhpur in May. With BSP and SP having announced their candidates, and Congress in the process of doing so, Gadkari informally announced that the Mahasangram rallies would be the key instrument in deciding the candidates. In the rallies, the 'crowd-collecting-capacity' of the would-be candidates was put to test. The candidate who could collect a bigger crowd was supposedly the taller leader. In this rat race to collect crowds, leaders with smaller fiefdoms of influence gained significant importance.

This rally was held at a ground outside the city. At some point on the way from Basti to Gorakhpur, the four-lane smooth highway turned into a narrow, potholed road. An earthen wall-like structure appeared on one side, which was actually a Bundor Dam to stop the flood-waters of the Rapti river from flooding the fields and entering the city. At the rally venue, both sides of the road were lined with buses, a few trucks and tractors, but they were all overshadowed by a huge number of the Mahindra SUV, Bolero. There were flags in front of these vehicles and flex-posters on the sides and back. The party symbol on these posters was small in size, but the names and faces of the local leaders were prominent. Some were more systematic and imaginative—they had pasted printouts of the registration numbers of vehicles, the total number of vehicles arranged, and the name of the leader who had made this arrangement to show how many vehicles a leader had brought to the rally.

Political rallies have a distinct 'transportation economy'. It changes from one region to another, from one party to another and, sometimes, from one candidate to another. In this region, the BJP voter is mostly middle or upper caste, a farmland owner who wants to be seen as different from others. He will not board a bus with more than fifty people from his village. Anyone who wants to take him along needs to cough up some more money and arrange for a Bolero which should have only three or four other people—not a crowd. For a candidate, it increases the cost, but having a well-known face from the village supporting him and sitting in a vehicle with his flag and poster is not a bad move politically. At times when one has to show one's political strength, such economic considerations never come in the way.

Many Boleros had arrived with just one or two people other than the driver, but they made the number of vehicles swell even if the volume of the crowds did not. The image of many vehicles crowding the roads leading to the rally venue is necessary, and if one can choke the town and the roads leading to the town—the rally would be considered a resounding success.

So on this hot May day the road entering Gorakhpur was blocked with buses, Boleros and other sundry vehicles. Bhagwa (saffron) flags were as visible as the BJP ones, and the rally exuded a visibly Hindutva flavour.

At the time, Nitin Gadkari was still not a familiar personality for the people of the region. People were not very sure about his caste but most knew what he looked like. Villagers have their own way of describing the physical attributes of public personalities, and Gadkari with his bulk was an amusing figure. A sixty-year-old man had specially come to see how a leader from Maharashtra spoke Hindi. People in UP perceived him as a leader who knew his work and who had been entrusted by the Sangh to put things in order for the BJP.

Those who are aware of the covert hand of the Sangh in the running of the BJP would tell you that Gadkari is a 'professional' and he has his own 'sources' through which he receives information about the work and performance of local leaders from even the remotest corners of Gorakhpur's rural areas. Many of the BJP leaders in these parts believed that Gadkari had invisible machinery that kept an eye on everything that the ticket-hopefuls did in their respective areas. In fact at many places throughout the state, when we tried to talk about political issues with people, they asked us, 'Aap Gadkari ji ka survey kar rahe hain kya (Are you involved in Gadkari's survey)?'

There are mainly two BJP power centres in this region—one is Gorakhpur MP Yogi Adityanath (who belongs to the Thakur community and is the mahant of the 'Gorakhnath Peeth', the famous Goraknath Temple Trust) and the other is Suryapratap Shahi (state BJP president), who belongs to the Bhumihar lobby within the party that also derives its strength from neighbouring Bihar, where BJP is a coalition partner in the government. Shahi is well-known in the region but his acceptability among the different castes and communities is not very high. He is not liked by the Thakurs and Brahmins, the two important communities of the region.

Yogi Adityanath is a staunch Hindu rightist and a maverick. Reportedly a short-tempered man, Yogi has survived on the plank of communal polarization in the region. BJP ticket hopefuls have to keep Yogi Adityanath in a good mood, as he has a decisive say in ticket distribution in the region. Yogi Adityanath, or 'Baba' as he is fondly called by his followers, has a considerable following among the Thakurs of this region. People say that for four and a half years Yogi is a Thakur leader in the region, but he becomes a Hindu leader six months before the elections. Thus, there is a natural political rivalry between Thakurs and other castes supporting the BJP, mainly Bhumihars and Brahmins. Infighting among various warring factions—the Yogi (Thakur) camp versus the Brahmin camp, the Brahmin versus the Shahi (Bhumihar) group, and the Bhumihar versus the OBC (Other Backward Castes) group—continues in the BJP, and it is this infighting that led to its poor poll performance in Awadh and Poorvanchal.

The rally ground had a huge stage where Gadkari, Shahi, Yogi and some other leaders of the party were seated. Gadkari was in a jubilant mood because of the huge crowd that had gathered and because all the factions were working together. In the end he announced that all those who had been working hard would get tickets and no one would have to come to Delhi, the tickets would come to their homes. This had a considerable impact in the field. When we spoke to some young leaders in the region about Gadkari's statement a few days later, they were convinced that Gadkari meant it.

In the course of their speeches, all the leaders made appeals to the public to remain united and help the party win seats in the region. The repeated calls for unity revealed the high degree of internal discord within the BJP in the region. The differences were also clearly visible in the crowd, with Yogi supporters being louder and rowdier than Shahi supporters.

But despite these differences, all factions worked together as they wanted the rally to be a success because they feared Gadkari's doots (messengers). However, once the tickets were distributed, and Gadkari's attention was drawn to other things, the infighting returned in full force, which deflated BJP's dreams of capturing Poorvanchal, as was evident from the results.

Scene 2: Har Har Mahadev at Bhinga, Bahraich

Political experts in UP agreed that this time, the Muslim vote in the state was expected to be divided for two reasons: one, the arrival of many new claimants like the Peace Party, Ulema

Council, and Ittehad-e-Millat Council, along with old parties like SP, BSP and Congress; two, the weakening of the fear pyschosis attached to a BJP victory. Every year, after the Babri Masjid was demolished on 6 December 1992, Muslims in UP have voted en bloc to make whichever party win that could prevent BJP from coming into power. Such phenomenal unity was missing this time, as BJP appeared too weak to stake its claim to form the government.

In the absence of the possibility to engineer a state-wide communal polarization, the party tried to use the imminent split in minority votes in its favour by orchestrating Hindu-Muslim tensions, wherever possible. One such place was Bhinga in the Shravasti district of Poorvanchal.

When a Brahmin girl from Dhanni Deeh village (a Muslim majority village) eloped with a Muslim boy in July 2007, a mob of Hindus attacked the village, allegedly under the leadership of Ashok Mishra, brother of the local BSP MLA and minister Daddan Mishra. The mob thrashed the Muslim residents of the village, set some houses of the community on fire, and allegedly paraded the women of the accused's house naked through the village. In response to this attack, some Hindu huts were also set ablaze later on, allegedly with the backing of Congress leader and 2007 election runner-up Aslam Raini. When denied a ticket from the BSP, Daddan Mishra joined the BJP and, with Aslam Raini from the Congress in direct contest, the election took a heavy communal turn.

We witnessed a street meeting of Daddan Mishra in Bhinga constituency, where mahant Ramvilas Vedanti of Ram Janmabhoomi Andolan was also a speaker.

Unlike other market meetings which make little difference to the normal goings-on, this meeting virtually stopped all business for the day. Whether they supported BJP or not, everyone listened attentively to the speeches. People with red tilaks on their forehead thronged the venue, and the meeting started with cries of 'Jai Shri Ram' and the war cry of 'Har Har Mahadev'. Elaborating on the reasons behind his ousting from BSP, Daddan Mishra said, 'Mera apradh ye tha ki jis Bahusankyay Samuday ne mujhe jitaya, uske khilaf uthne wali ungli ko kaatne ka kam maine kiya, aur ye main karta rahunga (My crime was that I had tried to cut the fingers that were raised against the majority community that had helped me win, and I will keep on doing so).'

Warning the Hindus about the dangers that would follow if the 'Muslims got powerful', Mishra said, 'Unka ek hi uddeshya hai, kattar wala, aur isiliye kai ummidwar hokar bhi unhone ek ke piche hi taakat laga di hai, unka vote nahin batega ab (They have only one agenda—fanaticism. Despite many Muslim candidates, they have united behind one so that their votes will not get divided).'

Asking Hindus to unite, he said, 'Agar voh 70,000 hokar ek ho sakte hain, to aap dhai laakh hain, ek ho jaiye to kisi ka garda nahin milega (If seventy thousand of them can unite, then you are two and a half lakh and if you unite they will be reduced to smithereens!).'

While the speeches were going on, we could sense an imminent tension building in the locality. In Rajnath Singh's rally in Bhinga, the same frenzy was built up, and the party made all attempts to cash in on it. However, this time 'history repeated itself as a tragedy', with SP's Indrani Devi Verma (who was well outside this communal polarization game) winning the seat while Mishra finished third.

Scene 3: Charkhari—The Homecoming of the 'Daughter'

Considering what we had witnessed at remote places like Bhinga, we wondered what the condition would be at Charkhari, the constituency of Hindutva's firebrand leader, Sadhvi Uma Bharti.

Charkhari is one of the two assembly constituencies of the Mahoba district in Bundelkhand, which borders Madhya Pradesh, and has a sizeable Lodh population, the caste to which she belongs. One could expect the fiery leader to provoke fierce communal feelings. Things however, proved to be very different.

We reached Charkhari on the day before the polling began, when she came to Charkhari Bazar for a paidal jansampark (connecting with the masses on foot). Nothing exceptional could be sensed, except for a group of BJP activists (identifiable by the lotus badges pinned to their Nehru jackets and shirts) huddled together at one end of the market. A cavalcade of not more than four or five vehicles arrived after some time, and Uma Bharti stepped out of one of them, in her traditional bhagwa or saffron attire. Surprisingly, none of the vehicles included luxury SUVs like Fortuner, Endeavour or Pajero, but were all simple Boleros and Ambassadors, an exception to the current political culture in UP. The activists rushed to offer garlands, but no one shouted slogans; maybe out of fear of the Election Commission, as the official campaign had ended the evening before.

As soon as she arrived, the till then sleepy market jumped to action; people everywhere stood up and rushed to fetch flowers they had arranged for well in advance. Children rushed to nearby lanes to pass on the message of her arrival, and girls and women emerged from their homes with pooja thalis. The Uma Bharti we saw here was very different from the one that appeared on TV screens. Unlike the virtual avatar, here she appeared more mature, a bit tired but at ease with the people, smiling at everyone and talking with the ones she knew, blessing all those who touched her feet, caressing the cheeks of children and girls to display her affection.

At a small stationery shop, she stopped and touched the feet of a very old shop owner, a Vaishya by caste, who was overwhelmed by her act. When we asked him if he knew her from before, he replied in a voice full of fatherly affection, 'Ve hamari beti jaisi hain. Jab aath saal ki thin aur pravachan karti thin tabse yahan aati rahin hain (She is like my daughter. She has been coming here since she was eight years old to deliver religious discourses).'

When asked if he thought she would win or not, he smiled and said, 'Ye bhi koi poochne ki baat hai (Isn't it evident?).'

What was remarkable was that despite the palpable excitement, the people did not raise their voices or shout slogans. Like the activists, the people too were aware that shouting slogans could create problems with the Election Commission, and so exhibited exemplary self-restraint and discipline. The atmosphere was relaxed and the whole event felt like an important family function.

As Uma Bharti slowly moved ahead, with security guards and activists huddled around her, people standing on their roof-tops showered flowers on her, covering the narrow market street with flower petals. When she entered the Muslim-dominated locality, she walked on in the same manner. People here were less prepared for her reception. There were no flowers, but there was a lack of opposition and hostility as well. However, a sense of being overwhelmed was tangible. During the 2012 election campaign, Rahul Gandhi termed Uma Bharti an outsider, who came to Bundelkhand only during elections for petty political gains, while he had continued to raise the issues of Bundelkhand consistently. A witty Uma asked him to call his own mother an outsider (an Italian) and not his bhua (father's sister), who is the beti (daughter) of Bundelkhand. What we saw in Charkhari proved that the Sadhvi was not being unrealistic while making that claim.

Samajwadi Party (SP) Rallies

The Samajwadi Party, founded in 1992, has its roots in the socialist politics of Ram Manohar Lohia and Raj Narain.

From the opposition to English to its unique ways of protests (Thooko Virodh or spit protests, Ingit Karo or point out the corrupt protests and a lot of Putla Dahans or effigy burnings) it has always redefined the grammar of politics.

Unperturbed by Opposition critiques of being uncouth, it has always stood by its street-fighting stance and rustic manners. But over time, a party that had steadfastly opposed the dynastic rule of a single family (the Gandhis) was stung by the same vice itself, with Mulayam Singh Yadav's (fondly called Netaji) family being elevated to the status of the 'First Family of UP'. Further, the street-resistance character of the party lost its political content, and outright criminal elements took over the organization. The ideological content diminished at a rapid pace, and once popularly known as the peasants' own party, SP was lost in the glittering glamour of Bollywood, Ukrainian belly dancers and five-star hotels.

Being the biggest Opposition party, all eyes were set on it during the 2012 elections. The campaign was primarily led by Akhilesh Yadav, Mulayam's son. Mulayam started his election campaign from Etah on 16 November 2011 because of the party's superstitious belief that whenever he starts an election campaign from here, SP ultimately captures power in the state.

Azam Khan, his old trusted lieutenant and the Muslim face of the party was with him after rejoining the party. (He had been ousted from the party during Amar Singh's dominance, when he opposed party candidate Jaya Prada in the Lok Sabha elections.) The crowd in the rally was quite encouraging and Mulayam came into his own once he started talking. He spoke in detail about the Kanya Vidya Dhan Yojana (Girl Child Education Programme) and the unemployment allowance provided during his regime. After criticizing the BSP government and Mayawati for a while (he barely spoke two or three sentences about BJP and Congress), he started talking about the promises his party would fulfil once it returned to power.

In a similar fashion, at the rally in Barabanki on 8 January 2012, Mulayam (once again accompanied by Azam Khan) began by criticizing the BSP government: 'Pichle paanch saal is mukhyamantri se koi mil nai paya. Masheen laga rakhi hai aur khali note ginne ka kam kiya hai isne (In the last five years nobody has been able to meet this chief minister. All that she has done is set up a note-counting machine and has done nothing but count notes),' said Mulayam, while making a note-counting gesture with his hands. His poll promises included, 'Agar hamari sarkar aayi, to kheton main jaane wala paani muft, dawa muft, padhai muft (If our party comes to power then water for irrigation will be free, education will be free and medicine will be free).'

According to the SP campaign plan, Mulayam was not supposed to attack political opponents. This task was left to Akhilesh and others. Netaji was asked to make promises to the people, as people would have more faith in them if they were made by 'Dhartiputra Maulana Mulayam' (Cleric Mulayam, son of the soil), since he was said to have a reputation of always fulfilling his promises. Mulayam made it a point to end all his addresses with the emphasis that law and order would be taken care of and nobody, including SP leaders, would be allowed to break the law. All criminals would be sent to jail. This was aimed to allay the public's fear of the last SP regime when lawlessness had become the order of the day. Compiled as a holistic package this gave a positive aura and sense of euphoria to the SP campaign.

In district after district the following-day newspapers carried headlines such as 'Mulayam ne lagai vaadaun ki jhadi (Mulayam makes an array of promises)', 'Chote se sambodhan main Netaji ne khola ummidon ka pitara (Netaji opens a box of freebies in a short address)', 'Sabhi vargon ko kuch na kuch aas bandha gaye Mualayam (Mulayam promises to give a breather to all classes)'. The strategy, of course, worked.

However age seemed to have taken its toll. The ex-schoolteacher and wrestler-turned-politician addressed a small number of rallies (ninety-one in total), mainly at the district headquarters. In a huge rally at Bijnor in February, Mulayam forgot the name of the district: 'I want you to make all our Moradabad candidates win,' he proclaimed. Puzzled candidates looked helplessly at one another as nobody dared correct the leader on the dais. The reason for this was Netaji's short temper, which had increased with age. The candidates had a taste of it during the same rally.

A fatigued Mulayam was not in a very good mood on stage. When Bijnor Sadar candidate Ruchi Veera tried to show him some papers, he first shook his head and then visibly irritated, pushed her hand and the papers away in utter disregard. Similarly, during his address when Netaji asked people to raise their hands to make SP win, a party candidate standing beside him raised his hand right in front of Netaji's face. Mulayam caught his hand in an angry gesture and pulled it down forcefully.

With such incidents taking place quite often, speculations were rife within the party and outside about who the chief minister would be if the party won, as Netaji did not appear to be in a condition to handle the responsibilities and stress that went with the job. One thing was quite clear from these developments—Netaji was not leading and directing the campaign due to his ill health. In such a scenario a generation shift within the party organization appeared imminent even to observers like us.

Indian National Congress Rallies

The entire Congress campaign in UP revolved around just one person—Rahul Gandhi. In the absence of grassroots leadership, the Gandhi scion first ran from pillar to post to build a general hawa (environment) for the Congress in the build-up to the UP elections, and then worked tirelessly to lead the formal election campaign of the party from the front.

His campaign officially started from Phulpur in Allahabad on 14 November 2011 and continued till 29 February 2012 in Bareilly. The sheer scale of his labour can be understood from the fact that in 42 days the All India Congress Committee (AICC) general secretary in-charge (youth affairs) addressed 211 rallies and conducted 18 'road-shows' in cities like Lucknow, Kanpur, and Bareilly covering more than 375 of the 403 assembly constituencies in total. Heavy security arrangements marked his rallies with the Special Protection Group (SPG) keeping a hawk's eye on the venues. However, two things never left him since the very first day of his campaign—controversial remarks or gestures, and black flags.

Scene 1: The Beginning at Phulpur

The reason why the party chose Phulpur in Allahabad to begin the campaign on 14 November, Jawaharlal Nehru's birth anniversary, was to highlight Nehru's association with Phulpur (his constituency in the first general elections) and to signify the homecoming of Congress in UP through Rahul Gandhi, the worthy successor of Nehru's legacy. The party prepared many days in advance to make the rally a success, with many leaders camping in Allahabad. The rally was well attended, but became known for two other reasons.

As soon as Gandhi's helicopter landed at the rally ground, three or four activists of the Samajwadi Party's youth wing came from behind the landing venue with black flags in their hands. Led by Allahabad University student leader Abhishek Yadav, the youth were protesting against Rahul's inaction on the issue of student union elections at Allahabad University, which had not been held since the last four years. The activists maintained that since it is a Central university, elections could have been held there if Rahul Gandhi had done something about it.

As the police rushed in to stop the activists, Central government ministers Jitin Prasad, R.P.N. Singh and Congress legislature party leader Pramod Tiwari charged towards the youths and started kicking and beating them while trying to snatch the black flags. Later, a case was registered against all three leaders and the Opposition made it an issue alleging the Central ministers of indulging in goondagardi (hooliganism), while the Congress leaders made a hue and cry about the breach of security.

The second incident that overshadowed the official beginning was a remark made by Rahul Gandhi on migrants from UP working in Maharashtra and Punjab. In an attempt to play the 'angry young man', fed up with the state of affairs in UP, Gandhi highlighted the atrocities of the police at Bhatta-Parsaul and the misuse of money on statues, while welfare schemes suffered, asking 'Aapko gussa nahin aata hai (Don't you feel angry)?' Continuing further in this vein, he asked the people of

UP, 'Kab tak aap Maharashtra main bheek mangoge? (For how long will you beg in Maharashtra?)', to emphasize the need to change things in UP rather than migrating to other states. While the puzzled crowd stood still, not knowing how to react to this outburst, Congress leaders like Pramod Tiwari raised their hands over their head and began to clap, to encourage the people to cheer on Gandhi's 'genuine' outburst on the sorry state of affairs in UP. Though the audience appeared uninspired with these comments, Opposition parties could hardly hide their jubilation, as their leaders and spokespersons repeatedly highlighted this issue to beat down Congress, emphasizing that the people of the state had been insulted.

Since then, rally after rally, Gandhi's words, gestures and actions created one controversy after another. In Lucknow, after tearing a piece of paper symbolizing the fake poll promises of SP and BSP in every election, he stood in an angry posture with an elbow on the dais. The act invited a lot of criticism. Black flags also chased him across all the regions in the state: he was shown black flags in Orai (Jalaun district, Bundelkhand) on 18 January, in Duddhi (Sonbhadra district, Poorvanchal) on 22 January, in Kanpur (Awadh) on 20 February, in Bilaspur (Rampur district, western UP) on 27 February, in Bareilly (Rohelkhand) on 29 February, in Azamgarh and at many other places. At some places the flag-bearers were far-rightists like Baba Ramdev supporters, while at most other places they comprised Muslim youth demanding a judicial enquiry in the Batla House encounter that had occurred in Jamia Nagar, Delhi, where two boys from Azamgarh were killed. The presence of the black flags was so inevitable that the photographers arrived at Gandhi's rallies with a special briefing from the bureau chiefs: 'Keep an eye out for black flag photo-ops.'

Scene 2: Charisma at its Best—Road Show in Kanpur

Kanpur is a multi-cultural city with a tradition of having a Congress-BJP contest on most of the seven urban seats. Rahul Gandhi's road show was scheduled for 20 February 2012. A bus, with 'Utho, Jago, Badlo Uttar Pradesh (Get Up, Wake Up, Change Uttar Pradesh)' written on it, was present for the event and plans were made to cover all seven urban assembly constituencies in the district. Starting from the airport, the road show covered a distance of thirty-five kilometres in the city in some five hours. The Gandhi scion either sat near an open window, or stood on the foreboard at the entrance with party candidates. Some SPG men were on the bus along with him, while others ran along the door covering him from all sides. As the bus moved slowly, people tried to touch Gandhi's hands. Rahul Gandhi shook hands, waved, said 'namaskar' and exchanged smiles.

Women and children sat on the rooftops and balconies, waiting patiently to have a look at the 'future prime minister'. Young girls showered flowers and waved the tricolour as the cavalcade went past. Youth Congress activists moved with the bus on motorcycles, and school children, grown-ups and old people all vied to get close to him. In the Dalit-dominated area of Bajaria, he got off the bus to garland the statue of Baba Saheb Ambedkar.

The road show choked the roads, bringing traffic to a standstill. At every turn, hundreds of people stood on the roads to greet the Gandhi scion. People from the Ulema Council ran along the bus at a few places with black flags, but nobody tried to beat them or stop them this time. No one, other than the media gave them a second look. The noise of protest got lost in the buzz of jubilation and euphoria. However, the euphoria failed to work its magic, as the Congress won only one out of the seven urban seats in Kanpur.

Scene 3: The Limits of 'Anger'

Despite much controversy, the party continued with its unnecessary aggressive posturing, self-righteous approach and 'Kab jagoge logon (when will you wake up, people)?' sort of speeches. Highlighting the condition of poor people and repeated appeals to the youth were also a regular feature. Explaining the reason behind this strategy, eminent journalist and *India Today*'s editorial director at the time, M.J. Akbar, wrote in an article: 'In the Rahul calculus, eternal youth plus dynastic charisma plus poor politics equals hundred plus seats in UP.' The mission however failed miserably with Congress winning only twenty-eight seats.

Jumping on to the bandwagon was younger sister, Priyanka Gandhi Vadra. Focusing exclusively on Rae Bareli and Amethi districts, she imitated her brother's style to pitch perfection. Equipped with the charisma and natural style associated with the Gandhi name, she could charm anybody. However, when it came to the speeches the typical aggression and arrogance made its customary appearance here as well. Addressing a Congress rally she told the people, 'Mere bachche achche school main padhte hain, unke pas sab suvidha hai, apke pas kya hai (My children study in good schools, enjoy all facilities, what do you have)?' This was followed by the regular scolding, 'Agar aapke bachchon ka bhavishya is haalat main kharab hai to aap ise badalte kyun nahin (If the future of your children is so bad, then why don't you change it)?'

With the two members of the Gandhi family setting the tempo for the campaign, the UP Congress leadership joined the chorus with full enthusiasm. Political commentators kept pointing towards the ridiculously foolish aggression and arrogance in the statements of the UP Congress leadership during the election campaign. The electorate was not impressed. Citing reasons behind this, M.J. Akbar wrote: 'Rahul Gandhi's slogan for UP is a curious defensive feint disguised as an aggressive jab: "Hum Jawab Denge". It is the sort of phrase that looks more convincing in an advertising agency than a village tea shop. It is a subliminal plea by a new leader, eager to answer questions that no one has asked.'

When 'Babuji' Had to Keep Quiet

Beni Prasad Verma, popularly known as Babuji, is considered a stalwart Kurmi leader of the Awadh and Poorvanchal regions. Originally from Barabanki, the Gonda MP from Congress and minister for steel in the Central government, Beni Prasad Verma was an old associate of Mulayam Singh Yadav, who left SP and joined Congress prior to the 2009 Lok Sabha elections.

Though his supporters keep calling him 'Vikas Purush', Mr Verma seemed to have little interest in trivial things like development. When we toured Gonda in April last year, we were told by people that after the 2009 elections he had come only three times to his parliamentary constituency; that too for very brief intervals. A massive public resentment had built up against him in the district. Even the Congress party members were not very happy with him, charging him for taking money from bogus candidates in return for party tickets, at the cost of genuine candidates. Some people alleged that the leader had no command over the electorate and that he was way past his 'expiry date'.

On 1 February, Sonia Gandhi came to Gonda to address her first election rally in UP. Being the local MP, Beni Prasad Verma also graced the venue. However, he had to face the ire of voters this time as the moment he rose to speak people started hooting at him, shouting 'Baith jao (Sit down)!' When the uproar did not stop, a helpless Mr Verma was asked by party leaders to sit down and only after Sonia Gandhi rose to speak did the crowds stop shouting.

In the elections, Congress candidates lost all seats in the Gonda district and Babuji's son, Rakesh Verma came in third in Dariyabad (Barabanki).

Shayari for Nagma's Zulfein

Things took an ugly turn in the Bijnor district of western UP when film star Nagma addressed the rally of Barhapur Congress candidate, Hussain Ahmed Ansari in February 2012. Ever since she got there, Ansari kept making attempts to touch the actress, a star campaigner and AICC member, in an attempt to show his supporters how close he was to her, something he had earlier boasted about in public. Nagma took strong exception to this and asked him to return to the dais. Despite the rebuff, Ansari kept trying to touch her. When on stage, to the horror of all present, Ansari read the following sher over the microphone, in Nagma's honour:

> *. . . chhedti rahti ho, rukhsaaron ko,*
> *Tumne zulfon ko sir par chadha rakha hai*

> What ails you that you seem to be in such bad shape,
> You are not wearing make-up, your hair is not styled
> You keep teasing your fans
> And have pampered your tresses with the care you give them.

During the whole episode, senior Congress leader Rashid Alvi was present beside the actress. A furious Nagma reprimanded Ansari on stage, telling him, 'Kya aap bakwas karne aaye hain (Have you come here to talk rubbish)?' The meeting ended abruptly as a visibly-upset Nagma finished her speech in a few minutes and left.

Ansari came in third with 39,000 votes, compared to his debut when he had polled around 60,000 votes in 1996 on a BSP ticket from Afzalgarh (as the constituency was previously known).

Rallies in Western Uttar Pradesh

Western UP is quite prosperous in comparision to Awadh and Poorvanchal, e.g. the Muzaffarnagar district has the highest per capita income in the state. Shamli, the district headquarters of the newly-carved Prabuddha Nagar district (now Shamli), is said to have the highest LIC premiums in the country. The Jat-dominated districts of Meerut, Ghaziabad, Muzaffarnagar, Baghpat, Mathura, Bulandhshahr, Hathras and Saharanpur come under the western UP region. Other than the Jats and Gujjars, Dalits and Muslims also make up a sizeable part of the population here. Despite massive production of sugarcane and sugar, the local dialect is far from sweet and can be described in one word: 'Lathmar' (ruthless).

The other things this part of UP is known for are its fertile soil, its proximity to the national capital, the assertive peasant politics of Chaudhary Mahendra Singh Tikait that rocked Delhi and Lucknow in the eighties and early nineties, and very high crime rates. We came to know that the day before our arrival in Shamli, a son had strangled and killed his father over a 'property dispute'. People said such things were not rare here.

Ajit Singh's Rashtriya Lok Dal (RLD) is an important political force here. This is the 'Janmabhoomi' (land of birth) and 'Karmabhoomi' (land of work) of his father, Chaudhary Charan Singh, UP's biggest-ever Jat leader. His Bharatiya Kranti Dal (BKD) is now known as the RLD.

Since Jats consider themselves to be an egalitarian caste, the different factions are highly susceptible to infighting. According to a Jat we spoke to they believe that 'equals fight, unequals don't'. In every election it would seem that this infighting among the Jats costs RLD dear.

However, in Baghpat, the epicentre of the RLD power, there is a famous tale. A local leader told us that on the night before polling, Chaudhary Sahib (Chaudhary Charan Singh) appears in the dreams of all Jats of the region, personally asking them to vote for RLD. All Jats then follow the great Chaudhary's directive and help RLD win. However the dream diktat did not work this time as RLD lost two of the three seats in Baghpat (earlier it had won all four).

One important difference that marks the rallies here is Ragini, traditional folk songs associated with the local peasant culture. Marriages, family functions, and even political rallies are considered incomplete without them. Over time and with growing prosperity, women dancers became an integral part of Ragini. In many political rallies in western UP, candidates arrange for women dancers, mainly brought from Haryana, to pull crowds. In these rallies, women dance to obscene songs and people pass lewd remarks while throwing money. On most occasions, arrangements for male-female interaction are made, where someone from the audience or a person on stage will make suggestive or sometimes openly obscene remarks to the dancers and the latter will reply in the same tone. During such sessions, things often take an ugly turn and on some occasions the situation goes out of control.

In Meerut south, RLD candidate Manzoor Saifi organized a rally on 17 February 2012 and arranged for women dancers to pull in crowds. Ajit Singh graced the rally with his presence. The dancers included a girl in her early teens. To make matters worse, a session of obscene comments was also held before the dance. Though the exercise helped in pulling in the crowds, it failed in making much difference, as Mr Saifi polled fourth in the contest, while BJP won the seat.

In Sardhana in Meerut, similar arrangements were made by Haji Yaqoob Qureshi of RLD. Mr Qureshi, an ex-MLA and ex-minister in the BSP government came to limelight when he offered a reward of fifty-one crore rupees to the person who could behead the Danish cartoonist, Kurt Westergaard, who was deemed guilty of blasphemy for creating a cartoon of the Prophet Mohammad with his turban in the shape of a bomb.

In a rally organized by Qureshi at Falalda, dancers were present to draw crowds in the name of Ragini. Ajit Singh again graced the rally with his presence. However, as soon as he left the venue, the dance started again in the name of 'manoranjan' (entertainment). A crowd of lumpen elements jumped onto the stage and pulled the dancers down. All hell broke loose; the goons tore the dancers' clothes and molested the helpless women, who tried to run towards the leaders on stage to save them. The police finally had to lathi-charge the mob and escorted the women to a businessman's house. A case was also registered in the Falalda police station with the police taking suo motu cognizance of this incidence.

Haji Yaqoob too lost to BJP's Sanjeet Singh Som by approximately 12,000 votes.

Unruliness and hooliganism was not limited to these places only. In Baraut, Baghpat district, when BJP star campaigner Hema Malini could not make it to the rally of the local BJP candidate as announced, an angry mob that had gathered for a glimpse of their 'Bhabhi' (sister-in-law; Hema Malini's husband Dharmendra is a Jat) ran amok and vandalized the venue, breaking chairs and pulling down the decorations. In Shamli, Prabuddhanagar district, where the 'Dream Girl' finally arrived to address the crowd at another BJP rally, an excited mob on touching the actress created such a ruckus that the police had to resort to lathi-charge once again and an obviously shaken Hema Malini had to be escorted out of the venue under police protection.

What is remarkable is the fact that such incidents were not reported from Poorvanchal and Awadh, the regions known for their history of raja-rajwadas where 'mujra' (traditional dance performed by professional female dancers) is not uncommon. They were reported in the western part of the state, which boasts of an egalitarian society and peasant culture. The Election Commission too appeared inactive, taking no action to prevent such incidents, despite the furore in the media. Though the Election Commission was quite effective in preventing such malpractices in the earlier phases at Poorvanchal and Awadh, it became a bit sluggish and ineffectual by the time the last phase rolled up, which was when the election process had started in western UP. Whatever be the reason, election rallies in western UP were somewhat terrifying, not just for the observers but for the 'star campaigners' as well.

Leaders Lecture Empty Chairs, School Children in Rallies

During the 2012 elections, while some leaders set records in the number of crowds drawn to their rallies, some others proved adept in repelling them instead. This time two tall UP leaders launched their parties with much fanfare: Amar Singh, who launched the Rashtriya Lok Manch (RLM) with a 'bucket' symbol, and ex-chief minister and ex-BJP stalwart Kalyan Singh, who launched the Jan Kranti Party (Rashtrawadi) with an 'almirah' symbol. Both leaders were ill and ageing. Both drew a zero in the elections within the state.

Amar Singh is known as a blabbermouth. In the build-up to the elections he announced that he would spoil the chances of SP to win even a single seat. SP won a record number of seats in this election, while Amar Singh's party won none. He did manage to gather some crowds in his rallies due to Jaya Prada's presence, but it was evident that people had come to see her and not to listen to Amar Singh. At places where the actress was not scheduled to make an appearance, the party candidates announced that she would be present in the hope that once people arrived to see her, they would not go back. But this trick did not work all the time.

One of Amar Singh's rallies was scheduled at a place in Firozabad district. The candidate had announced in the advertisements that Jaya Prada would come to the rally. A large number of people turned up at the rally venue but when Amar Singh arrived alone, people realized that they had been cheated and started to leave. The organizers rushed the proceedings so that the event could finish before the venue was completely deserted. However, by the time Amar Singh started his speech, not more than fifty people remained. Amar Singh finally lectured to the empty plastic chairs about the wrongdoings of Maya and Mulayam, appealing to them to cast 'their' votes for his party.

But even Jaya Prada was not very successful in pulling in crowds at some places. In January 2012 at the rally of RLM candidate Satya Narayan Bind in Handiya (Allahabad), most of the chairs were empty despite Jaya Prada gracing the venue. To compensate for this, the organizers made an arrangement and a nearby school declared a half-day holiday. After this, the more than happy school children, mostly girls from the seventh grade and below, filled the chairs at the rally venue and clapped happily at the poll promises made by Amar Singh and the party candidate, Mr Bind, who polled 729 votes.

Tears for Votes

Bizarre scenes kept emerging in the course of the 2012 UP election campaign, as the candidates were hell-bent on employing all sorts of tactics, ranging from 'money-muscle' to emotions, to score a victory. In such a situation, leaders did not forget to invoke the support of the electorate by citing that their lives were being threatened by powerful people. Babu Singh Kushwaha is one such example.

Kushwaha was a tall OBC figure and minister of state for family welfare in BSP's cabinet when the successive murders of two chief medical officers in broad daylight rocked the state capital. These murders put the spotlight on the state health ministry and family welfare ministry, which were allegedly involved in massive corruption in the disbursal of funds related to the National Rural Health Mission (NRHM), a Central government scheme to ensure healthcare in rural areas. When further newspaper investigations and RTI inquiries revealed a scam of some thousand crore rupees in this case, a political storm was created by the Opposition, making it necessary for some heads in the cabinet to roll. True to her style of functioning, Mayawati tried to silence the upheaval by sacking two ministers—Babu Singh Kushwaha and Anant 'Antu' Kumar Mishra.

Kushwaha alleged that BSP was trying to turn him into a scapegoat and joined the BJP. However, inner-party opposition to the inclusion of such a tainted face, mainly by Uma Bharti and Yogi Adityanath of Gorakhpur, prevented his formal inclusion in the party. Even so, he kept campaigning independently in favour of the BJP. Rally after rally, he cited the atrocities committed upon him by the BSP government along with the threat to his life from Mayawati and her lieutenant Naseemuddin Siddiqui, appealing to his fellow caste people (Kushwahas or Kachis) to vote for the BJP. During one such rally in February at Atarra (district Banda), an emotional Kushwaha began weeping in front of the public while narrating the same story of being hounded by the BSP government.

But Kushwaha was not alone in doing so. Mulayam Singh Yadav's samdhan (mother-in-law of his nephew Dharmendra Yadav, an MP from Badayun), who had rebelled against SP to contest on a Congress ticket from Karhal (Mainpuri district), also could not control her emotions at a rally here. While addressing a rally in Karhal, Urmila Yadav broke into tears when AICC general secretary Digvijay Singh reached the venue. 'Aap meri har galti maaf kar dijiye aur apna samarthan dijiye (Forgive my past mistakes and give me your support),' a teary-eyed Urmila appealed to the people with folded hands.

However, the case of another BSP minister, Avdhesh Kumar Verma is more dramatic. A minister of state for backward class welfare in the BSP government and an MLA from Dadraul, Shahjahanpur, Verma was denied a ticket by the BSP after which he joined the BJP. On 2 January 2012 when Verma joined the BJP, he broke into tears while talking to the media: 'Maine use apna maa-baap maana, apna sab kuch maana, mere khilaf koi FIR nahin hai, phir mujhe kyun ye saza dene ka kam kiya gaya (I considered her my mother and father, there is no FIR against me then why did she punish me like this)?' the ex-minister complained about Mayawati, weeping like a child asking his mother the reason for the punishment being meted out to him.

However, in none of these cases did the theatrics work, as Urmila Yadav and Avdhesh Verma both lost, not making it even to second position, while the BJP candidate in Babu Singh Kushwaha's constituency Naraini (SC) polled third after SP and BSP.

The Candidate Goes 'Tel Lene'

On one hectic campaign day in Basti, a helicopter landed at the GIC grounds in the city, the venue for most of the political rallies. People were not sure about who was coming, as no party had announced a campaign. Even so, about fifty people had gathered around it, just to look at the helicopter from a close range. This was possible as no barricades had been put up, unlike at other party rallies. A man jumped out of the helicopter and asked the people gathered, 'JD(U) ki rally yahin hai? (Is this Janta Dal United's rally?)' The people replied, 'Hamein nahi pata, hum to helicopter dekhne aaye hain. Aap udhar poochiye (We don't know, we have come to see the helicopter, please ask someone there),' gesturing towards the other end of the ground where a lone man in a white kurta pajama stood on the stage.

The man who had jumped out of the helicopter went up to the stage and asked the same question to the person on stage, who said that indeed it was. 'Ummidwar kahan hai (Where is the candidate)?' the first man asked. 'Ji mike chalane ke liye generator lagaya hai, us mein tel nahin tha to woh tel lene cycle se gaye hain (Actually there was no fuel in the generator to operate the mike, so he has gone on bicycle to get it),' was the matter-of-fact reply.

Muttering to himself, the man walked back to the helicopter and spoke to the man sitting within, who finally decided to come out. This man was none other than Sharad Yadav, the national president of JD(U), and the National Democratic Alliance's (NDA) convenor. Choosing not to deliver a speech from the stage, Mr Yadav walked towards the people and started to chat with them casually. After a while, an old man with very thick glasses appeared at the entrance of the ground, pedalling a bicycle with a canister of oil in one hand. This was Fazlur Rehman, JD(U) candidate from Basti. Sizing up the situation, Yadav told the people, 'Inhe kahiyega jo paisa-rupya inhe mila tha, woh party karyalaya mein zama kara aaein (Tell him to return the money given by the party to contest the elections),' and turned back towards his helicopter.

Fazalur Rahman polled last among twenty candidates with 279 votes.

PART TWO

WAR ROOMS AND OPEN FIELDS

WHEN THE ELECTION PROCESS IS UNDERWAY, POLITICAL PARTIES inevitably have to perform different functions. From writing the script for party manifestos to the challenging task of selecting candidates, strategizing and chalking out the line of action, booth management during the actual polling and so on. They have to demonstrate varied experience and professionalism to successfully fulfil these assorted but critical functions. Not surprisingly, political parties find themselves sometimes moving in an anticipated manner and sometimes in unexpected ways.

It is here that the war rooms and think tanks come into play. Equipped with senior, experienced leadership and with the rational allocation of functions and tasks, these places are the nerve centres of political action and hubs of crucial information. With the advent of information technology, it became possible to keep a tab on activities in an entire state from one centre. This development also marked the arrival of non-party professionals into war rooms, who undertake crucial functions such as devising the print and electronic advertisements for the campaign, managing booth level data, keeping track of everyday activities, making future plans, and performing other such functions. In these elections, almost all parties had taken the help of professionals for different tasks, usually for their media campaigns.

It is important to keep in mind that the electoral campaigns, movements, rathyatras and poll promises launched by different parties are not just random, persona-based leadership decisions, but carefully-grafted tactics and strategies with some objectives and target constituencies in mind. The war of words that the leaders of different parties engage in is also more often a calculated game than just spontaneous outbursts of political rhetoric. However, the ultimate testing ground for all the calculations and strategies devised within 'closed rooms' are the 'open fields'— the streets, mohallas (small neighbourhoods), villages, colonies, and work places where the power of the people matters.

Evolution of the War Room

Echoing the recent trend in Indian politics, most political parties—national and regional—have tried to put together a modern system of communication and information technology, which has become an important component of these war rooms. Surprisingly, the political party which places great emphasis on 'local' and 'swadeshi' and appears to staunchly oppose the 'new' and the 'modern' has been at the forefront in this regard. It was BJP's Pramod Mahajan who started the trend of 'war rooms' or 'central commands' in election management with the introduction of a 'remote-control central command' to micro-manage elections in remote constituencies. For the 2009 elections, Sudheendra Kulkarni managed a well-equipped, highly-sophisticated 'war room' for the BJP from Delhi.

L.K. Advani was the first national leader to launch his website in the run-up to the 2009 Lok Sabha elections. The technological interface was inspired by the US presidential election campaigns and even their communication models bear strong similarities to American models of communication.

However, after initial success in assembly elections in Rajasthan and Madhya Pradesh, BJP war rooms did not bring any major results to the party, although they were not the prime factors in the failure or even in the prior success. They failed in the 2004 elections when their 'India Shining' campaign failed miserably. Later in 2009 too, they could not bring the party to power.

The BJP, under the leadership of Nitin Gadkari tried to put a new face of the party forward in the recently-held assembly elections in Uttar Pradesh as well as in some other states. The party hired the services of many professionals, PR companies and social and market research agencies to manage the elections. Gadkari had made a popular appeal to his party men in Uttar Pradesh to not bother coming to Delhi or Lucknow for tickets, as he had his own system of surveys and political intelligence. However, the number of seats won (forty-seven) remained far below the number that the BJP leadership had hoped for.

When BJP had taken a lead in technology and 'war rooms', one could assume that the Congress would incorporate technology into its campaign on a larger scale. But this was not the case. The Congress has not incorporated much technology in political management although its 'young' leader Rahul Gandhi has been flaunted as a laptop-savvy politician. In the 2012 elections, the Congress was way behind BJP and even SP in the adoption of technology in election management.

In the pages to come, we will talk about not only the war rooms, but also the broader election strategies of the four main parties in UP, the reasons behind choosing them, and the final result of these strategies in Battleground UP 2012.

Samajwadi Party

The Uneven Ride to Power in Lucknow

The Samajwadi Party had retained power in UP from August 2003 to May 2007, though the road had been far from smooth. Despite emerging as the largest party in the 2002 assembly elections (143 out of 403 seats) it fell short of the magic number of 202. Since BJP (88 seats) and BSP (98 seats) too were not in a position to form the government on their own or with a coalition and since no party was ready to ally with the other, President's rule was imposed from March to May 2002. It ended after the central BJP leadership asked the state leadership to join a coalition government led by BSP with BJP as a junior partner. This third alliance of BSP-BJP (earlier two were in June 1995-October 1997 and March 1997-September 1997) died an untimely death after Mayawati was caught in the Taj Corridor controversy. Taking the offensive, on 28 July 2003 Mayawati rubbished all allegations levied against her and alleged that the Jagmohan, who was tourism minister in the Central government, was the real culprit. She also demanded his resignation while BSP MPs raised a furore in both houses of Parliament for the same. On 25 August 2003 she severed all ties with BJP and recommended to the governor to dissolve the house and hold fresh elections.

A shocked BJP mustered its cunning and retaliated by allowing

Mulayam Singh Yadav to form the government in UP, supported by Rashtriya Kranti Party leader Kalyan Singh, Rashtriya Lok Dal leader Ajit Singh and UP Congress chief Jagdambika Pal.

With the might of the state government in his hand, the erstwhile pehelwan flexed his political muscles and lured MLAs with ministerial portfolios to engineer more defections, breaking as many as thirty-seven of the ninety-eight BSP MLAs within a period of ten days.

The new SP government, which was formed by employing not just political cunning and mean calculations but also illegal procedures and neglect of the prescribed norms, remained true to its foundational principles from day one. While the SP cadre made it a habit to break the law whenever possible, cases like the Nithari (where dozens of children were murdered and raped by two men in a Noida home) sprang up. A whole 'apaharan udyog' (kidnapping industry) thrived under political protection and many scandals involving the MLAs rocked the state, such as the Kavita Chowdhary murder case in Meerut involving RLD ministers.

Mulayam Singh would occasionally tell his supporters to invoke caste pride: 'Virodhi kahte hain ki UP main Jungle raj hai, par jungle ka raja kaun hota hai (The Opposition says that there is jungle raj in UP but who is the king of the jungle)?'

People in UP were fed up with the situation and the empty rhetoric. At the next possible opportunity, the 2007 assembly election, they threw SP out and brought in Mayawati, whose BSP captured power with a thumping majority of 206 seats, the only party to do so since the 1991 elections. The Samajwadi Party was reduced to ninety-seven seats, while BJP was down to a historic low of fifty-one seats with Congress tailing behind with twenty-two seats.

The Bitter Taste of 'Satta Parivartan'

The erstwhile second-in-command of the state, Shivpal Yadav, had a taste of the regime change, when a police constable slapped the SP state president on 8 January 2008 in Lucknow. The event was SP's protest against Mayawati's ban on holding student union elections across the state. Mayawati's main mass-base, the Dalits, are less assertive in educational institutions due to their background, and since BSP does not have a student or youth wing to address their issues too, student unions were of no use to Mayawati.

On the other hand, for SP, student union elections served as a recruitment exercise to induct not just future leaders but also future organizers and muscle men. In this situation, the Samajwadi Chatra Sabha, SP's student wing that has a massive following within the state, decided to hold state-wide demonstrations demanding the ban to be lifted. Sunil Yadav, Akhilesh Yadav's would-be lieutenant and a student leader from Unnao, engineered the agitation. The Mayawati government instructed the police to handle the agitation with an iron fist across the state.

In Lucknow, students of a post-graduate college belonging to the Samajwadi Chatra Sabha were brutally lathi-charged by the police during the agitation in which many students and SP activists suffered serious injuries. However, instead of allowing them to recover from their injuries, the Lucknow police threw them all into jail. Shivpal Yadav along with Akhilesh Yadav and other party activists started a dharna outside the residence of the Lucknow superintendent of police and stayed there till late evening, demanding that their activists be released. When the agitators refused to end the dharna and vacate the venue, the police used force to take them into custody. Both Akhilesh and Shivpal were detained along with the other SP activists.

As the news of the incident spread through the state, SP

workers took to the roads in almost all major cities, demanding the chief minister's resignation. Mayawati's government was determined not to bow down. The result was a riot-like situation in Uttar Pradesh. Vehicles were set ablaze, government offices set on fire and the police officers were pelted with stones.

Though the agitation cooled down later, it provided the SP rank and file with the necessary motivation and desperation required to make an attempt to return to power. For the first time, a leader, Akhilesh Yadav, had led the party activists from the front, charging them with new confidence and energy. Echoing the general sentiment, Akhilesh's trusted-comrade Sunil Yadav said, 'Pahli baar aisa hua ki neta aage tha, janta piche thi, aur isse karyakartaon main nayi urja, naya vishwas paida hua (For the first time, the leader was ahead and the people behind him. This has inspired a new energy, a new confidence in the activists).'

Three Days that Shook the State
(Oust BSP Movement: 7–9 March 2011)

In early 2011, the Samajwadi Party looked like a worn-out force, incapable of taking on their old political rival, BSP. The BSP under Mayawati had had a lion's share in almost all elections (the Lok Sabha elections being the only exception) held in the state since the 2007 assembly polls. A number of Mulayam's trusted comrades had also left him, like the Kurmi leader of Barabanki-Gonda, Beni Prasad Verma, who had joined Congress, and the firebrand minority leader and SP founding member, Azam Khan, who left the party on the issue of inclusion of ex-BJP leader Kalyan Singh (who was considered guilty of having a hand in the Babri Masjid demolition). Azam Khan was also critical of SP's decision to support UPA-I on the nuclear deal.

While a large number of party leaders were against the inclusion of Kalyan Singh, Mulayam sidelined them all under Amar Singh's influence. Mulayam hoped that Kalyan Singh's Lodh voters (the OBC caste to which he belongs) would support SP in the 2009 Lok Sabha elections, and the party could improve its tally of thirty-nine MPs in the state. However, the results revealed that Azam Khan was not the only Muslim who was angry with the inclusion of the 'Hindutvavadi' leader in the party. A large number of Muslim voters rejected SP and its tally came down from thirty-nine to twenty-three in the Lok Sabha. SP became a laughing stock in political circles when its general secretary, Amar Singh, gatecrashed into UPA-II's inaugural dinner hosted for the coalition partners and was allegedly asked to leave the venue.

SP suffered other defeats: Raj Babbar from the Congress party defeated Mulayam's daughter-in-law and Akhilesh Yadav's wife, Dimple Yadav by over 85,000 votes in the November 2009 Ferozabad parliamentary by-election. Later, BSP virtually swept the panchayat polls held in late October 2010. Aditya Yadav, Shivpal Yadav's son, was defeated in Etawah zila panchayat elections, a former SP bastion.

These humiliating defeats created a furore within the party as SP's rank and file cried out for Amar Singh's head, blaming him for all of these failures. Amar Singh finally resigned on 6 January 2010. On 2 February 2011, Amar Singh and his close associate Rampur MP Jaya Prada were formally expelled from SP as the SP spokesperson, Mohan Singh, stated that they were a 'communalist (anti-Muslim) and casteist intrusion' within the party.

It is not clear whether Amar Singh was solely responsible for the problems and the weakening of the SP, but it seems unlikely. He has never really been associated with the rogue image of the SP and its patronage of criminals, which took a heavy toll on the party's performance in the 2007 elections. However, with his industrial and Bollywood connections, he was definitely responsible for luring the party towards the world of glamour and riches. Under his influence, the Saifai Mahotsav, an annual rural carnival held in Mulayam's hometown Saifai, was transformed into a high-glamour affair, with Ukrainian belly dancers and Bollywood divas being flown in to perform. Old socialists fondly remembered the days when rural folk songs and local culture dominated the mahotsav, but they were sidelined during the party's 'Amar Days'.

The ouster of Amar Singh proved highly beneficial for the party as he was turned into a scapegoat and blamed for all the misfortunes that had befallen SP in the recent past. It also eased the way for a regime change in favour of Akhilesh Yadav, as both Shivpal Yadav and Amar Singh, considered to be stalwarts when Mulayam Singh was in power, proved to be inefficient. Akhilesh, who had till now led the four frontal organizations of the party—the Samajwadi Chatra Sabha, Lohiya Vahini, Samjwadi Yuvjan Sabha and Mulayam Singh Youth Brigade—was now seen to be ready to take on bigger responsibilities.

It is around this time that the Yadav scion commissioned a series of surveys about the party's public image. These studies confirmed that though people were angry at BSP, they were also afraid that if SP came back to power, it would bring back goonda-gardi (hooliganism). That was when Akhilesh Yadav realized that SP was fighting not just a battle at the grassroots but also a 'war of perception'.

Amar Singh was once again made the scapegoat and all charges of aligning with communal forces and forgetting the 'Samajwad' (principles of socialism as defined by Ram Manohar Lohia and Jayaprakash Narayan) and turning corporate were squarely placed on his shoulders. This also energized the party from within to overhaul its reputation and return to its original philosophy, and finally, to hit the streets with renewed energy. The party demonstrated this new energy in the three-day state-wide 'BSP Hatao, Pradesh Bachao Abhiyan' (Oust BSP, Save UP Movement) from 7 to 9 March 2011.

The decision to launch this agitation was taken at a conference of the SP state executive on 26 February 2011, where a new strategy was outlined to revamp the party organization. A decision was also made to start an early campaign with the intent to apply sustained pressure on the ruling BSP until the elections next year. The new office-bearers and executive members were inducted into the party in SP's recently-concluded state conference at Gorakhpur (10-12 February), the highest decision-making body of the state party unit, which formally elected Akhilesh Yadav as the UP state president of the SP.

According to the new SP leadership, the movement was targeted at the 'all-round deterioration in law and order, crimes against women—particularly the involvement of ruling party MLAs in rape and the rampant corruption in the BSP government'. It was aimed at bringing the state machinery to a grinding halt by laying siege to government offices and locking the offices of district magistrates.

A cautious Mayawati tried to control the agitation by putting Mulayam Singh and Akhilesh Yadav under house arrest on the first day of the protest on the grounds of maintaining law and order. This further boosted the movement. Everywhere, SP cadres stormed the streets in thousands. With the government hell-bent on crushing them, the resultant mayhem was termed by the media as a 'full-on political war' as the Opposition and the government were out in the streets with 'daggers drawn'. Reporting on the first day of the protests, the *Indian Express* wrote on 8 March: 'Netaji followers set streets afire' and 'Day One of SP's three-day protest against the BSP government creates ripples from Allahabad to Delhi'.

In Lucknow, several leaders, including Bhagwati Singh, leader of the Opposition in the Vidhan Sabha, Shivpal Singh Yadav, and MP Sushila Saroj were detained. Three busloads of SP activists were sent to the Lucknow jail and the police resorted to lathi-charge to disperse the mobs. Protests, traffic disruptions, government office closures and police lathi-charge and detainment were reported from across the state—from Meerut to Gorakhpur and Lakhimpur Kheri to Banda. At many places, women led the protests with red-cap-wearing party activists.

The BSP was forced to lift Mulayam's and Akhilesh's house arrest when SP MPs raised a furore in parliament. On 9 March 2011, the last day of the protest, Akhilesh Yadav was detained in Lucknow as soon as he landed at Amausi airport. The police resorted to extensive use of force and the Yadav scion was virtually lifted up by policemen and forcefully shoved into the police vehicle under the command of IPS officer B.P. Ashok. Akhilesh was later sent to Lucknow jail.

The following day, on 10 March, SP workers gathered to protest outside the jail and at the time of Akhilesh Yadav's release, a battle ensued between both parties.

Summing up the feelings of his party activists and sympathizers, Akhilesh Yadav said, 'Hazaaron crore rupya barbaad ho gaya yahan par, lakhon acre jamin kabja ki inke logon ne, kitna bhrashtachar hua hai, kitni loot hui hai, kitna balatkar hua hai, log kitne apmanit huye hain (Thousands of crores of rupees have been wasted here, their people have acquired lakhs of acres of land, so much corruption has been going on, so many robberies and rapes have taken place, people have been insulted so much by this government)!'

Later on 17 March, as a sequel to this agitation, massive effigy burnings of Mayawati were organized by SP all over the state. Akhilesh Yadav was once again placed under house arrest, but the government could not control the thousands of SP workers who had come out in the streets in various cities to burn Mayawati's effigies, despite police threats. Sitting in his party office, Akhilesh Yadav was flooded with phone calls from across the state informing him about the protests held by Samajwadi activists. Yadav looked elated with the success of his party's show of strength. And there was a sense of contentment within the party as well. The new leadership had finally delivered. The party had shown its strength with the rank and file coming together to brave the jails and the blows of Mayawati's government. What was more important was that the people of the state had now seen them on the streets, braving blows, arrests and being framed in fake cases. There was hope that the people, who were already angry with the government, would sympathize with the protesters and if they wanted to get rid of this government, they would know which political party was capable of defeating the ruling party.

Reaching Out to the People—Samajwadi Kranti Rath Yatra

Keeping up the momentum generated by the 'Oust BSP Movement' in March, the Samajwadi Party declared its first list of 162 candidates on 9 April 2011, far ahead of the BJP and the Congress but a little behind BSP's 'unofficial' declaration. The street protests had helped the SP in energizing its cadre and orienting the whole party towards political success in the coming elections. The leadership had established a direct connection with the activists and the new SP now exuded confidence, well aware of its organizational might. The challenge now was to establish the same connection with the people of Uttar Pradesh. This required two things—a clear plan and a clean face.

The party decided to launch the Samajwadi Kranti Rath Yatra along the same lines as the one that Mulayam Singh had launched on 14 September 1987, which saw him becoming the chief minister of the largest Indian state for the first time in 1989.

A specially-designed bus with an internal lift was prepared for the yatra and Akhilesh Yadav was chosen to be the official face, as health problems did not allow Mulayam Singh to take the stress of the strenuous yatra. The party wanted Akhilesh to be the face of the yatra as it served two purposes: One, to counter the Congress's youth icon, Rahul Gandhi, with one of its own, and two, to project the new image of the party that reflected not only a generational change, but also a positive change towards governance, technology and politics. The party that had opposed computers and English in its 2009 election manifesto now projected an English-educated, Australia-returned leader who was always visibly engaged with his two BlackBerry phones.

Much before any other party had begun its poll campaign, the rath yatra was flagged off by the Muslim face of the party, Azam Khan, on 12 September 2011 from the Samajwadi Party headquarters in Lucknow. The yatra was to be conducted in different phases, with each phase covering a set of neighbouring districts, going through almost all the assembly constituencies of the district. The advertisements that appeared in newspapers about the yatra popularized the catchy tag line: 'Vikas ki Ganga bahane ko, Ab bhrashtachar mitane ko, Kranti rath par ho sawar, Nikal pada hai Samajwad (To unleash the river of development and put an end to corruption, socialism has embarked upon its march atop the chariot of revolution).'

Few people know that this new tag line was not a product of a professional team, but was written on Akhilesh Yadav's Facebook page by a party sympathizer. Judging the potential catchiness of this tag line, Yadav junior incorporated it in the official campaign of the rath yatra. Furthermore, in response to Rahul Gandhi's anglicized 'Mission 2012', the yatra tried to present its own alternative, 'Vijay 2012' (Victory 2012) which appeared simpler, more rooted and effective. The yatra campaign advertisements echoed the same: 'Parivartan janta ki pukar,

Vijay 2012 ki hai Hunkar (People cry out for change, which is echoed in Victory 2012).'

The route chart of the yatra was meticulously planned and the party machinery left no space for any malfunction. The course of the yatra and Akhilesh Yadav's complete date-wise programme was given to the Vidhan Sabha Ikai (assembly units) well in advance, so that they could promote the yatra and make arrangements for the meetings at the designated places. Conveyance was arranged so that people from nearby areas could attend it.

As the yatra reached the border of a new district or assembly constituency, party workers and candidates welcomed it and a motor cavalcade escorted the yatra to the meeting venue, where crowds would be waiting to look at and listen to the Yadav scion. After the ceremonial welcome and slogan shouting, Akhilesh Yadav would address the crowd from the top of his rath. The speeches were more focused on the promises that the party would fulfil once it came to power, rather than the political rhetoric of making allegations against BSP and other parties.

During these meetings, SP state secretary Naved Siddiqui remained by Akhilesh's side and spoke to the crowd before and after his speech, creating the right atmosphere for the leader's speech. Siddiqui, former Radio Mirchi jockey and a former chairman of the culture wing of the Congress party in the state, joined SP at the behest of Akhilesh Yadav and compensated for the lack of rhetoric in Akhilesh's oration. The rath would then move through the assembly segment with the party activists escorting it in other vehicles, till the activists from the next assembly segment took charge at the border.

At the end of every phase of the rath yatra, the team would take a few days of rest, plan upcoming phases, and review the progress before moving ahead to the next phase. Vijay Chauhan, the IT in-charge of Akhilesh's team procured photographs of the yatra at the various assembly constituencies and updated them daily on the party website and Facebook page.

The Yadav scion addressed on an average, four meetings a day and by 25 October 2011 (he had started on 12 September) he had covered more than fifty assembly constituencies in fifteen districts, covering a distance of many thousand kilometres. None of the other parties had started campaigning yet. 'By the time they start, we will be 100 constituencies and 5000 kilometres ahead of them,' a confident Akhilesh Yadav told the media in October 2011.

Although the electronic media—national and regional—did not cover this rathyatra and its rallies sufficiently, the number of people that turned up to listen to Akhilesh Yadav was a clear indication that the magic of the new SP leader was working at the grass-root level. Known for his humility, Akhilesh would not hesitate to have tea at a roadside dhaba or talk to people in nearby vehicles when caught in a traffic jam. These measures not only boosted his image but that of the party too, encouraging the till-now wary people of the state to trust the party. The yatra continued till February finishing in Mainpuri, the parliamentary constituency of SP chief Mulayam Singh. Approximately 9000 kilometres were covered across 300 constituencies. A cycle rally of around 250 kilometres was also organized from Noida to Agra from 21 to 23 October 2011.

The Youth Brigade of Akhilesh Yadav

While the media kept talking about Rahul Gandhi and his youth leadership in UP, it was Akhilesh Yadav's team of young people that actually delivered. Unlike the Gandhi scion's team, most of the members of Akhilesh's team were grounded party workers who rose to prominence on the basis of their struggle.

Anand Bhadauria, national president of SP's youth

organization Lohiya Vahini, was a trusted comrade of the state SP president. The youth leader made headlines when he was mercilessly thrashed by the UP police on 9 March 2011 when he was leading a protest at Lucknow's Hazratganj. The then Lucknow DIG D.K. Thakur not only beat him up but also tried to crush his face with his boots. This was covered by the media and the picture made it to the newspapers the next day. The National Human Rights Commission took suo motu notice of the incident, seeking an explanation from the state government.

Similarly Sunil Yadav, the Samajwadi Chatra Sabha leader not only engineered state-wide protests in January 2008, but also led the protest in Lucknow. In the course of these protests, not only was Yadav beaten up by the police along with other activists, but he also spent a couple of days in jail. Later, in the three-day Oust BSP movement in March 2011, he was targeted by the police again and was beaten up so badly that he fractured his hand. But this brought him to Akhilesh Yadav's attention. Today, he is considered to be Akhilesh Yadav's closest confidante. Coming from a humble farming background in Unnao, Sunil had no prior political connections when he joined the party in 1999.

Two other student leaders who made it to Team Akhilesh on their own steam are Nafis Ahmed, former president of Aligarh Muslim University Students' Union and Naeem-ul Hasan, former student leader of Jamia Millia Islamia in Delhi. Two other names are Naved Siddiqui and Vijay Chauhan. However, their actual roles were quite limited. While Siddiqui addressed rallies and defended the party on English news channels; Chauhan, an Australia-returned native of Mainpuri, was involved to a lesser degree in the day-to-day politics. He efficiently managed Akhilesh's and the party's websites and the Facebook pages. Another young Turk is Abhishek Mishra from IIM, who is now a minister in the SP government.

It is this versatile team, comprised of street fighters to radio jockeys and foreign-returned techno-geeks that helped the Yadav scion in achieving his spectacular success.

Media Discovers Akhilesh Yadav

'After six months of hard work, it looks like Delhi has suddenly discovered me,' said the youngest UP chief minister taking a dig at the sudden change of heart of the national, mainly electronic, media. As recently as November-December 2011 people in the Delhi media were not very keen on Akhilesh Yadav, who was leading his party's poll campaign through the Kranti Rath Yatra. The media was more concerned about what Rahul Gandhi was doing or saying in Uttar Pradesh and then in Priyanka Gandhi Vadra's activities.

When *The Hindu*'s senior correspondent Vidya Subramaniam accompanied him on his yatra in November 2011, Akhilesh indirectly complained about the media's obsession with Rahul Gandhi. He said, 'As far as the media is concerned, there is only one yuvraj (prince, meaning Rahul). They don't understand that every son is a yuvraj for his family.' His complaint was not unjust or baseless for despite covering thousands of kilometres and dozens of constituencies, the national media was not interested in giving due coverage to his party's campaign and the yatra. In fact, if one wants to dig out information about the yatra, there is virtually nothing on the websites of the national English language media. Most of it is available in the Hindi print media. One has to rely upon photographs posted on SP's Facebook pages to build an opinion about the yatra's details and success.

Prior to the results of the opinion polls, no news channel or English language newspaper was even talking about SP's 'Ummeed ki Cycle' (cycle of hope) theme. However, as soon as the initial phases of polling indicated that SP was leading due to high voter turnout, the media started anticipating Samajwadi success, finding innumerable qualities in the Yadav scion.

When the final results came out, the media went berserk blasting its old favourite Rahul Gandhi ('incapable, immature, ineffective') and showered praise on Akhilesh Yadav ('new hope, young Netaji'). In the coming days, it dug up virtually everything it could find about the party leader—what he likes to eat ('likes idlis'), what he listens to ('Metallica fan'), what his pet name is ('the adorable Tipu'), his humility ('you know, he said hello to a truck driver'), his A-team, his B-team, his childhood photos, his favourite sports, his daily exercise regimen and so on.

Even his father Mulayam Singh, who was till a few days ago regarded as the guardian of crooked politicians and criminals, suddenly became the perfect candidate for a future prime minister as the leader of a 'hypothetical Third Front', and on some channels, he became the precursor of a 'Fourth Front'.

Two Years, Two Leaders, Two Manifestos and a Top-Down Change in the Same Party

While releasing the Samajwadi Party Manifesto on 11 April 2009 in the run-up to the May 2009 parliamentary elections, the party's national president, Mulayam Singh Yadav stressed that 'expensive English education must be abolished and the use of computers must be brought down so that more jobs could be created for the unemployed'. Almost all Opposition parties criticized Mulayam Singh and the SP, declaring it 'regressive', 'backward' and 'living in the nineteenth century'.

Within a period of approximately two years, on 20 January 2012, Mulayam Singh Yadav released the SP manifesto for the assembly elections in the state. Unlike the last time, Akhilesh Yadav was prominently visible at his side. The manifesto promised free tablets to all students who passed Class 10 exams and free laptops to all students who passed Class 12 exams from government schools. The party which had vowed to discourage the use of computers just two years back was now openly endorsing their use and even promising to promote the number of computer users with state patronage.

Amar Ujala's Lucknow edition captured the moment of evident change in the party with a catchy one-liner. The photograph of a beaming Akhilesh and a serious Mulayam releasing the manifesto with Gurjar leader Chowdhary Yashpal was captioned: 'Muskuraiye, Hum Badal Gaye (Smile, we have changed).'

Ummeed Ki Cycle Wins the War of Perceptions

The surveys commissioned by Akhilesh Yadav and his team way back in March 2011 revealed that the Samajwadi Party was a victim of its own image—it was the party that brought lawlessness and anarchy to the state during its 2003-07 tenure. The people of UP wanted to get rid of the BSP government, but they feared that if the SP came in its place, it would bring back goonda-gardi. Allaying the fears of the people and replacing past memories with a new image of the party was the most critical task at hand. The party strove to do so by picking a team of professionals that included people like Arjun Sablok, Neelesh Misra and Sonu Nigam. The party also did not create a hype about its campaign or the people involved, although these details were not deliberately kept a secret either.

Arjun Sablok is a Hindi movie director who has worked on movies like *Na Tum Jaano Na Hum* (2002). He was asked to prepare the TV commercials (TVCs) nine or ten months in advance. The brief was focused: find out what the people in UP aspire for, what they want their future to be, what their dreams are, and then relate all of this information to the party's poll promises. Political attacks on opponents or any negativity were a big no-no. The reason was simple—the party did not need to portray a political combatant's image, as the people were already aware of the fact. What it needed to portray was the image of a development-oriented, futurist party committed to the progress of the state, as opposed to the political culture of revenge that was present in the state so far.

Sablok toured the state and pinpointed jobs, infrastructure, electricity, education and irrigation as the main issues. On the basis of these issues, Sablok created eight TVCs representing the hopes of different sections, namely weavers, the unemployed, rickshaw pullers, farmers, people dependent on the tourism industry, girls, youth and families of migrant workers. Every TVC represented the ummeed (hope) of an individual, for example, 'Raju's Ummeed' or 'Neetu's Ummeed'. The approximately thirty-second TVCs narrated the dreams or needs of the protagonist and then related it to SP's poll promises. It ended with an appeal to vote for SP.

In 'Kaushik ki Ummeed', a youth says, 'Mera naam Kaushik hai, naukri dhundh raha hoon (My name is Kaushik, I am searching for a job).' Then there is a voice-over which talks about unemployment allowance given by the SP's old government and the party's promise to start it once again. 'Jab tak naukri nahin milti, koshish kar rahe hain kisi tarah gujara ho jaye (I am trying to make both ends meet till the time I get a job),' says Kaushik while the ad ends with: Poori hogi Kaushik ki ummid, Samajwadi Party ko vote dain (Kaushik's hope will come true, Vote for the Samajwadi Party).' The same sequence is repeated in Ritu ki Ummeed (promising to restart the Kanya Vidya Dhan Yojana for girls' education), Budhiram ki Ummeed (promising electricity for irrigation) and so on.

The remarkable thing about one of these commercials was that it was completely in English, talking about the party's vision to create jobs, build parks, universities, and stadiums, asking the youth to make it all a reality by voting for SP with the tag line, 'One vote, Your vote, can make it happen, Vote for Samajwadi Party'.

A ninth TVC titled 'cycle race' is the only ad that speaks of political competition albeit, without uttering a single word. It shows a boy on an elephant trying hard to make it move, when a cyclist races past the elephant with the SP's anthem playing in the background. This anthem 'Yeh Samajwadi Jhanda' written by SP leader Uday Pratap Singh and sung by noted playback singer Javed Ali was popularized by the party via mobile ringtones.

The tag line 'Ummeed ki Cycle' was conceptualized by Neelesh Misra. Misra is an award-winning journalist and former deputy executive editor with the *Hindustan Times*. He has written four books and edited three, is a photographer and member of a band called Nine, which blends story-telling with songs. Misra is also a lyricist who has written songs for films like *Jism*, *Krishna Cottage*, *Gangster*, and many more. He wrote the lyrics for the longest SP TVC, the 'Musafir' (traveller) TVC. In this eighty-second TVC directed by Sablok, Neelesh recites a poem about his hopes for a jubilant, progressive and peaceful UP under the Samajwadi Party—while an Akhilesh look-alike rides a bicycle through different terrains, finally moving towards the gates of the Vidhan Sabha as a new day begins to dawn.

It has to be admitted that the TVCs of the SP were far ahead of anything the other parties came up with, not only in terms of beauty and simplicity, or dramatic efficacy, but also in terms of capturing the hopes and aspirations of the people.

It is this carefully-crafted strategy that enabled SP to project a positive image of itself, which succeeded in allaying the fears of the common people, enabling them to trust the party. The result, as they say, is history; SP won a complete majority of 224 seats in a house of 403, a feat that no party has achieved since the last three decades.

The Final Blow: Double Precision till Booth Level

The Samajwadi Party has a deep-rooted organizational structure that reaches all sections of society in the state. For a successful performance in any election, regular feedback from the field is required, so that the party can keep tabs not only on the activities of its opponents, but also on the activities of rebels, dissatisfied elements, and traitors among its own members. Other than that, the booth committee plays a crucial role on the polling day. It not only brings people out from their homes to the booth, but also keeps a check on the activities of the opponents—whether they try to lure or intimidate its voters. Successful electoral performance can hardly be ensured without efficient booth committee management.

Earlier, the assembly and booth-level management in the Samajwadi Party would be the responsibility of senior leaders in the party with frontal organizations working under their directives. This time, Akhilesh Yadav's team made a different arrangement. Without disturbing the teams of the Samajwadi Party, the four frontal organizations developed their alternative teams, going as deep as booth level in all assembly constituencies. The phone numbers of all the people involved in the booth committee were kept in the Lucknow office and the people in charge were deputed to look after specific segments—all on the behalf of the four frontal organizations under Akhilesh Yadav's command.

This resulted in the rise of an effective parallel structure within the party, which could not be easily influenced by others as it was difficult to identify and single out the committee members. This structure gave regular feedback from the field to the party's new leadership and made it possible for them to access their actual locations, weak links and the response of the people to the party candidates. On the basis of this feedback the party even changed some of its candidates.

Talking about the accuracy and precision of this structure, Samajwadi Chatra Sabha national president Sunil Yadav said, 'We could tell the candidates how many people welcomed them at how many places when they visited the constituency and they would be shocked by the accuracy of the facts. This helped the party in doing double-micromanagement and much before the final phases of polling, we were sure that the party would work wonders.' It indeed did.

Nothing Succeeds Like Success

If your only source of information is the media, you will be bound to believe that it was the regime change in SP which led it to the use of professional PR agencies who prepared the TVCs for the party with professional excellence. One more common theme was of the highly positive nature of the campaign, which kept all negative attacks on the Opposition at bay. As a matter of fact it was not the first time that the SP had taken the help of professionals in devising its TVCs and other campaign material. Nor was the 'Ummeed' theme used for the first time in this election. Political commentators remember that in 2007 also, a professional hand was evident in Samajwadi Party TV and print advertisements. Amitabh Bachchan graced those advertisements and the tag line was: 'UP main Mulayam, to Ummeed Kayam (Hope is alive if Mulayam rules UP).' However since the party performed badly in that election, nobody talked of the positive content of those ads but criticized both the SP and Amitabh Bachchan for mocking the people of UP who endured SP's 'jungle raj'. With remarkable success this time, things changed completely.

Change: Perceptional and Real

When the national electronic media was going overboard with Akhilesh Yadav after the magnificent Samajwadi victory in UP, it never tired of talking about the changes which Akhilesh brought about in the party. One such change was in improving the party's record in law and order by 'refusing tickets to criminal elements' to salvage the image of the SP which was considered to be a party of rogue elements till recently. As proof of this, and almost all channels, newspapers and magazines would go into great detail with one and the same story—how Akhilesh refused to give D.P. Yadav an entry into SP despite the mentorship of veteran Azam Khan and spokesperson Mohan Singh in early January 2012. D.P. Yadav, a known history-sheeter (he currently has six cases pending against him including four under sections 302 and 307 of the Indian Penal Code (IPC) and sitting MLA from Sahaswan (in the 2007 assembly) made his political debut with the SP when Mulayam Singh gave him a ticket from Bulandhshahr in 1989. Later, he went to many parties: became an MP on a BJP ticket in 2004; made his own party, Rashtriya Parivartan Dal, in 2007 and joined BSP. However, while the D.P. Yadav part was over-emphasized by the media to back the image projection and 'change' rhetoric of the SP, what was overlooked was the number of criminal politicians who were given tickets by the SP.

Meet Shribhagwan Sharma alias Guddu Pandit, now an MLA from Debai (Bulandhshahr) on an SP ticket who made headlines in 2007 when he defeated Kalyan Singh's son Rajvir Singh from the constituency by a margin of over 15,000 votes; Pandit was in BSP at that time. He made news again in 2008 when his paramour Shital Birla, a research scholar at Agra University accused him of rape, intimidation and fraud. Birla alleged that after an intimate relationship the MLA had married her in a temple, not telling her about the fact that he was already married and had children. When she confronted him, she was threatened, tortured and raped several times. 'He wanted to keep me as his concubine. This was just not acceptable to me,' alleged Shital. An ex-driver of Purvanchal's criminal politician Amarmani Tripathi, his history-sheet was 'officially' destroyed from the Noida police webpage, as the then Noida SSP R.K. Chaturvedi confirmed in 2008: 'The history-sheet of Pandit is not missing. It has been officially destroyed.' On 22 November 2007 Dr C.P. Gupta, principal of DAV College, Bulandhshahr, was stabbed to death by three men in the college premises. Less than a month ago, he had registered a complaint with the police against Guddu Pandit who allegedly threatened to eliminate him if he did not give admission to the students he had recommended. Later the BSP suspended Guddu Pandit and denied him a ticket, after which he joined the SP in August 2011. Defending the decision to take him into the party, Akhilesh and Shivpal Yadav told the media, 'Guddu Pandit has told us that the criminal cases registered against him were politically motivated and the charges levelled were baseless.' Akhilesh Yadav, the 'crusader against criminalization of politics' was speaking a very different language here, for against the six cases registered against D.P. Yadav, Guddu Pandit had thirteen against him. According to Guddu Pandit's election affidavit, many of them were under sections like 376 IPC (rape), 384 IPC (extortion), 364 IPC (abduction in order to murder), 147-48 IPC (rioting), 420 IPC (fraud), and 325 IPC (voluntarily causing grievous hurt). Not only was Guddu Pandit given a ticket but his brother Mukesh Sharma, allegedly his partner in crime, was also given an SP ticket from Shikarpur (Bulandhshahr); both won.

Meet Mehboob Ali, another SP strongman from western UP. Currently an MLA from Amroha (Jyotiba Phule Nagar) on an SP ticket, Ali has fifteen cases against him including two related to use of unfair means in elections under section 171 D and 171 H. Other decorations in his (history) 'sheet of honour' include cases under IPC sections 395 (dacoity), 392 (robbery), 364 (kidnapping in order to murder) and 307 (attempt to murder). Local residents in Amroha claim that there is virtually no big crime that he has not committed. During the course of elections in 2012, an FIR was registered against him and his supporters for allegedly making an attempt on the life of a rival Peace Party candidate in March. After his victory, he was sworn in as minister of state (MoS) for silk and textile in the new SP cabinet. When he reached Amroha after the swearing-in on 18 March, his supporters brandished guns in his victory rally resorting to heavy celebratory firing, after which the police had to register an FIR against them citing law and order issues.

Then there is Abhay Singh. Said to be one of the biggest mafia dons of Poorvanchal, Singh was accused in the murder of the then Lucknow jail superintendent R.K. Tiwari in 1998. During the last SP regime when Abhay Singh was in BSP, he and his supporters blocked the then additional director general of police Umapati Rai's vehicle at Rudauli on the Lucknow-Gorakhpur national highway in Faizabad and threatened him, after which he was arrested. Later in December 2009, Abhay joined SP with his wife and supporters citing 'BSP's takeover by capitalists' as the reason for his change of heart. He was welcomed in the party by Shivpal Yadav, who said, 'the common people never lodged any complaint against Abhay and he was not a criminal but a victim of government's frame up'. The police had suspected Abhay Singh's role in the murders of two CMOs in UP the previous year. According to a report in the *Indian Express*, Abhay Singh's history-sheet (No-1 A) at the Maharajganj police station of Faizabad district shows thirty-two cases pending against him. Out of them, five cases of murder were reportedly registered against him in Lucknow. Surprisingly, his election affidavit shows 'only' eighteen cases against him. The variety of different IPC sections in which these cases are registered is hard to reproduce here due to shortage of space but they virtually include all minor and major sections from the Arms Act to the Gangster Act, attempt to murder, murder and the like. In these elections, he was fielded by SP from Gosainganj (Faizabad) and he defeated his nearest rival, Khabbu Tiwari of BSP by 59,000 votes approximately, polling 122,235 votes.

We will not elaborate this list further with names of people like Raghuraj Pratap Singh alias Raja Bhaiya (against whom SP did not field a candidate) but the names discussed till now have two things in common—all of them had a higher number of cases in comparison to D.P. Yadav and all of them won while Yadav did not. Perhaps this factor, 'winability', was more important for SP than criminal image, for everyone in Badayun was talking of the diminishing impact of D.P. Yadav. In this situation, the SP's decisions appear more calculated than based on noble intentions of cleansing the party.

What is more questionable here is the role of the media. Without raising questions, they took SP's media briefings at face value. They did not try to cross-verify SP's statement of denying tickets to criminals, by checking the criminal credentials of other SP candidates. In their haste to create a hero out of Akhilesh, they resorted to the exercise of 'D.P. Yadav bashing' while showering praise upon Akhilesh Yadav. This also shows the decline in standards of journalism as it avoids hard 'home-work' in the rush to catch hot 'breaking news' thus producing almost similar stories across all channels.

Though there may not have been much difference from 'the good old days' in terms of fielding criminals, the party's image-projection mechanism did succeed in preventing such facts from emerging in common discourse. Added to this, its political initiatives and strategies did hit the bull's eye, and the welfare-focused, people-friendly, development-oriented image of SP under Akhilesh Yadav enabled it to beat all opponents in the final contest.

The Curious Case of the Congress

War Room or Call Centre?

If one were to talk about Congress' war room and Central Control Command in the 2012 UP elections, one would be more concerned about its absence rather than its failure. For unlike SP's two-tiered structure, Congress did not have a sound war room, at least not in the UP elections.

The Congress established a sort of war room in Lucknow in mid-January that was manned by the Poonawala brothers, who had been involved with Congress' media cell in Delhi. But all that the brothers were asked to do was to run an unsophisticated and technologically bankrupt control room that was mainly used to transmit essential information from the central party organization to all its candidates in different parts of the state. Their main task was to coordinate this flow of information via SMS and phone calls.

They had a database of the contact information of all the candidates. If the candidates needed any information on the rules and regulations or the Election Commission's directives, this call centre was to provide them with the relevant information. It did not have any other mandates. They were not involved in planning a campaign, or countering the Opposition's propaganda, or taking real-time feedback and acting upon it. They were just a simple call centre that was used to dispense the limited information they got from the central command. Other than having a centralized team for this, the Congress has a culture of independent, personal teams of big leaders like Rahul Gandhi, Digvijay Singh and state chiefs who operate secretly and are never in sync.

As there was no set or 'institutionalized' mechanism in the Congress to coordinate the feedback from the ground up and counter the Opposition's propaganda, the party and mainly its leader, Rahul Gandhi, suffered. The common people in UP had initially trusted Rahul Gandhi's words and loved the way he came down to their level. After all, in the recent political history of independent India, no other national leader had actually raised the issues of farmers so vehemently and walked on foot for such long distances, as Rahul Gandhi had done in his five-day yatra along the Yamuna Expressway. But the lack of organization and planning was reflected in the fact that none of the Congress spokesmen highlighted this event either while it was happening or later on during the elections. The organization and its communication system (in the form of advertisements) also never highlighted this yatra.

Political commentators, journalists and common people always held the opinion that whatever efforts Rahul Gandhi had been putting in at the grassroots level, could not be taken forward by the organization. A sort of disconnect between the leader and the organization was clearly visible. A lot of people we talked to told us that they trusted Rahul Gandhi but not the Congress candidates for the state: 'Woh to badi badi baatain karke chunav ke baad vapas chale jayenge, humain to yahin rehna hai. Aur yehan par unka koi dhang ka aadmi hi nahin hai (He will go back after making big promises as soon as the elections are over, but we have to live here, and he does not have a single good person here),' a middle-aged farmer told us in Barabanki.

It was only in the much later phases of Rahul Gandhi's campaigns, that he personally tried to address this concern of the people by saying that he would stay in UP even if the party lost the election. But the people were not convinced as by this time, they had made up their minds about who to vote for.

Anti-Incumbency Despite Being Out of Power in State

When people in the Congress-represented parliamentary areas were asked if they were satisfied with their MPs, their replies were mostly in the negative. A sense of dissatisfaction was prevalent among a number of them. The spectacular performance of the Congress in the 2009 Lok Sabha elections in UP resulted in twenty-two MP seats for the party, which was largely because of the farm loan waiver and the Mahatma Gandhi National Rural Employment Guarantee Act (NREGA). Trusting the words of the Gandhi scion, the people of UP had elected turncoats like Beni Prasad Verma and Raj Babbar, even unknown faces like Kamal Kishore Commando, who did not have any political background except for the fact that he was once in the security staff of the Gandhi family. The trust however withered away soon as most of the newly-elected MPs did not bother to even visit their constituencies. Just as in the case of Beni Babu, the people of Moradabad too complained that, after the 2009 elections, Mohammed Azharuddin, the former cricket captain-turned-politician, appeared in Moradabad only during the 2012 elections. Some reported that even the Congress activists in Moradabad were unhappy with him, and had staged a protest against his neglect of the constituency, while others had pasted 'missing' posters carrying his photograph. Those who had trusted the Gandhi scion once were not willing to trust him again, mostly because of the actions of the party's own MPs.

The people of Uttar Pradesh did not return a single MLA from the assembly segments in the parliamentary constituencies of most of the MPs, who they had elected just two and a half years ago. Even the kith and kin of the MPs were not favoured, leave aside their aides or supporters. Wives of three sitting MPs joined the fray—Farrukhabad MP Salman Khurshid's wife Louise Khurshid finished fifth from Farrukhabad, Bahraich MP Kamal Kishore Commando's wife Poonam Kishore finished third in Balha in Bahraich, and Bareilly MP Praveen Aron's wife Supriya Aron lost in Bareilly. Sons of two of the sitting MPs and so-called big leaders of their respective communities lost too. Beni Prasad Verma's son Rakesh Verma came third in Dariyabad and Jagdambika Pal's son Abhishek Pal lost in Basti.

Over all, this was a communication failure. Rahul Gandhi failed to convey to the people of Uttar Pradesh that he had any command over the organization or its people. A tea-stall owner just outside Gonda told us, 'Bhaiyya, ye pradhanmantri jo kuch nahi hai ground pe, woh to inke bas mein hai nahi, kahe nahi petrol-diesel ka kimat rokte hain? Jab use nahi kuch kah sakte tab Beni Babu jaisa neta kaise inki sunega? Yeh unhe chahe jo bana de, woh karenge apni hi (When the PM, who commands no popular support at the ground level is not in their control, as they failed to stop him from raising petrol-diesel prices, how can a leader like Beni Babu be expected to heed their advice? Whatever portfolio they give him, he will do as he wishes).'

A Word with a Congress Old Guard

When you enter the Allahabad Coffee House, the third table on the left is bigger in size. It is actually three tables joined together to seat ten or twelve people at a time. On one of the chairs in the centre sits Jagpat Dubey, the octogenarian Congressman. Jagpat Dubey comes to the coffee house every morning at half-past ten and convenes his 'house' for about an hour. Many established and wannabe leaders join this table for discussions and debates on several issues—local, national and global—which may or may not appear in the day's newspapers. The panwadi in the shop just outside the coffee house told us to meet Jagpat Dubey if we wanted to know the realpolitik of Allahabad. We approached Mr Dubey who was listening to someone arguing about the prospects of BSP in the upcoming elections and the distribution of tickets in the Congress party. He asked us to meet him at another restaurant across the road a little away from the coffee house.

Jagpat Dubey is eighty-two years old but does not appear to be so. Jawaharlal Nehru had gifted him a Willy Jeep that Dubey still drives every day from his home in Civil Lines to the coffee house. During our conversation he told us many stories about Nehru, Indira Gandhi and Rajiv Gandhi, and how the Congress leadership would miss the bus this time too. It was July 2011 and he had already announced the fall of the Grand Old Party in the state. He told us how the present leadership of Gandhis had failed to gather the right people in the party, despite Rahul Gandhi leading a high-decibel campaign. He declared that Rahul Gandhi would never be able to succeed if he continued with the same Doon School coterie around him and that he had even warned Rajiv Gandhi about 'these' people, telling him that they had ulterior motives and would eventually malign his name. Jagpat Dubey had been a constituency representative of Jawaharlal Nehru, Indira Gandhi and Rajiv Gandhi till the time he quit (as representative—he remains a Congressman to this day) in 1987. He was a student leader in Allahabad University and Nehru had set his eyes on him to take care of his work in the constituency. When Nehru asked him to join the party and offered him a salary, Dubey refused. He told Nehru that he came from a landed family and his parents had asked him not to do a naukri (job) so he could not accept any payment for the work. Nehru accepted. He went on to tell us, 'Nehruji knew he was about to die, so a few weeks before he passed away he called me and asked me what I wanted in return for my service. I told him that I wanted to continue serving and look after Priyadarshini's constituency work. He agreed and called Indiraji to say that she should keep me on and take care of me. Congress ka graph kewal hawa mein utha hai, yeh votes mein convert nahi hoga (Congress's graph has gone high only due to hype, and has no connect with the ground reality. It will not get converted into votes).'

According to him, while the present generation in the party lacked the courage to tell Sonia and Rahul Gandhi about ground realities, the Gandhis had no faith in the older generation; the Congress had turned into a 'corporate body' that had lost touch with the common people. At the peak of the election run-up, such words from a Congress old guard were quite startling. Are the Gandhis listening?

The Grand Congress Orchestra: Cacophony not Symphony

Congress and Rahul Gandhi's failure was not so much about the actual work at the ground level as about the lack of communication. They did not have a system in place which could communicate in one tone and language. There were internal differences within the party and among the leaders, which exist in every party. The only difference with the Congress was that it was not able to quell these differences and they spilled out into the open.

Different leaders were speaking in different voices and there was no one who could command them and keep them in line. There was an ongoing war of words between Beni Prasad and P.L. Punia. On the other hand, Prakash Jaiswal was busy in his own world, saying that he would be proud if the party high command designated him as the chief minister of Uttar Pradesh, while in reality the party did not win any seat in Kanpur city, except Ajay Kapoor, who managed to retain his traditional seat.

An arrogant Jaiswal also created a furore when he stated that there would be President's rule in the state if Congress did not come to power. This statement gave the Opposition and the media plenty of ammunition to start Congress-bashing.

This was in stark contrast to BSP and SP, both of which had a very elaborate chain of command and an effective control on the statements of the local leaders. In many instances, the senior SP leadership, like Ram Gopal Yadav, Shiv Pal Yadav and even Azam Khan, had chosen to keep their mouths shut (or were sternly asked to do so), rather than contradict official party positions. Whenever there was any confusion over an issue or a statement, their spokesperson or leaders were asked to quell the doubts and confusion to stop any damage. When there was confusion over D.P. Yadav's inclusion in the Samajwadi Party, Akhilesh Yadav made it a point to clear the air very firmly. They did not shy away from the fact that they are a family-controlled party, removing old guard Mohan Singh at Akhilesh's behest from the official position of spokesperson, though the manner in which it was done was uncalled for but was so smooth that even Mohan Singh could not make any noise about it.

Similarly, everyone knows that the Congress is a party controlled and run by the Gandhi family but in these elections, the Gandhis tried to project it as otherwise by not taking a firm stand on anything, thus making matters worse. Throughout these elections, with no one to control them, the top Congress leaders made speeches as they wished, creating a cacophony of statements in place of a well-practised political symphony, antagonizing many constituencies and attracting none.

When Digvijay Singh declared that the Batla House encounter was fake and injustice had been done, with the intention of attracting a chunk of the minority groups who genuinely felt this way and wanted a judicial inquiry to probe the issue, P. Chidambaram came on air within hours and declared that it was genuine. Then, when Salman Khurshid said that Sonia Gandhi cried after looking at the Batla House encounter photos, Digvijay soon snubbed him, saying that she did not cry. In such a situation, while the Hindus were irritated by the over-use of the Batla House issue, considering it an obvious case of minority appeasement, the Muslims did not feel placated as the home minister of the same party was quite unsympathetic to their concerns. The party thus antagonized both communities and won the support of neither, ending up in a 'lose-lose' situation. There was no clarity even about who the official spokesperson was. The Antony Committee, which was asked by Congress central leadership to probe into the reasons for the UP debacle, mentioned 'controversial campaigning' among other reasons for the poor show.

One could also argue that it was Rahul Gandhi's failure as a leader—he could not keep his party people in control. He looked like a commander who had no control over his forces. Just before the elections, the infighting over ticket distribution grew and newspapers reported Rita Bahuguna Joshi storming out of a meeting in Delhi.

We were sitting at Varanasi's Assi Ghat on the day that the newspapers reported this incident, when we overheard an elderly person, saying, 'Ab iee sab bhi bhav dikhawa lagaa hua, tab bhaiyya hui gaya Rahul Gandhiwa aur uke missun dui hazar bara ka bum-bum (Now even these people are throwing tantrums. It seems now that Rahul Gandhi and his Mission 2012 are destined to doom)!'

This shows that the common folk in the state also felt the leadership's lack of control. And unfortunately, Rahul Gandhi did not have any mechanism in place that could give him such factual information from the grassroots level.

After the elections, the leadership indicated that some heads could be expected to roll for the debacle. However, months have passed since then and nothing has happened. Perhaps this is the Congress style of functioning, where damage control is unheard of and disciplinary action is taken against grounded leaders only, with a number of unpopular, ungrounded and non-performing leaders continuing to cling close to the party organization. A close friend told us about a statement by an important Congress leader (now a Central cabinet minister) about the party. In a personal conversation, the leader had told him, 'You know, the grand old party is like a leviathan. It works at its own pace. You can't make it leave its style and speed up for you, so not getting desperate and restless is the first key. The second key to gain power here is to remain associated for a long time, even if you do nothing. If you follow this advice, it will be very difficult for you not to become an MP or MLA.'

The 'Virtual' Party

The Antony Committee, appointed to find the reasons for Congress's poor performance in the 2012 UP elections also highlighted a 'lack of grounded organization' as one of the reasons. Knowing your status every moment and having a firm control over the situation is the key to electoral success, but Congress lacked an organization in UP to do so. This also severely undermined its performance in another significant aspect of the electoral game—booth management. Anyone who has a little political experience, even at the student's union level in one's college, would know that the most significant part of any election strategy is to bring voters out of their homes to the booth to cast their votes.

Most candidates either have their own mechanism—paid or volunteers from their castes in place, or the party structure helps them manage the booths on polling day. It is usually through the booth-level activists that the candidate or the party knows beforehand which areas in a town or village or which houses in a locality are voting for which party, and they prepare their plans accordingly. At least two or three days before the voting begins, the booth team is ready with parchis (slips) with the names of voters and prepares the voter list of the area in order to bring them out of their houses on the voting day.

While other parties had invested a lot of energy in this, most of the Congress candidates were busy cajoling the senior leaders to bring Rahul Gandhi to their constituencies, thinking that his charisma alone would make them win. Though people turned up in large numbers in his rallies to listen and see Rahul Gandhi out of curiosity, the charisma could not turn the rally turnout in votes.

Rahul Gandhi was a crowd-puller because of the 'Gandhi' surname and because of the antics he had been using, like staying in poor homes, eating with Dalit families and the like. So people wanted to see him and know what he looked like. As far as votes were concerned, the people of Uttar Pradesh were neither confused nor misguided. They had assessed both young leaders—Akhilesh and Rahul—even before the vote for the first phase was over. And from the second, and in some places by the third phase, they knew who was winning and whom they should vote for. They all knew that charisma alone would not give them jobs or even an unemployment allowance (which the lesser 'yuvraj', Akhilesh Yadav, had promised—Rahul Gandhi didn't even speak of that).

Moreover, since all parties give a good amount of money along with the party symbol to their candidates to contest elections, a number of Congress candidates resorted to hired workers to campaign for them, due to the lack of working teams of party cadres at a number of places. The efficiency of such hired workers, who are more concerned with making money in every election, most often does not equal that of committed and experienced party cadres. This time, while the cadre of the SP was desperate to seize power again and was not leaving any stone unturned, knowing full well that they would be doomed in case these elections were lost, this factor was missing in the case of parties like the Congress and the BJP as they had been out of power for too long and their cadre did not have any such motivation or incentive. It may seem incredible to those who see democratic politics as just a part of citizenship rights, but at the local level, it is greatly the favours (tenders, auto-permit licences, political patronage, handling police cases) doled out by political parties to their cadre and workers that matter.

In the absence of an elaborate party structure, frontal organizations like the National Students Union of India (NSUI) or the Indian Youth Congress (IYC) could have eased the party's woes, but the very model on which they were being built in recent times, on the directives of the Gandhi scion, appeared 'impractical' to many activists themselves. One of the young IYC leaders of Kanpur told us, 'Rahul Gandhi chahte hain ki Youth Congress ke worker apne kaam ke liye Youth Congress ka naam aur influence kaam mein na le; tab log hamare pass kyun ayenge? Woh dekhenge ki jab inke kaam hi nahi ho rahe hain to hamare kaam ye kya karayenge? Hamare naam ke peeche to Gandhi nahi laga ki hamare kaam na ruke (They want us to be honest and to not use our influence in getting our or our supporters' work done. Then why would people want to join our organization? They will think that when we can't get our own work done, how can we help them with theirs? After all, there is no Gandhi surname attached to our names to ensure that our work does not get interrupted).'

The 'democratic election system' introduced recently has further worsened the situation. Under the new system, after a membership drive, elections for all IYC or NSUI positions are held, with members voting through secret ballot to elect new office-bearers. The party claimed that this process allowed hard-working and popular leaders to emerge in the organization, but the actual result is completely the opposite. Since the membership drive requires a lot of technicalities and money in the IYC (two-digit membership fee, photos, Xeroxed documents of candidate members along with a lengthy form to be filled by them), most of the rich or influential people make huge investments in the membership drive, paying the fees of all candidates they get enrolled, along with arranging Polaroid cameras and Xerox machines in cars to get the formalities done at the candidates' doorsteps. In return, all they ask for is a vote in the elections. Thus, in this contest, those with scarce resources but more potential are actually left behind. Compare this complicated process with the membership drives of the frontal organizations of other parties, where all you need to do to become a member is pay an annual fee of two or five rupees, and give your name, phone number and address. Whatever Rahul Gandhi and his Delhi lieutenants like Meenakshi Natrajan and Jitendra Singh claim about the successful democratization of the Youth Congress, they cannot give a satisfactory reply as to why most of the 'elected' IYC office-bearers are from political families or from a 'certain' background.

A Team Akhilesh member told us that in every district, all those influential youth activists or leaders who were unhappy about being denied a ticket were told by Akhilesh Yadav himself that they would be accommodated in one profitable avenue or another once the party came to power. The SP leadership is never shy of the fact that the 'cadre-first policy' is how contracts, tenders and privileges are distributed in its rule. The SP, thus, had a very strong cadre that worked hard at the ground level.

The Congress leadership on the other hand, has always been non-committal on these grounds. In the absence of a genuine grounded organization and weak or 'virtually' present frontal organizations, it remained a 'hawai ghoron par sawar' (riding imaginary horses) party. Its election campaign ran primarily through the electronic media and newspapers, with its leaders being remembered mostly for making controversial statements that offended many and soothed none. It is for these reasons that it fought well in the virtual war on the media, but fell flat in the real one that was fought on the ground.

Bharatiya Janata Party

Riding High on an Anti-Corruption Agenda

On 31 March 2010 the Comptroller and Auditor General of India (CAG) said that there were large-scale irregularities in the allocation of 2G licences by the telecom ministry.

On 28 July 2010 the Central Vigilance Commission (CVC) released a report showing irregularities in up to fourteen Commonwealth Games projects, alleging massive corruption and financial irregularities.

On 6 May 2010 the telephonic conversation taped by the income tax department under suspicion of foul play between telecom minister A. Raja and corporate lobbyist Nira Radia was made public by the media. In November 2010, the CAG submitted a report alleging that the government exchequer had suffered a loss of Rs 1,76,000 crore due to corruption in the 2G licence allocation.

All these controversies created a storm on the political scene with the Opposition collectively calling for the head of the UPA II government at the Centre. The BJP saw their opportunity and grabbed it. With these scams of hitherto unprecedented scale rocking the nation, it started talking about the collapse of UPA II and early general elections.

At the same time, allegations of corruption and misuse of public money had started being levelled at the Mayawati government in Uttar Pradesh. The BJP tried to kill two birds with one stone. It decided to launch nationwide anti-corruption rallies called Mahasangram rallies and planned to have a large number of them in Uttar Pradesh as part of its strategy for the 2012 state assembly elections. This line of action was started in Delhi, where the first Mahasangram rally was organized on 22 December 2010. Immediately after this the second rally was organized in Kanpur on 4 February 2011. Though L.K. Advani could not attend this rally due to bad weather, Rajnath Singh and other state leaders addressed this massive rally and its turnout encouraged the party to continue its campaign along the same lines.

A list of one hundred scams that had allegedly taken place in both, Mayawati's and her predecessor Mulayam Singh Yadav's, regimes was released. Mayawati was also charged with involvement in the 2G Spectrum case as the Enforcement Directorate (ED) alleged that her principal secretary Vijay S. Pandey was involved with Hasan Ali, one of the prime accused in the scam.

On 17 April 2011 BJP state unit president, Surya Pratap Shahi, told the media in Varanasi that the issue of corruption taking place in the regimes of the UPA government at the Centre and the BSP-led government in the state would be highlighted as a priority in BJP's poll campaign.

The Meerut Mahasangram rally on 9 April 2011 and the Varanasi Mahasangram rally on 18 April were the next steps in this direction and in terms of crowds, they were a huge success.

At this time the general mood across the nation was against corruption as Anna Hazare was on a hunger strike at the Jantar Mantar in Delhi, demanding a strong Lokpal Bill. Boosted by the success of these rallies, the party decided to tow this line and in the Meerut rally, Surya Pratap Shahi said that BJP would fight the next elections alone, without forming alliance with any other party.

Finally on 27 August 2010, after a two-day marathon meeting of top leaders at the Delhi residence of the former national president of the party, Rajnath Singh, the BJP declared that it would fight the 2012 UP elections on the issues of corruption, crime and lawlessness.

The party did not miss a single chance to highlight the issue of corruption, portraying itself as a champion of anti-corruption forces. It raised a hue and cry at the national level and all over UP when Baba Ramdev's agitation was forcefully suspended by the Delhi police at midnight on 4 June at the Ramlila Maidan. BJP also attempted to cash in on the next anti-corruption stir launched by Anna Hazare in August 2011 at a number of places in Uttar Pradesh; BJP activists took to calling themselves Anna supporters, actively joining and leading such protests. However, such issues could not be dragged on for eternity in politics, especially during electoral contests marred by identity and welfare agendas, and both BJP and Anna learnt this the hard way.

BJP Takes Refuge in the Rath

On 13 October 2011, BJP leader Lal Krishna Advani launched a nation-wide anti-corruption rath yatra with the intention of bringing BJP back at the Centre. The party simultaneously launched two parallel Jan Swabhiman Rath Yatras (public esteem chariot marches) in Uttar Pradesh, intended to bring BJP to power in the state. While one yatra started at Varanasi under the leadership of Kalraj Mishra, Rajnath Singh led the other one from western UP. According to BJP state president Surya Pratap Shahi, the yatra was to be launched in two phases—from 13-22 October and 9-17 November—with the objective of unmasking the Mayawati government that was involved in large-scale corruption and other misdeeds. The plan was that the yatra would go through 61 districts, 370 state assembly constituencies and reach around 4.31 crore voters, covering a distance of around 5,000 kilometres to finally conclude in Ayodhya at the 'Vijay Sankalp Samagam Sammelan' in November.

Other than these, Uma Bharti also wanted to launch a Ganga Bachao Yatra (Save Ganga Yatra) that was supposed to take place mostly through boats, with the purpose of winning the trust of the Mallah and Nishad (fishermen castes of UP) communities. However, due to internal rivalry and indifference of senior party leaders, who did not want to give her much exposure, the yatra could not take place. Later during the elections when Uma Bharti tried to start her yatra again, she could not do so because of the restriction by the Election Commission. Though the party succeeded in energizing its cadre to some extent through these yatras, in the absence of any popular appeal and grounded booth-level preparation, it failed to make any difference in the electoral contest.

Targeting All and Hitting None: The Case of 'Bhay Bhook Bhrashtachar' Campaign

BJP was one of the first parties to take professional help in election management and PR campaigning and most of the credit goes to the late Pramod Mahajan. Continuing with the August 2011 declaration that the party would contest these elections on the central theme of corruption, crime, and lawlessness; The Hive, an agency that has been designing BJP's campaign lines since 1998 was given the task of chalking out party slogans around this theme. Making good governance its USP and hitting all vices of all three adversaries in one line, the party banked on the slogan, 'Na Ugahi, Na Gundayi, Na Bhrashtachar, BJP Degi Saaf Suthri Sarkar (No extortion, no hooliganism, no corruption, BJP promises good governance).' While a dig was made at BSP by pointing a finger at the massive government-sponsored extortion during Mayawati's regime, SP and Congress were attacked for the hooliganism and corruption during their respective regimes. The catch-line was accompanied with the photographs of Atal Bihari Vajpayee to symbolize good governance and a decent image of the party through a moderate and acceptable face.

One other strategy was devised by BJP to counter Congress' campaign of consistently attacking BJP's 'India Shining' campaign in speeches and statements. In Congress' advertisements of Sochiye Jara (think a bit) people from different sections of society would talk of its welfare programmes asking voters to think what more could be accomplished if they brought Congress to power in UP. Countering it, BJP brought in 'Humne to Soch Liya' (we have made a decision), which showcased the successful governments of BJP in Madhya Pradesh, Gujarat and other states, ending with people from different walks of life saying they had decided to vote for BJP. Talking about the campaign, Sushil Pandit of The Hive told the media, 'We are not promising the moon in our advertisements but just plain and simple good governance.'

This virtual mode of rivalry through attacks and counter-attacks in advertisements may be interesting for corporate houses or ad professionals, but the villages and towns of Uttar Pradesh did not give these gimmicks a second thought. It made no difference to their lives, as no concrete assurance for their future was offered. The campaign line lacked a positive orientation and whatever promises of good governance were made to them, they could not understand what it meant other than a disavowal of the vices of the other parties—SP, BSP and Congress. Finally, by attacking all opponents in one go, the party lost its focus and ended up looking rather confused instead.

Other than this, people also rejected BJP's brand of 'copy-cat' welfare-ism. When SP declared that they would give free laptops and tablets to tenth and twelfth grade students in its agenda, after criticizing it initially, BJP too declared the same, with one difference. In its agenda, the party promised to give the tablets and laptops to the same set of people at a cost of Rs 3,000 and Rs 5,000 respectively. However, despite these announcements, the party failed to make any difference. The people of Uttar Pradesh refused to take the sub-standard 'duplicate' (BJP) when the 'original' (SP) was available to them and that too for free.

History Repeats Itself as Tragedy: Ram Mandir Fails BJP

The Ram Mandir agitation which was aggressively started by BJP since the mid-1980s is considered the primary reason for their rise to the upper echelons of power both at the Centre and in UP. BJP raised the issue of the construction of a Ram temple at Lord Ram's assumed birthplace in Ayodhya where the Babri Masjid was built by Mughal emperor Babar in the 16th century, allegedly by demolishing the original Ram temple. Its aggressive posturing on this issue and success in communalizing the majority voters helped the party in getting a clear majority in UP in 1991 but the demolition of the Babri Masjid by karsevaks (volunteers) on 6 December 1992 alienated the party in political circles for years to come.

The temple issue continues to appear in party manifestos and speeches of leaders, election after election, and the party has continued talking of building a grand Ram temple at the disputed site, come what may. However, a substantial change took place this time.

On 30 September 2010 while giving its judgement on the future of the disputed site at Ayodhya, the three-judge special bench comprising Justice S.U. Khan, Sudhir Agarwal and D.V. Sarma of Allahabad High Court ruled that the disputed land be divided into three parts—with the central portion being declared as Lord Ram's birthplace, the second portion being given to the Wakf Board and the third to Nirmohi Akhara. This ended all roadblocks in the path to building a Ram temple at the disputed site and robbed BJP of the agenda that had characterized it. Now it became impossible for it to fan the passions of Hindus by pitching the temple issue to polarize Hindu votes in its favour. Despite this change in the situation, BJP decided to give the temple one more try.

On 26 April 2011, BJP organized its Mahasangram rally at Faizabad. The assembly constituency which consists of Faizabad city is called Ayodhya and the disputed site comes under this constituency. Since 1991, BJP's Lallu Singh Chauhan has been winning this seat. The Mahasangram rally was addressed by BJP's national president Nitin Gadkari, state president Surya Pratap Shahi, firebrand Hindu leader and national vice-president Vinay Katiyar, Ravi Shankar Prasad and Kalraj Mishra. Dropping the campaign line of making Mayawati's misrule a central issue, all leaders took refuge in the temple issue once again.

The first to start talking about this issue was Gadkari, who stated that Tuesday was the proudest day of his life as he finally had the privilege of visiting the Ram Lalla temple. Playing the temple card once again he pledged before the assembled people that the 'displaced deity' would be housed in a magnificent temple beyond the Panch Kosi Parikrama Marg, asking 'others' (Muslims) to cooperate in the good work. However, even if they did not 'cooperate' the task would be completed at all costs, said BJP's national president.

Banking upon the old RSS strategy of portraying Hindus as an exploited community, enslaved for hundreds of years (first by Muslims and then by the British) Surya Pratap Shahi told the people how 'upset' he was at 'beholding the token of slavery', when he visited Ayodhya before 1992. Indirectly commending the demolition of the disputed structure in 1992, he expressed satisfaction over the fact that the 'token of slavery' was no longer there. He added that the scenario in Mathura and

Kashi continued to cause him pain, implying that the disputed structure in Mathura and Kashi needed to meet the same fate. Vinay Katiyar was at his best in the rally. 'Babar got the mosque constructed by using brute force,' he thundered, asserting that, 'We will build the Ram temple at the spot by resorting to the same method.' He also promised that he was ready to sacrifice everything for this objective.

What was puzzling here was the fact that after the court order, the path for constructing the Ram temple at the proposed site was clear and not much 'force' or 'sacrifice' as suggested by the BJP leaders was required. BJP however refused to acknowledge the fact. Releasing its manifesto on 27 January 2012 in Lucknow, the party again reiterated the issue of building a grand temple at Ayodhya in the hope that like old times, history would repeat itself and the temple issue would help leverage BJP hopes. However, this time BJP won only forty-seven seats against fifty-one in 2007. It also suffered a below-the-belt blow in Ayodhya, where Lallu Singh Chauhan, its sitting MLA since 1991, lost for the first time to SP's young face Tej Narayan Pandey alias Pawan by approximately 5,000 votes.

The Fall of the Divided House

'Bharatiya Janata Party has fifty-five chief ministerial candidates,' said BJP leader and Pilibhit MP Varun Gandhi while talking to NDTV in February 2012. Though Mr Gandhi later tried to deny this, saying his words were fabricated, this insider's statement characteristically defines the internal situation of BJP in the state, amid a very crucial election. BJP always opposed the 'dynastic rule' of Congress and other parties and believed in plural leadership and internal democracy. However, the unabated development of this plural leadership within the party in UP led to a situation where there was virtually no central leadership that could unite the different camps within the BJP. Infighting within BJP's UP unit has been going on for years; when Kalyan Singh was chief minister of the state, he had allegedly conspired to get his own party leaders defeated in the 1998 general elections. Not being in power for years in UP, the aged leadership of the BJP had grown so desperate that the moment it got a chance of having a say in the state, the party leaders immediately start fighting for hypothetical future benefits if the party were to win.

The same situation emerged this time too, prior to the polls. As soon as some political pundits started saying that BJP would hopefully do better in 2012 due to the anti-BSP sentiment, weak Congress and SP's goondaraj still fresh in public memory, different BJP leaders started laying claim to the chief ministership, trying to underplay claims from other camps. In May 2010 itself, when Surya Pratap Shahi was appointed the state unit's president, from the very first day of his appointment he tried to 'set up' his people with important positions within the party, throwing out people of other factions, thus inviting the wrath of the Vinay Katiyar, Lalji Tandon, Kalraj Mishra and Rajnath Singh camps. Then there was Yogi Adityanath of Gorakhpur (who is said to be more of a Thakur leader and less a BJP leader) who never missed a chance to fire a salvo against the senior leadership to show his own worth. *Amar Ujala*'s Lucknow edition did an eight-column story on the infighting within BJP in May 2011 and its title beautifully conveyed the real situation in eight words: Apnaun ko hi niptane main nipat rahi bhajpa (BJP is getting settled in the wake of leaders settling each other).

Uma Bharti was re-inducted into the BJP by the high command on 7 June 2011 to revitalize the faction-ridden party in Uttar Pradesh. Bharti was brought back into the fold after a five-year hiatus and the party tried to project her as a clean, outside face and a future chief ministerial candidate, but the greatest opposition to her came from within BJP itself. First

Gadkari and later on 24 January 2012, senior BJP leader Sudheendra Kulkarni said that Uma would be the future chief minister of Uttar Pradesh if BJP came to power. The BJP old guard in the state raised its swords against this statement, as in 2011 the party had projected Kalraj Mishra as the candidate for chief ministership.

The BJP also lagged behind other parties in poll preparations. Out of the four major parties, it declared its candidates after everybody else had declared theirs. That it is a divided party with desperate oldies fighting for some imaginary gains, became a joke in political circles. The infection that had marred the party for more than a decade ultimately became gangrenous and the BJP finally got 'settled' in the 'score-settling' game that its leaders were playing against each other.

In Poorvanchal which is considered a BJP stronghold and which has important party leaders like Surya Pratap Shahi, Ramapati Ram Tripathi, and Keshri Nath Tripathi, BJP performed poorly. People rejected the factional satraps of the BJP here. While both Ramapati and Shahi lost from Siswa (Maharajganj) and Pathardeva (Deoriya) respectively, Keshri Nath polled third in Allahabad. Such was the situation that Yogi Adityanath was making a greater effort to make Fateh Bahadur Singh (a Thakur) of the NCP (Nationalist Congress Party) win at Campiyarganj (Gorakhpur), rather than his own party's candidate. As a result, BJP finally won only three out of the nine Gorakhpur seats. The situation in Awadh was the same. Lucknow became the centre of a political tug-of-war between BJP leaders with Lalji Tandon and Kalraj Mishra claiming to be the Kshatrapas of Lucknow.

Lucknow is considered a BJP citadel as it was the parliamentary constituency of ex-prime minister Atal Bihari Vajpayee. However, the infighting cost BJP dear this time and it won only one out of the nine Lucknow seats, while Lucknow MP Lalji

Tandon's son, Ashutosh Tandon 'Gopalji' came third in Lucknow (North). This was the first time since 1991 that BJP's tally in the Lucknow district was less than four seats.

The only two areas where BJP performed well were Bundelkhand and western UP, regions where BJP didn't have any 'tall leaders'. In the dry-lands of Bundelkhand, which was left to Uma Bharti and where no other 'would-be-chief minister' of BJP was interested to go, BJP won three out of nineteen seats; in the last elections it had won none. In western UP and Rohilkhand, BJP won nineteen seats and this area became BJP's saving grace. The only area in the west that has an important BJP leader is Ghaziabad—Rajnath Singh is an MP here. The results—BJP won none of the eight seats in Ghaziabad and Hapur.

The senior state BJP leadership finally proved that it was worthless. It is obvious that if the party wants to make a comeback in UP, it needs to develop a fresh leadership, with a new orientation and newer vision towards politics and people.

The Muslim OBC Quota Row

In an attempt to gain lost ground in UP by attracting Muslims, the Congress promised 4.5 percent sub-quota for Muslim OBCs within the 27 percent OBC quota just two days before the declaration of the election schedule. The Election Commission intervened to stop the Congress leaders from making such declarations during their poll speeches citing the code of conduct. However, a desperate Congress refused to comply. Trying to show their commitment to the community, its leaders adopted a ridiculously aggressive and unnecessarily stubborn posture. Leading this was the Union Law Minister Salman Khurshid, who dared the Election Commission to stop him from 'working for the welfare of the Muslims'. In an election meeting in February in Farrukhabad, his wife Louise Khurshid's constituency, he asserted that he would ensure that the Pasmanda (backward Muslims) get their share, even if the EC 'hangs' him. Though nobody at the meeting seemed moved by these theatrics, a clearly emotional Louise was seen wiping her tears at the possibility of her husband's 'supreme sacrifice'. Continuing this tradition, Beni Prasad Verma, while addressing a meeting in February in the same Farrukhabad district in the presence of Salman Khurshid and the Congress general secretary Digvijay Singh said, 'Reservation for Muslims will be increased and if the EC wants, it can now issue a notice to me.' Such arrogance failed to make a good impression on the voters or other parties.

Seeing an opportunity to polarize the Hindu OBCs, the BJP jumped into the sub-quota controversy pledging to do away with any attempts to 'deprive' the Hindu backward castes of their 'rightful share'. An advertisement frequently appeared in newspapers on BJP's behalf where the division of the share of Hindu OBCs in the 27 percent quota that was proposed by the Congress was shown as a chapatti.

The whole jamboree of BJP's OBC leaders ranging from Uma Bharti to Vinay Katiyar made repeated attacks on the Congress, which happily replied back in the same tone. Both parties hoped that the issue would help them in polarizing Hindu and Muslim OBCs in their favour, leaving SP and BSP at the losing end.

However, SP proved to be far smarter, promising a separate 18 percent quota for Muslims and not dividing the pre-existing 27 percent OBC quota, providing a fair solution for both communities. This finally worked as evident from the results, while the divisive politics of BJP and Congress failed to make an impact on Muslims and OBCs.

Despite the election loss it is good news for Mr Khurshid in one respect; if SP maintains its 18 percent separate minority quota promise, he need not 'sacrifice' his life for the 'kismat of the garib (lot of the poor)'.

Bahujan Samaj Party

Sarkari Stamp on the Campaign

The Bahujan Samaj Party is an ideological party and its campaign line reiterates the Dalit-Bahujan agenda. The songs and audio campaign cassettes of the party have always reflected this agenda and its audio campaign cassettes were the best this time around too. Some of the songs were sung by renowned singer Kailash Kher. However, when it came to TV commercials, the sarkari stamp on them was quite visible. The TVCs virtually lacked any creativity; they were like the advertisements made on bulk contracts by government departments for upcoming welfare schemes. All of them included a heavy dose of data regarding progress during Mayawati's tenure. While a background voice narrated these figures, most of the screen time was dedicated to either the monuments or parks built by the government or to Mayawati herself. Mayawati's 'hero worship' was also evident here: she would be shown in different poses—sitting, reading, signing files, walking, looking skywards like a visionary and so on. The BSP functionaries and sycophants might have been awe-struck by these ads, but the people found nothing awe-inspiring or interesting in them.

Another theme of the BSP's ads was 'Shukriya Behenji' (Thank you Behenji). In these ads, people from different walks of society, such as Muslims, sugarcane farmers, students and so on talked about how Behenji had done so much for them, concluding the ads with a 'Shukriya Behenji'.

The party's decision to convert government policies into ad films and print ads exhibited a sarkari attitude of being non-creative and these ad campaigns failed to give any perceivable advantage to the ruling BSP.

BSP's print ads were very much like the UP government ads that were seen at all the government offices in the state. Along with a large photograph of Mayawati, these ads included hundreds of lines talking about government schemes in such a small font that it was impossible for anyone to read and understand anything from a distance. It needed a couple of minutes to understand what was written and the general voters clearly did not feel the need to do so. As far as Mayawati's photos were concerned, people were habituated to seeing them over the last five years and they no longer held any fascination for them. Though the party officially denied the need to hire professional PR agencies, it was reported in some newspapers that the services of a local ad agency, Isha, had been engaged on a low-cost basis. The quality of the ads only gave credence to this theory.

Although the ad campaign was a reflection of the casual attitude of BSP towards the voters, there were many more significant reasons that led to BSP's decline in these elections. How did a party, which was the beacon of hope for the people of UP, just five years ago, turn so villainous? What had failed the thus far invincible Mayawati in her ambitions? How did the 'future PM' Mayawati get reduced to just another Rajya Sabha MP within such a short period? These are some of the bigger questions that need to be answered in any analysis of the 2012 UP elections in a detailed manner. We will try to answer them in the next chapter.

In Lieu of a Conclusion

Booth and the Basta—Actual Drill on the Polling Day

As discussed earlier, booth committee management is a *sine qua non* for any successful election. Experienced and grounded parties generally conduct their booth-level committee meetings two to three months before the election campaign. A basic drill is followed to manage the booth committees across the country.

The booth committee comprises five to six local people of the area where the polling booth is located. At any given time at least three people are present in the booth. While the polling agent of the party or candidate sits inside the booth, keeping an eye on the proceedings in order to check for any discrepancies, two to three people sit outside the booth (generally at a desk with relevant documents like the electoral roll) to assist their voters and keep a tab on who has come to vote and who has not. This information is passed on to the other members of the team working in the locality, who go to the homes of missing supporters and bring them to the booth to cast their votes. Earlier, the outer-desk team would also give a slip to their voters, tearing it from the electoral rolls, which would say that their name appears on so and so page, so that the poll officials could allow the voter to vote without wasting much time in searching for their names. However, this time this task was undertaken by the Village Development Officer (VDO), thus freeing the desk team of the booth committee from this job.

The inside polling agent's job is very important as he is the only person inside the booth to check any malpractice. He needs to fill a form for this purpose, which is authorized by the presiding officer of the booth and this whole process needs to be completed well before 7 a.m. on the polling day, thus making it necessary for the agent to be committed enough to reach the booth early in the morning. Some extra manpower is also required to replace the working team during refreshment, breaks and so on.

To sum up, a booth committee is the basic mechanism that translates one's popular support into concrete votes, and only in the situation of an extreme wave can a party or candidate win without having efficient booth management. Further, if one party or candidate has efficient booth committees throughout its constituency, it can even calculate the approximate number of votes it has polled prior to the results.

The phone numbers of the main people at all booths are made available at the assembly war room by the party leadership. The phone numbers of all the concerned administrative and police officers of the assembly constituency are also listed. The constituency war room remains in direct contact with the state or zonal war room. Talking to activists at every booth, it gathers information regarding the conduct of polling and passes the same information to the state or zonal war room. If any problem or threat comes up, the booth-level committee reports it to the constituency war room, which passes the information to the relevant administrative and police officers asking them to take action. The same information is also passed on to the higher war rooms from where the senior leaders of the party interact with state level officers to ensure proper action in this regard. It is for these reasons that, on polling day, a large section of the senior leadership remains glued to their phones, tracking the management of elections through their respective war rooms.

'Basta' is the most important component of the booth management system. Prior to polling every party arranges two copies of the electoral rolls, stationery, relevant forms for the polling agents and so on in a bundle to be sent to all the booths. These bastas are given to the booth-level party unit two to three days before polling begins so that relevant arrangements for the poll day can be made. Some veterans have told us that every basta also includes some money so that arrangements for liquor, refreshment for the team, bribes/incentives for voters, and conveyance expenses can be made on the night before the polling day.

Almost all parties spend money on this count but it is effectively spent only by grounded parties as it is their committed booth-level activists who make sure that the money is used efficiently, and at the right place. On the other hand, when parties do not have an efficient grounded organization, a number of fake workers at the booth level spring up to lay claim to the basta, because of the money involved. Such people eat up the money and do nothing for the party. Sometimes, people from grounded parties ask their people to lay claim on the basta of such 'hawai' parties. These dummy workers enter the booth as agents of the 'hawai' party they have targeted but once inside, act in favour of their original party.

It is on this count that parties like Congress and BJP lost to BSP and SP and it is for these reasons that a grounded organization is required to make a difference in electoral contests.

PART THREE

WHY THE JUMBO CRASHED

Yamuna Expressway:
The Road to Despair, Destitution and Deaths

This chapter is the story of BSP's downfall in the 2012 assembly elections. It tries to explore how Mayawati, the invincible chief minister of UP, failed in recapturing power once again in the state. It engages with the question as to how all the factors that led to BSP's historic win in the 2007 assembly elections failed to work this time. Since there is a specific chapter on social engineering and caste-community calculations in UP, the failure of her social engineering will not be dealt with here. But other than that, this chapter tries to go into detail about how Mayawati's Jumbo finally crash-landed this time, reducing the once 'would-be PM' to just another political leader in UP.

*

On the evening of 14 August 2010, fourteen-year-old Prashant Sharma was ironing his clothes at home in his village for his school's Independence Day function the next day, unaware of the imminent tragedy. Suddenly, a call went through the village, 'Neta kaun uthay lao, neta kaun uthay lao (The leader has been taken away)'. The 'neta' was Ram Babu Kateliya, a Jat peasant leader from Mathura who was sitting on a dharna in Tappal (Aligarh district). It was an agitation by farmers demanding greater compensation for their lands which were being taken away for the Yamuna Expressway and Tappal Township projects of the Jaypee group.

Jaypee group, a corporate house owned by Jai Prakash Gaur who is said to be close to Mayawati, was given the contract to build a multi-lane 165-kilometre expressway between Greater Noida and Agra. As it was a build-operate-transfer (BOT) contract, Jaypee did not charge anything to build it but received the right to collect toll on the road for thirty-five years before handing it back to the government. More importantly, the UP government agreed to give it 6,000 acres of land on either side of the road on a ninety-year lease to develop townships at five locations: two in Gautam Buddh Nagar (Greater Noida) and one each in Noida, Aligarh and Agra. The corporate house plans to build residential and office complexes, an international airport and a luxurious sports complex on this land. Jaypee's executive chairman Manoj Gaur says that the development of these projects could yield Rs 135,000 crores in revenues over the next twenty years. Political commentators allege that other than the Jaypee group, some BSP leaders were also going to share these huge profits. One such township was proposed near Tappal.

The farmers who were supposed to lose their land in the project were never consulted. The BSP government invoked the Land Acquisition Act 1894 to acquire the land. This was the same infamous colonial law which had been used in Singur and Nandigram (West Bengal) to acquire agricultural land for industrial projects, leading to widespread protests and, finally, the ouster of the CPI(M)-led Left front government after thirty-five years in power.

'We came to know about this thing only when the lekhpals (revenue officers) started showing up, telling us that our land is going to be taken for the project and we have to sign and give it away,' said Raju Sharma, an affected farmer. The farmers challenged this in the Allahabad High Court but could not get a judgement in their favour. With this setback in the high court, some 30 percent of the agitating farmers gave up their land and signed the papers. Charged with these victories and confident of the patronage of the UP government, the Jaypee group destroyed ready, standing crop in the fields of non-complying farmers with bulldozers. Some farmers then filed a petition in the Supreme Court but that too did not make any difference. Left with no choice, the farmers started a dharna at Tappal in July 2010 led by Ram Babu Kateliya.

The farmers demanded higher compensation, highlighting the discrepancies in the system. 'Yahan ek varg metre ka 436 rupaye mil raha tha, lekin bagal main Noida jile main usi jamin ka lagbhag 700 rupaye diya ja raha tha. Kai jagah to aisa tha ki khet ke is taraf ki jamin 436 main, aur us taraf 700 main li ja rahi thi. Hum baraabari chahte the (The compensation for one square metre of land was Rs 436 here, but it was approximately Rs 700 in Noida. At some places, land on one side of the field was being taken for Rs 436 while that on the other side it was being taken for Rs 700. We wanted parity),' said Jai Narayan Sharma, a Tappal resident.

Another point of dispute was the fact that the farmers were not ready to give up all their land. 'Hum byapari nai hain, paisa te paisa banano nai janta hain. Paisa ke badle sari jamin de denge to khayenge kahan te, kyunki paisa tau kha pi ke khatam kar dego kisan (We are not businessmen, we don't know how to make money from money. If we sell all our land in return for money then how will we feed ourselves? This compensation money will be spent very soon).'

Highlighting the truth in the statement, Ghanshyam, another affected farmer, spoke about a number of farmers who had taken the compensation money and had already spent almost half of it in building houses, on marriages or other lavish expenditures.

Further, the farmers objected strongly against giving their land for real estate townships. 'Hum bhi desh ka vikas chahte hain, sadak ki jamin to humne bina na-nukur ke de di, lekin raison ke bungley banane ke liye hum apne khet kyun dain (We too want the development of the nation and gave the land meant for the expressway without raising a problem, but why should we give up our fields for the bungalows of the rich)?'

For all these reasons, the farmers thought that they were fighting for the right cause and the agitation started picking up momentum. Work on the project site had to be stopped due to furious protests, causing a daily loss of millions to the Jaypee group. It pulled some strings in the government asking for police action to crush the protests. On the evening of 14 August 2011 when most of the farmers had returned to their villages in the evening for their daily chores, the police and RAF (Rapid Action Force) under the leadership of Tappal station officer Udaiveer Singh forcibly removed Kateliya from the dharna spot.

As soon as the news of this incident reached the farmers of nearby villages, they geared up to protest, marching towards the dharna site. The youth and children reached there ahead of the elders and when the police did not allow them to go near the actual dharna site, a stone pelting contest started between both the parties. With clear briefs from the government to crush the movement, the police later resorted to firing, killing three protesters. A policeman was also killed, while a boy, Rafiq, went missing, thus raising the toll to five. Out of the three protesters who were killed, two were children below fourteen years of age, Prashant being one of them. He was in the fifth standard at that time.

The next day as the news of the killings spread, thousands of farmers from the affected and other neighbouring villages reached the venue. Later, under heavy political pressure the government agreed to increase the compensation amount to Rs 570 per square metre, while earlier it had not been ready to give more than Rs 450 per square metre. An ex-gratia compensation of Rs 10 lakh for the families of all three victims (and for Rafiq's family, whose body was never found) was also announced.

Similar protests on the issue of greater compensation sprang up at other places through which the expressway was going to be laid. In Agra, Mathura and Gautam Budh Nagar (Noida) farmers came out onto the streets, blocked highways and resorted to arson, demanding greater compensation or refusing to give up their lands for posh housing projects meant for rich people.

The Bhatta-Parsaul case of Jewar district made it to the national headlines in May when a violent confrontation between the protesting farmers and police led to the death of four people on both sides. 'We were being paid Rs 800 for one square metre but the government was selling the same land for Rs 6,000 per square metre. Was that justified?' asked Ravinder Singh Malik of Parsaul village.

Manveer Singh Tewatiya led the protest here. On 7 May 2011, when the protesting farmers took a UP Roadways bus driver and conductor hostage, police resorted to the heavy use of force, thus leading to four casualties, two from both sides. After this, the police laid siege on both villages, not allowing anyone to leave or enter.

On 11 May 2011, Rahul Gandhi sneaked into the villages early in the morning, riding on a motorcycle with Congress' would-be candidate from Jewar, Dhirendra Singh. The national media rushed to cover the incident and so did the UP police, which arrested Rahul Gandhi later in the evening. The issue became a turf war for settling political scores between different parties, and in the clamour, the original demands of the farmers were forgotten. Later, under pressure from all quarters, the Mayawati government raised the compensation by an average of 60 percent and an ex-gratia compensation of Rs 10 lakhs was given to the families of the dead. A government order was also issued, promising that the lands of unwilling farmers would not be taken forcefully.

When we reached Tappal just before the elections, we found that work on the Yamuna Expressway township was at a standstill. People informed us that only a small number of farmers who had not given up their land remained, but they were facing threats to comply. Many of them had received notices from an enquiry commission (set up to enquire about this incident) in Lucknow, asking them to come and present their views before the commission. However, no travel allowance was promised to them. The farmers at Jehangarh, an affected village, were very apprehensive. 'Yadi je sarkar aai gai, tau kisan phir maaro jayego (If this government comes to power again, then the farmers will be penalized again),' said one farmer.

Being a largely Brahmin dominated village, the residents of Jehangarh are mostly BJP voters but they decided not to vote for BJP this time. 'Hum vote barbaad nai karenge, jo BSP kau harayego tai vote denge, je hatyari sarkar nai aani chahiye phir (We will not waste our votes, but will vote for whoever can defeat BSP. This murderous government must not come to power again).'

In the Khair (SC) assembly constituency in which the affected village of Tappal falls, this tactical voting by the farmers and other common people led to the victory of the RLD candidate Bhagwati Prasad who secured 93,470 votes, defeating BSP's Rajrani by more than 39,000 votes.

Prashant's father, Chandrapal Sharma, is determined that he will not give up his land come what may. His greatest concerns, as of now, are securing a job for his eldest son Jai Kishore, who has studied up till the 12th standard, and marrying off his four daughters. When we asked Prashant's mother Ramwati about the incident, she started crying, 'Sab hamai hi galti hai bhaiyya jo humne jameen daibe tai mana karo), woh to becharo choudeh saal ko baalak tho jo tamasho dekhbe chalo gao, baane to kisi ko kuch nai bigaro tho, phir kaye maar dalo bai (It is all our fault that we refused to give our land. He was a mere kid of fourteen years who went to see what was going on. He had not harmed anyone, then why did they kill him)?'

On the question of the government's compensation she had this to say, 'Inke dus lakh ke badle main inhe pachis lakh dungi, puri jindagi chahe bhik maang ke dun lekin dungi, je ka mero ladika wapas kar denge badle main (I am ready to give them twenty-five lakhs in return for their ten lakhs, even if I have to beg my entire life, but can they return my boy alive to me)?'

She said that her only wish now was to see the fall of BSP's 'hatyari sarkar' (murderous government).

Witnessing this agony of a mother, we felt a sense of helplessness and grief. We could imagine that there were innumerable people who had suffered such atrocities at the hands of Behenji's government at different places in the state. At that moment we had a very strong intuition that BSP wouldn't be able to make it again this time in Lucknow. Eventually, it did not.

From Bahujan to F1: Hobnobbing with Big Business

The instances of political parties supporting and acting as a corporate group's strongmen are not rare. On 7 July 2006, the then SP government of Mulayam Singh Yadav had resorted to heavy police action against the farmers of Bajhera Khurd, Dadri (Ghaziabad) who had demanded a higher compensation for their land. Their land was being taken for Anil Ambani's proposed 8,000 MW gas-based power plant in Dadri. Mulayam's government had acquired 2,500 acres of land on Ambani's behalf citing 'public purpose' but later under political pressure he had to back down.

Though the Yamuna Expressway and the SP-Ambani combine appear similar, as a continuation of the politician-corporate houses nexus, the former is quite different in some ways. It was not an exception in the BSP regime but a persistent phenomenon. It also shows how Behenji, who once spoke of the sufferings of the Dalits and the common people, gradually distanced herself from them, aligning herself more and more with the select few who had better resources. Jaypee group's chairman Jaiprakash Gaur and Wave Inc' slate Gurdeep Singh, alias Ponty Chadha, are two of the most prominent luminaries of that selective coterie. After the fall of BSP regime, Ponty Chadha managed to develop a good rapport with the SP government as well and continued to enjoy state patronage. However, his life came to a tragic end in November 2012 when he was killed with his brother in a shootout at his own farmhouse at Chhattarpur (Delhi).

In the case of Jaypee's expressway, Mayawati's government not only acted as the agent of a private company in procuring agricultural land, but also as its strongman in crushing all opposition to it, be it at Tappal or at Bhatta-Parsaul or Agra or Mathura. The same situation was repeated in Karchana (Allahabad), where the police firing upon protesting farmers on 21 January 2011 left one dead and several injured. These farmers were demanding greater compensation for their lands, which were being taken for a power plant the Jaypee group proposed to build.

With strong connections within the government, this corporate house flourished in UP, most of the time at the cost of the common people. The group, whose revenue grew at the pace of 5.9 percent between 2001-02 and 2006-07, shot up to 33.5 percent between 2006-07 and 2010-11 under BSP's rule. Samajwadi Party spokesperson, Rajendra Chowdhury, alleged that Jaypee was favoured brazenly during BSP's rule and procedures were bent for them, because Mayawati's brother Anand Kumar had benami shares in the group.

Instead of caring about the funding of needy sports persons in UP, the Mayawati government went on to promote the Formula One races in Greater Noida, a game well beyond the reach of millions of people in the state. The contract for organizing this was given to the Jaypee group, which named the racing track 'Buddha International Circuit', to please its political masters. A more-than-pleased Mayawati not only awarded trophies to the winners herself, but also relieved the Jaypee group from paying entertainment tax, thus again giving them a sop worth crores of rupees.

The other big beneficiary of the Mayawati government's patronage was the late Ponty Chadha. In an exceptional move in 2009, the Mayawati government handed Chadha's company the wholesale rights to distribute liquor in UP as opposed to the traditional system of district-wise bidding. Making full use of this favour, Chadha resorted to all sort of tactics to increase his profits, ranging from selling alcohol above the maximum retail price to the exclusive sale of his own brand of beer through a number of retail stores, while the UP government looked the other way.

Other favours to him included help in procuring over 4,500 acres of land in Ghaziabad and using it to develop perhaps the largest integrated township in India. The group also managed to get 152 acres of commercial land in the heart of Noida for real estate development. As anyone knows, getting hold of such tracts is not possible without government patronage.

Behenji's blessing to Ponty Chadha didn't stop here. In 2010 he bagged five of the eleven sick sugar mills sold by the UP government. Congress leader V.M. Singh alleges that Chadha got them for Rs 276 crore while their market price was between Rs 1,000-1,500 crore. The Mayawati government had allegedly manipulated the bidding process to favour him.

Despite maintaining a low profile, Chadha had been on the radar of a number of different political parties in UP and the new chief minister Akhilesh Yadav had criticized the Mayawati government for protecting him during his campaign. We were surprised to see Chadha's 'popularity', when a Peace Party candidate in one of Azamgarh's assembly constituencies said during his speech, 'Bhrashtachar mitana hai to Chadha ki chadhi utarni hogi (If you want to eliminate corruption, you have to unmask Chadha).'

Despite a highly competitive political environment in UP, Mayawati kept giving her opponents multiple chances to attack her by protecting these two particular business groups. A set of political commentators assert that her high-handedness in dealing with farmers is because her mass-base, the Dalits, own very little land in the state, while the landed castes, mostly the OBCs, have been quite hostile towards the BSP and Dalits, who work as agrarian labourers in their fields. However, this theory could not be given much weight as it misses one fundamental fact: any party in an agriculturally-dominated state like UP could not hope to stay in power if it is hostile towards farmers, and BSP is too smart a party not to have known this fact.

In such a scenario, the allegations of the Opposition accusing BSP of making money through its association with these corporate houses, seems closer to the truth. Though Mayawati tried hard to portray every act of hers as an act for the empowerment of the Dalits, the Dalit Bahujan was nowhere to be seen at the Formula One jubilation in Noida. And when Behenji left the people for the elite, the people too left her.

Mayawati Chooses F1 for 'Sports Promotion' as Sportsmen in UP Sell Milk and Vegetables for a Living

Varanasi is most famous for the Ganges, Baba Vishwanath, Banarasi saris and Banarasi paan. But what about judo? Just ten kilometres away from Varanasi, along the railway line lies Bhatthi village, the home of aspiring judokas that has produced about fifteen national-level judo players, who have won more than a hundred medals at state, national and international events, a gold at the Commonwealth Judo Championship in Mauritius in 2008, and a silver in the Asian Judo Championship in 2009.

A small hamlet of mostly Yadav peasants, the village produced its first international player in the form of German Yadav, now a CRPF personnel. Both Yadav and his younger brother, Ram Asray, have won between them about thirty medals in state, national and international events. German, an athletics enthusiast, who used to go to Varanasi's Sampurnanand Stadium to practise running, was drawn into judo by Lal Kumar, a National Institute of Sports (NIS) certified coach, who worked there on an ad hoc basis. After German managed to get a job in the CRPF through his judo performance, many more unemployed youth were driven to the sport; Lal has been a source of inspiration to all of them.

German's brother Ram Asray Yadav, a Commonwealth gold medallist, and an Asian Championship silver medallist recalls the days when Lal used to coach him, saying he will always remain his disciple. Lal's latest disciple, who has carved out a niche for himself is Subhash Yadav, a 2008 gold medallist in the 50 kg category at the National Junior Championship. He was selected for the World Cadet Judo Championship at Budapest.

Lal coaches a number of judo enthusiasts of all age groups with complete devotion. And all he earns is Rs 7,000 per month for ten months of the year, as he is only an ad hoc coach. He started working here in the same role in 1993, earning Rs 300 per month. Even after so many successes, he has still not been given a permanent job. The only respite came during Rajnath Singh's chief ministerial term when his salary was increased to Rs 7,000. The condition of his students isn't better, as coming from peasant backgrounds, most of them sell milk or vegetables in Varanasi to make ends meet.

Impressed by their talent, Japanese director Fujimoto shot a thirty-minute documentary film 'Asian Smile' based on this village, which was telecast by a première Japanese channel, NHK BS1. The documentary brought Bhatthi to the notice of four-times world champion and 1984 Olympic gold medallist Judoka Yashuhiro Yamashita, who sent a couple of premium Judo-Gees (judo gear) to the players as a gift. The players and their coach were very excited with the gift. They are in such dire need of resources that they practise in a badminton hall, as they lack a separate judo hall.

While Japan was discovering Bhatthi and its talent, Mayawati was busy 'promoting sports' through the Formula One race, giving tax concessions worth more than a hundred crore rupees to the race organizers. With only one percent of the concession money, the judokas of Bhatthi could have worked wonders.

Flop Show: Mayawati Suspends 110 MLAs, and Fails to Reach Benchmark of 100

In the last five years, one of the biggest problems that hounded Mayawati involved her own MLAs. Time and again, BSP MLAs kept hitting the headlines for criminal activities or unruly behaviour. BSP MLAs like Shri Bhagwan Sharma, alias Guddu Pandit (Debai), Yogendra Sagar (Bilsi), Purushottam Naresh Dwivedi (Banda) were alleged to have raped and harassed women, while Anand Sen (Milkipur), Shekhar Tiwari (Auraiya) and others were arrested and convicted for murder. Other 'feathers' in BSP's cap include Haji Yaqoob Qureshi, Naseemuddin Siddiqui, Babu Singh Kushwaha, Badshah Singh and dozens more who were either implicated in cases of massive corruption or were known history-sheeters.

Whenever a complaint regarding any MLA emerged, Mayawati would act like a stern administrator, suspending the concerned MLA in most cases. This helped her in two ways—firstly, it communicated the image of a just and strict chief minister, who did not excuse even her own party MLAs, and secondly, in the absence of any other meaningful disciplinary action, the MLA in question could still reap all the benefits of being an MLA, vote for the party in the house, conduct all necessary activities, and being satisfied with this situation would not think of leaving or going against the party.

This was thus a strategy that pacified public resentment, prevented rogue MLAs from acting against the party and helped in BSP's image management. And when it came to favourites like Naseemuddin Siddiqui, Yaji Yaqoob Qureshi and Ramveer Upadhyay, even the suspension drama was not resorted to. Despite repeated complaints from the Lokayukta, the party refused to take any action against Upadhyay or Siddiqui in corruption cases. Similarly, when a police constable was publicly beaten and insulted by Haji Yaqoob in Meerut, the party decided to ignore the incident and the victim could not even lodge an FIR against the MLA.

Additionally, in the case of one-time close ministers, such as Babu Singh Kushwaha (whose name appeared time and again in the NRHM scam and the murder of two chief medical officers), stern action was not taken against them till peak election time. Only hopeless cases like Shekhar Tiwari, Anand Sen and Purushottam Naresh Dwivedi were dealt with very sternly. As there was very strong evidence against them, it was virtually impossible to save them in the media-hyped Opposition furore that rose against them.

Given these facts, it is quite clear that the 'clean governance' rhetoric that Mayawati espoused when she denied tickets to 110 sitting MLAs on charges of criminal activities and corruption, was less idealistic and more opportunistic. This decision was first made in respect of four ministers and other MLAs towards the end of December, after the elections notification had already come out and the elections were going to be held within two months. This also made a mockery of BSP's candidate declaration exercise that had occurred a year ago in 2011, as a large number of former candidates were changed.

Party spokesperson Swami Prasad Maurya told the media on 31 December 2011 that a confidential survey was conducted by the party and on its basis, those who had not been performing well were denied a ticket. Finally, concluding this exercise on her birthday, 15 January 2012, Mayawati released a new list of candidates, denying tickets to about 110 sitting MLAs including about two dozen ministers. BSP tried to portray that it had taken this step, motivated by its urge to provide a clean, corruption-free, decent political alternative to the people.

BSP tried to gain much leverage from the fact that even powerful ministers like Babu Singh Kushwaha (minister of family welfare), Fateh Bahadur Singh (forest minister), Daddan Mishra (MoS for ayurvedic medicine), and Anant Kumar Mishra (health minister) were denied tickets. However, Ramveer Upadhyay and Naseemuddin Siddiqui, two of the biggest names in the last government were given tickets, despite repeated complaints of massive corruption from the Lokayukta. Two other prominent ministers, Rangnath Mishra and Rajesh Tripathi, both of whom were also indicted by the Lokayukta for the misuse of authority, were given party tickets.

Ramveer Upadhyay was so confident of Behenji's patronage that not only did he threaten to remove the Lokayukta, Justice N.K. Mehrotra, from office but also went to the extent of boasting about his threat at a rally in Hathras during the election campaign. His brother was also given a ticket from Bulandhshahr district.

The party thought that after making 'use' of such MLAs, it would deny them tickets at the last possible moment, to prevent the angry public from voting against the party. The BSP would then claim that it had purged itself of all criminal and corrupt elements, hence the people must give it another chance. In fact, this was the line of argument in Mayawati's election speeches at a number of places, where she accepted that due to general criminalization of politics, such elements had entered BSP too, but the party had expelled all of them and hence was worthy of being given a second chance.

The initial response to her speeches was quite encouraging. On 16 January, newspapers reported it in a very positive light. While *Indian Express* used the headline, 'Maya clean-up: 110 MLAs denied ticket', *Jagran Post* reported, 'BSP adopts "clean image" with minor changes in social engineering'. *Amar Ujala* wrote, 'Operation Clean ke chalte Basapa main ulatpher (Big Reshuffle in BSP due to Operation Clean)'. However, the people of UP seemed less impressed with BSP's instrumental rationality.

In 2007, out of the eight seats in Balia, BSP had won six, reducing SP to only two seats in what was once SP's pocketborough. BSP denied tickets to all six sitting MLAs just before the elections. The party hoped that this 'sudden change of heart' would help in checking people's resentment against these MLAs, and as a result they would not vote against Behenji.

However, the former MLAs had something different in mind; barring two, the rest contested either as independents or on other party tickets. Both parties (BSP-rebels and the BSP) went into overdrive, trying to impress upon the people that they were really interested in doing good things for them, but because of the other 'evil' party, they could not do so.

The fed-up Balia electorate rejected both the BSP and the rebel candidates, and except for the Rasara seat, BSP lost all the other seats, while the rebels could not even achieve runner-up positions. In all, the ticket denial-image improvement exercise proved to be a big flop.

UP Under Mayawati:
Corruption in a Police State

Since India is a democratic country, it allows people a range of rights, including the right to protest peacefully, which also includes the burning of effigies. These rights are guaranteed to the people by the Constitution of India, which the BSP faction of the Dalit-Bahujan movement considers to be the sole product of Dalit icon, Dr Bhimrao Ramji Ambedkar.

Throughout the length and breadth of the nation, people use effigy burning as a method of protest. However, during the Mayawati government, if one dared to burn her effigy, the police would forcefully stop it. If one succeeded in burning an effigy of hers, IPC sections from breaking the peace to non-bailable offences would be slapped upon the culprits. All of this just served to show how narcissistic and insecure Behenji was.

We were told by a senior Congress activist that in 2011 at Kannauj, when they had burnt Mayawati's effigy a few months ago, not only were the participants sent to jail, but some very senior party leaders, who were as old as 70-80 years, were booked under non-bailable sections of the IPC by the police. We met dozens of SP activists during our journeys, who had faced criminal cases and had been jailed for burning Mayawati's effigies. The police state that Mayawati had created was not limited to just punishment for burning her effigies. Just after assuming office, she issued orders that no protests could be held near or could pass by the Vidhan Sabha, which was a norm earlier. A place near Lucknow's Ambedkar University campus on the outskirts of the city was designated as the official protest site. Protests could be organized there only with prior police permission.

This new protest site was a unique place, for not only was it outside the city, but was also covered on three sides by huge iron grills with a narrow entryway. The Gomti flowing on the fourth side, made it a perfect replica of Jallianwala Bagh. Whenever protesters tried to march from here towards the Vidhan Sabha by crossing the nearby Gomti Bridge, the police blocked the entrance to the dharna sthal (demonstration site) and beat the protesters who had no other option but to run towards the Gomti to save themselves.

This is exactly what happened in December 2010, when the Village Employment Workers union tried to march to the Vidhan Sabha to put forth their demands before the chief minister. They were so brutally lathi-charged by the police that many jumped into the Gomti to save themselves. The aanganwadi workers and Class IV government employees, were all treated in a similar fashion. Whenever any group came to Lucknow to protest about an issue, it came prepared to face police batons and cases.

During her tenure, Mayawati virtually refused to meet any delegation of protesters, the only exception being farmer leaders of western Uttar Pradesh in 2011 after Rahul Gandhi's Bhatta-Parsaul episode.

Her supporters claim that Mayawati's tough stance on political protests was due to her urge to ensure law and order and good governance. In reality, though, the BSP government hardly made any significant achievement in this regard. As stated above, more than a dozen of Behenji's ministers were implicated by the Lokayukta on corruption charges, and BSP was also involved in corruption related to tenders awarded to the Jaypee group and Ponty Chadha. The NRHM scam is another 'feather' in its cap. Mayawati herself once admitted that police stations were being auctioned in order to earn black money.

The statue-installation spree undertaken by her government was also steeped in corruption. The red stone used to build the statues, parks and memorials across the state was all brought from Sonbhadra district, the only Maoist district of UP with a significant tribal population.

On our way from Varanasi to Sonbhadra, we had a tough time on the highway, as the roads were jammed with about a thousand trucks carrying sand from the Son river and red stone from the district. Local journalists told us that on any given day more than three thousand trucks leave the district carrying red stone, although according to them, the papers speak otherwise.

When a truck leaves a quarry carrying goods, a receipt called ravanna or departing permission is given to the truck after the required fee has been paid. Through this mechanism, the amount of mining allowed within the contract is also kept in check. However in Sonbhadra, though thousands of trucks left every day, not more than about a hundred ravannas were issued daily, indicating that more than half the mining going on in this district was illegal.

We were told by locals on the promise of anonymity that all the illegal trucks were counted by government officials, and that Naseemuddin Siddique and one of Mayawati's brothers, Anand Kumar, took a cut from each and every truck that went out of the mines. We also came to know that there were more than a thousand stone quarries in the region, while official permission was given for only about a hundred. This vast illegal mining empire was operated with full government patronage and Mayawati's own family was allegedly involved in it.

On the law and order front too, BSP government's performance was dismal as 7,875 incidents of rape allegedly occurred in the state from 2007 to 2011, with a total of around 6.66 lakh incidents of crimes occurring across the state from 2007 to 2010. According to a 2011 report of the National Crimes Record Bureau, UP recorded the highest number of cases of violence against Dalits. The police stations became centres of terror and policemen were caught in an attempt to cover up a number of crimes committed by them.

In the Nighasan police station of Lakhimpur Kheri, a minor girl, Sonam, was killed after a failed attempt at rape by the circle officer's bodyguard in June 2011. The Nighasan circle officer Inayatullah Khan initially tried to dub it a suicide and hanged the girl to save his bodyguard's skin, though photographs of the deceased girl clearly show her feet touching the ground. When this was exposed, Khan, said to be close to Naseemuddin Siddiqui, was 'punished' by being transferred to another district.

Within five months, in November 2011, a youth named Ranjeet was killed by policemen in the same Nighasan police station area after he was picked up by police on the pretext of a minor scuffle. Relatives alleged that the police were given money to kill him by a rival party wanting to settle scores with Ranjeet. When some villagers staged a dharna outside the police station in protest, they were lathi-charged and dispersed.

Such instances were not rare in Behenji's regime and on numerous occasions, the National Human Rights Commission (NHRC) had to send notices to the state, urging it to take action. *India Today* had reported that in 2008 alone, 295 people died in the state's jails. The reason for all this mayhem in police stations, claimed the report, was Mayawati's directive to police officers to decrease the number of 'reported' crimes, giving the perfect chance to the policemen to turn autocratic. According to another report by the NHRC, UP recorded the highest number of custodial deaths in 2011: 216 in total.

While the corrupt and favoured policemen enjoyed state patronage, the honest ones suffered. According to a report in *Tehelka* magazine, non-complying IPS officers would be punished by frequent transfers; from mid-2007 to mid-2009 more than ninety-five officers were transferred five to eleven times, with Bareilly having twelve senior superintendents of police during this period. The same report quotes a UP constable (a philosophy graduate from Allahabad University) saying, 'Aristotle said that man is a social animal. I am glad that he never met UP constables otherwise he would have said, "The UP constable is only an animal."'

It seemed that unlike the erstwhile regime of Mulayam Singh, where goonda-gardi (hooliganism) was the norm, BSP had started the practice of selective sarkari goondas (government gangsters), with the police playing an integral part. Nobody dared open their mouths against these government-patronized rogues, as they unleashed terror and amassed huge fortunes. In December 2011, a report in the *Indian Express* exposed how Naseemuddin Siddiqui's rich relatives cornered a chunk of tractor subsidies meant for poor farmers in the Bundelkhand region, using the money not for agriculture but illegal mining purposes.

When we were in Hathras, a local journalist told us about Ramveer Upadhyay, a local MLA and one of Mayawati's favourite ministers, who rose from being a Class IV roadways employee's son to becoming a millionaire. The local businessmen were allegedly forced to pay a fixed extortion amount to him if they wanted their work to run smoothly. At the time of the local Dauji fair in Hathras, a number of businessmen would flee the district so that they did not have to fork out huge amounts to Upadhyay to make it a success. While speaking about these things, the journalist kept pleading for anonymity. 'Please don't reveal my name,' he said, with terror in his eyes, 'otherwise Upadhyay will not leave me'.

Behenji Deserves the Best

During her brief chief ministerial stint in 2003, Mayawati celebrated her birthday as 'Swabhiman Diwas' (self-respect day) with lavish spending and grandeur. A 51-kg cake, one lakh laddoos, sixty quintals of marigold flowers and around 5,000 bouquets, many that included flowers brought in from Holland, are just some of the extravagances that marked the occasion. Justifying these events, she claimed that indulging in such extravagances for a Dalit ki beti's birthday gave self-confidence to the Dalits in the state, who could now proclaim with pride that such luxuries were not the exclusive privilege of the upper castes as 'one of their own' beat them at their own game.

After the 2007 victory, though the birthdays transformed from Swabhiman Diwas to Jankalyan Diwas (public welfare day), as public welfare plans used to be announced on this day, Mayawati kept using them as a way to raise funds for the party. It soon became a practice for BSP MLAs, government officers, and party functionaries to arrange for 'contributions' to the party and gift them to Mayawati on her birthday. This practice though proved fatal for Manoj Gupta, an engineer working in the Public Works Department (PWD), who was killed in December 2008 in Auraiya, reportedly by the local BSP MLA, Shekhar Tiwari and his supporters, when he refused to donate funds for Mayawati's birthday celebrations.

Whether such extravagant displays boosted Dalit pride or not is debatable, but Mayawati's obsession with them kept on increasing, reaching new heights once the BSP won a majority government in UP and the public resources were at its disposal. During the BSP government's reign, Behenji ensured that she got the best of everything. The fleet of Ambassador cars, meant for the chief minister's personal use, was replaced with six Toyota Prado SUVs that cost approximately Rs 60 lakh each. A super-specialized personal hospital was also established for

Behenji within the chief minister's official residence at a cost of Rs 75 lakh per year to the state exchequer.

Within a few months of coming to power, her government decided to add two aircraft—a six-seater Premier 1 Beechcraft and a 15-seater Bell 412 helicopter—to the existing fleet of four planes and two helicopters, making her the commander of the largest fleet of aircraft within any state in the country. Furthermore, for almost all the rallies organized by the BSP prior to the election campaign, special arrangements for air-conditioners were made on the stage for Behenji.

Her out-of-state visits were equally grandiose. In October 2007, Mayawati went to Chandigarh in a private jet to address her first out-of-state rally as the Uttar Pradesh chief minister. An anonymous blogger described the event on the Internet in the following words:

> Her convoy was made up of seven or eight Toyota Land Cruiser Prados—two of them bullet-proof. All of them were brought to Chandigarh from Lucknow. City residents had never seen such display of luxury, not even by the chief ministers of Haryana and Punjab. Given her Z-plus security, Mayawati enjoyed security cover from the Chandigarh police. Traffic was halted on roads whenever her cavalcade of 50-plus cars passed. Mayawati did not stay in either the Punjab or the Haryana Raj Bhawans, as most chief ministers do. She also avoided the state-owned Hotel Mountview—the only listed five-star property in the city. Instead, she opted for the luxurious Taj Hotel along with her entourage. Although she said the treasury of the Uttar Pradesh government was empty, that did not stop her from giving a grant of Rs 30 lakh to the Chandigarh Press Club.

To add to this grandeur, her security was increased from thirty-six to a hundred Black Cat commandos, and the VIP security models of twenty-five countries including Israel, UK, France and Germany were studied by her administration to enhance the quality of her security.

At one rally in March 2010 when some honeybees flew close to her stage, an FIR was registered and a proper enquiry by a DIG-level officer was ordered to 'uncover the conspiracy' behind it. When a government employee dared to say that it was quite a normal incident, he was transferred immediately.

One must also not forget the many imported handbags and footwear that Mayawati used to complement her attire, which were also replicated in her statues.

In February 2011, her DSP-rank, President's Medal awardee, personal security officer, Padam Singh bent down to clean Mayawati's sandals with his own handkerchief in full view of the cameras. Perhaps Behenji requires the best, not just in goods, but also in terms of sycophants.

Statues and Parks:
Empowerment or Narcissism?

On 29 June 2009, a PIL (public interest litigation) filed by advocate Ravi Kant was called for hearing in the Supreme Court. After collating information using the RTI (right to information) provisions, he told the court that more than Rs 1,200 crores was spent on erecting statues of Mayawati and Kanshi Ram in various parks in Lucknow—Dr Bhim Rao Ambedkar Samajik Parivartan Sthal, Manyawar Kanshi Ram Memorial at Alambag, Kanshi Ram Bahujan Nayak Park, Ramabai Ambedkar Rally Maidan, Kanshi Ram Sanskritik Sthal, Dr Ambedkar Samajik Parivartan Prateek Sthal, Manyawar Kanshi Ram Yaadgar Vishram Sthal, Buddha Sthal, Eco Park, Samata Mulak Churaha and Dr Ambedkar Chauraha, Buddha Shanti Upwan and Prerna Sthal. The PIL alleged that the Uttar Pradesh department of culture had spent almost 90 percent of its budget in this venture. The petitioner sought the justification for such misuse of public money when the state had the lowest literacy rate of 56.27 percent, the highest maternal and neo-natal mortality rate, largest child labour force (as per the 2011 census), largest number of people living below the poverty line, and only 59 percent of villages provided with electricity.

A non-apologetic BSP hit back via senior advocate and the party's national general secretary Satish Chandra Mishra, who asked why the monuments or parks built in the memory of upper-caste leaders never raised such concern and outrage. He gave the example of Teen Murti Bhavan in the national capital that had been converted into the Nehru Museum in Jawaharlal Nehru's memory, which at present is worth more than Rs 3,000 crores. 'It hurts when no one questions such memorials. But, if a memorial for Dr Ambedkar is built then objections are raised,' said Mishra.

Before the Supreme Court announced its verdict, Mayawati had inaugurated over a dozen projects comprising statues of Kanshi Ram and six of her own along with a number of parks, at hastily-organized functions, to prevent the Supreme Court from stopping her from doing so after the hearing.

Much later, all the Opposition parties brought it up as an issue during the elections. In an election rally in Noida, Akhilesh Yadav alleged that the Mayawati government had wasted Rs 40,000 crore on installing statues across the state. The war over BSP's statue fetish continued for long in the state and in national political circles.

Iconography, statues and symbols have always been an integral component of any ideological political stream in India, be it the Left, the Hindu right or the Dalit-Bahujan movement. The Dalit forces also came up with certain symbols to assert their rise, claiming their rightful share in all avenues of life—from public spaces to political opportunities.

The use of Jai Bhim as a greeting, the popularization of blue flags and BSP graffiti, and finally the emergence of Ambedkar statues first in Dalit-dominated areas and later in public places, is a part of Dalit assertion. The Dalits deemed the installation of Ambedkar statues as an important proof of their assertion, but the upper and backward castes considered it an assault on the space hitherto dominated by them, leading to violent clashes between the Dalits and other castes in many parts of country.

A number of such clashes erupted in Uttar Pradesh when the BSP first shared power in the state with the SP, after the 1993 elections. In one such incident at Shergarhi (Meerut) in 1994, the removal of Ambedkar's statue from public land led to riots, with two Dalits dying in police firing. Though the BSP did not do much in the interests of the protesting Dalits, the community spontaneously responded to this assault with massive and numerous protest actions and, according to local media reports, the demand for Ambedkar's statues to be installed in different districts of western UP reached such a height that it became virtually impossible for suppliers to fulfil the orders. That is how statues of Ambedkar sprouted everywhere after 1994— even in small villages and towns.

Installation of statues of Dalit icons by Mayawati's government is not a new phenomenon. *The Times of India* reported in July 1997 that during her six-month stint as chief minister in 1997, Mayawati's BSP-led government is said to have installed as many as 15,000 Ambedkar statues all over the state. One notable difference this time around was that Mayawati also began immortalizing herself, with her statues always being erected besides those of other Dalit icons. It is a fact that after Babasaheb Ambedkar and Kanshi Ram, Mayawati is the biggest Dalit icon of the nation, and not just Dalits, but even other common people in Lucknow were quite happy with these parks. We spoke to a number of upper-caste people (you don't need to ask which caste a person belongs to in UP, most upper-caste people always give you their caste along with their name) about these parks and most of them were happy with the fact that Mayawati had finally given the rajdhani jaisa look (look befitting a capital) to Lucknow, with a number of picnic spots and leisure areas.

People in Lucknow, even those who are staunch opponents of Mayawati and the BSP, admit that these parks have actually added an aesthetic grandeur to the new Lucknow. The Ambedkar Park on the banks of the Gomti is an architectural beauty. The sheer expanse of these monuments is historical and in the history of contemporary India monuments such as these have not been created, at least by a state actor. Mayawati, at the least, deserves praise for having the vision to conceive these monuments.

We believe that the official purpose for creating these statues and monuments, that is, creating a feeling of pride among the downtrodden and the Dalits was achieved to a great extent. We did not come across any Dalit who criticized these structures as wasteful expenditure, rather they argued that if statues of Nehru and Gandhi can be installed all over the country, then why not those of Ambedkar or Phule or even Mayawati? We saw people from rural areas coming to Lucknow and entering the Ambedkar Park with their shoes in their hands and touching their heads to the ground in front of the statues in these parks.

Samtamulak Chowk, a big complex that circles the Gomti river towards Gomti Nagar in Lucknow, is a good example of different sentiments and how they are reflected. Many worlds exist side by side in this chowk. If you are coming from the Lohia Path, you will find a huge stand in pink stone on your left. Phule and some other saints are standing in stone overlooking the main circle as if they are keeping a silent watch. This circle itself is an advertisement for the BSP and Mayawati. It has statues of different reformist saints appropriated by the BSP, of Baba Saheb and Behenji, and all the other structures, circles, their walls, their designs and motifs have the trademark style of the BSP era in Lucknow. Its construction work went on for years and locals have seen many roads and red stone walls constructed and removed many times.

Samtamulak Chowk presents an interesting intersection of different views and sections of society. Trying to get to know people's opinion of the present government and other parties, we asked a peanut vendor standing in front of a petrol pump at Samtamulak Chowk if he had ever read the nearby billboard installed by the BSP government? He told us, 'Bhaiyya, padhe-likhe to hum hain nahi jo ee boardwa padh sake, par haan ye jo murtiyan aur sab jo behenji banwayi hain, hamare sant logo ki aur Baba Saheb ki, ye sab to dikhat hi hai. Ye likhe bhi ihi sab ke bare mein hoi. Aur baki to hum ye janat hai ki behenji hum neechi jaat walon ka samman badai hai ki hamari beti ihan tak pahunchi to (Brother, I am not literate so I can't read what's written on the board but it should be about the saints, etc. whose statues Behenji has put here. But what we lower-caste people do know is that Behenji has earned us honour by reaching such heights).'

This was a completely different view from that of the man who sold Parag dairy milk on the other side of the road. When we asked him if he had ever read this board, he said, 'Ka hui? Wahi in sab logan ke bara mein hui jinki muratiyon pe u itna kharch kari hai? Hum ek cabin nahi bana sakte dudh bechne ko yahan par ye pratimaon ke liye jagah hai (What else could it be? It must be about these statues and their people. I can't put a cabin to sell milk here, but these statues get a place!).'

He was obviously a Yadav who wanted to construct a milk booth at the circle to sell his wares.

It was obvious that the hoardings, permanent structures and statues had a mixed effect. BSP's Dalit voters were proud of the statues and the huge hoardings in the heart of the state capital. It was a matter of pride for them that a 'Dalit-ki-beti' had reached such a stature. But this did not help Mayawati in the long run because what Behenji missed this time was, 'Combining samman ki rajneeti, or the politics of dignity—the core of Dalit politics thus far—and vikas ki rajneeti, or the politics of economic development,' as eminent political scientist, Ashutosh Varshney, noted. In the absence of genuine efforts to combine dignity with economic growth, her empowerment project proved to be just empty rhetoric, which was amusing and entertaining to start with, but not worth giving a second chance to.

NRHM Scam:
Money, Murder and Politics

On 26 October 2010 like any devoted Hindu wife, Dr Shashi Kumari Arya had been fasting all day on Karva Chauth, without drinking even a drop of water according to custom, till the moment the full moon appeared in the sky late at night. Only after worshipping her husband did she break the fast, kept to ensure that a long life for him; the gods however, were not pleased this time.

The next morning, her fifty-three-year-old husband, Dr Vinod Arya, a senior eye surgeon, left their home in Vikas Nagar for his daily morning walk along with his pet Labrador, at around 5:30 a.m. Dr Arya had lived in the same house in Lucknow for the past eight years and had been transferred from Kanpur to the city as the new chief medical officer (CMO), family welfare.

Most of the residents of the posh locality were still asleep; the few people on the road were either morning walkers or milkmen and hawkers on their early morning rounds. Two men wearing helmets on a black Splendor motorcycle, who had been waiting for a while on the side of the road, however had different intentions. The moment Dr Arya came out of the house, the men began to follow him at a distance.

At 5:40 a.m. when Dr Arya reached the Laxmibai Public School, a distance of about a hundred metres from his home, these bike-borne assassins rode up to him and the pillion rider fired three shots from behind. Showing the calm of professional hit-men, they stopped near the body and the driver asked his partner, 'Dekho mara ki nahin (check whether he is dead or not).' The pillion rider got off the bike to inspect the body only to find Dr Arya still breathing. He reloaded his 7.65 mm pistol and fired two shots at point-blank range at Dr Arya's temple, causing instant death. The assassins then drove away on the bike, threatening two dairy employees, who had witnessed the shooting and had tried to stop them from running away, with the weapon in their hands.

The gunshots alerted local residents who came out to see what had happened and somebody called the police. Station officer Gangesh Tripathi reached the crime scene with his team within a few minutes. In the city of culture, where it is said that everybody knows everybody, Dr Arya's body lay on the road for more than an hour, as none of the residents could identify their neighbour of eight years. It was only at 7:15 a.m. that worried family members came searching for him and identified him as CMO Dr V. K. Arya.

News about the murder of an important civil servant in broad daylight spread like wildfire in administrative and political circles, and soon senior officers of the government started coming to the crime scene, including additional director general (law and order) Brijlal, DM Anil Sagar, principal secretary of the health department Pradeep Shukla and DG, health and family welfare S. P. Ram. Both Ram and Shukla, who went there to express sympathy, did not know that within a year, their families would be the ones in dire need of sympathy.

As soon as the news of this murder reached the Provincial Medical Service Federation office-bearers, a meeting was convened that called for a state-wide suspension of all forms of medical services (other than emergency and post-mortem) the next day, in protest. The federation also demanded a Crime Branch Criminal Investigation Department (CBCID) inquiry into the incident. This murder turned out to be the lynchpin that triggered a domino effect leading to the unmasking of one of the biggest and most controversial scams in Uttar Pradesh's political history. While a number of people, from Opposition leaders to medical servicemen demanded that quick action be taken, they were unaware that history was going to be repeated very soon.

On 2 April 2011, the new Lucknow CMO (family welfare) B. P. Singh was on his routine morning walk with four friends in the upmarket Gomtinagar area of Lucknow. While talking, both Dr B. P. Singh and his friend Dr P. K. Singh left the other friends a little behind; the time was roughly 6:30 in the morning. Busy debating, they did not notice two men on a Pulsar bike coming from the other direction. While the driver was wearing a helmet, the pillion rider had hidden his face behind a handkerchief. The moment they crossed the doctors, the biker turned and stopped the bike while the pillion rider fired a shot at Dr B. P. Singh from one of the two handguns he was holding in both hands. Hearing the shot, while Dr P. K. Singh dived into a nearby drain, Dr B. P. Singh turned towards the assailants. One of them started firing indiscriminately at him from both handguns, hitting him more than half a dozen times. Like the last time, to confirm the kill, he went to Dr Singh and fired two shots point-blank at his heart and temple before running away with his partner.

Police recovered twelve empty cases and one live cartridge of the same 7.65 mm gun from the crime scene. This historically notorious cartridge, which was also used in the political assassination of Arch Duke Ferdinand in 1914 leading to the First World War, is a civilian bore and hence is easily available at all gun shops. Further, it is used in sleek and small weapons, which are easy to use and conceal in urban areas.

The post-mortem report revealed eleven bullet wounds on Dr Singh's body. It also confirmed that the bullets which killed Dr Singh were fired from the same weapon that had been used in the erstwhile CMO, Dr Arya's murder.

Two CMOs in the state capital had been murdered in the same fashion, just five months apart, and the police were clueless. The news created a political upheaval in the city, as the Opposition demanded the resignation of the chief minister for absence of law and order, even in the capital.

They were not wrong, for within the next thirty days, twenty-four people were murdered in Lucknow, most of them in broad daylight. Angry with the murder of Dr Singh, who was also the general secretary of the Provincial Medical Service Federation, doctors and medical employees of almost all government hospitals in Lucknow, stopped work and soon medical employees and doctors throughout the state followed suit. With the pharmacists, nurses and medical hospital staff supporting the agitation, government medical services throughout the state came to a grinding halt. By evening, the federation called for an indefinite state-wide strike till the murderers were brought to justice, and the post-mortem and emergency services also went on strike this time.

The public pressure took its toll and on 7 April, Uttar Pradesh family welfare minister Babu Singh Kushwaha and health minister Anant 'Antu' Kumar Mishra resigned from the Cabinet owning moral responsibility for the irregularities detected in their departments after Dr Singh's murder. Principal secretary (family welfare) Pradeep Shukla was also removed from his post.

This is when people started questioning the health and family welfare ministry in the BSP government, alleging foul play and a mafia-politician nexus behind the murders. Stories started appearing in the newspapers alleging scams worth thousands of crores in the health department. The Opposition cried for the head of the government and even the common people started questioning the law and order situation, which was considered Behenji's USP, equating it to SP's goondaraj.

The Youth Congress filed RTIs in different districts and on the basis of those reports, it charged the BSP government with orchestrating what later came to be known as the 'NRHM Scam'. Newspapers and Opposition parties alleged that thousands of crores of rupees given by the Central government under the National Rural Health Mission scheme (a Central government-funded scheme aimed at improving health facilities for rural people) were devoured by a nexus of ruling party leaders, ministers, bureaucrats and mafia dons. The post of chief medical officer, family welfare, was very significant in this respect, as it had a separate office, funds and work, other than the routine healthcare services under another CMO within the same district.

The annual budget of the CMO, family welfare, ran into crores of rupees in many districts, making it a profitable venture. Procurement and purchase of sub-standard items at inflated prices, inflated contracts of construction and repair, and forgery in accounting were some of the main ways of doing this. A news item in the *Indian Express* on 17 February 2012 alleged that the NRHM scam was worth more than Rs 10,000 crores. Pressure on the issue of the NRHM scam kept building around Behenji's government.

In the meanwhile, the police arrested Dr Y. S. Sachan, deputy CMO, alleging that he was the main accused in the murder of both CMOs. Three alleged shooters were also arrested on charges of being Dr Sachan's hired assassins. Since Dr Sachan was supposed to reveal significant details about the NRHM scam, indicting certain big sharks involved in this case, he was sent to a high-security prison in Lucknow, so that he could not be harmed by the influential people who had masterminded the scam.

Dr Sachan was supposed to appear in court on 23 June 2011. The day before his appearance, he was found dead, hanging by a belt in an under-construction ward of the jail hospital. There were lacerations on his wrists and neck, but no suicide note was found. However, the jail authorities and the police happily termed it a suicide, thus informally suggesting that all investigations would be ended, as the chief accused had died.

The station officer of the Gomtinagar police station filed a charge sheet on 6 July 2011 in the chief judicial magistrate, Lucknow's court in CMO Dr B. P. Singh murder case, holding deputy CMO Dr Y. S. Sachan responsible for hiring shooters to kill Dr Singh. Since Dr Sachan too was dead, it was more like a closure report.

Such a shameless attempt to cover up a case could not have been possible without the patronage of the state government. The government too officially declared that Dr Sachan had committed suicide, but succumbing to the huge political and social pressure, it had to order a judicial probe into the case, which later reported it to be a prima facie case of murder, much to the displeasure of the Uttar Pradesh government. Left with no choice, the state government ordered a CBI enquiry into Dr Sachan's murder in July 2011, but still turned a deaf ear to the Opposition's demand for a CBI enquiry into the NRHM scam. However, in November 2011, the Allahabad High Court while listening to a PIL filed in the case ordered the CBI to investigate all three murders as well as the NRHM scam.

As the noose started tightening around the BSP government's neck, it tried to create a new scapegoat in the form of former minister Babu Singh Kushwaha, Mayawati's erstwhile trusted lieutenant, to save the party and other ministers engaged in the scam. Sensing trouble, Kushwaha made advance preparations to repel these attempts by writing a letter to the prime minister, alleging that the troika of senior BSP minister Naseemuddin Siddiqui, principal secretary (home) Fateh Bahadur Singh and Cabinet secretary Shashank Shekhar Singh, were plotting to kill him. A furious BSP soon suspended him, blaming him for the entire NRHM scam, after which he quickly tried to join the BJP.

Though Kushwaha managed to save his life through these tactics, three more health department employees (involved with NRHM scam enquiries) were not so lucky. On 23 January 2012, Sunil Verma, a project manager in NRHM allegedly shot himself in Lucknow, while the deputy CMO of Varanasi, Shailesh Yadav, died in an alleged road accident on 15 February 2012. Mahendra Sharma, a clerk in the health department was found dead the very next day in Lakhimpur Kheri, thus taking the death toll caused by the curse of the NRHM scam to six.

The CBI has filed three charge-sheets up till now in the case (the enquiry is still on) and virtually all significant state-level medical officers and a number of BSP political leaders have already been implicated or are in the process of being implicated in this case. For in terms of looting the NRHM money, it allowed all sections of machinery to claim their booty, without any discrimination.

The NRHM scam was like a celluloid political scandal, where all-powerful villains prevent anybody from revealing their names by eliminating all possible 'weak links' and plugging all loopholes using the immense resources at their disposal. In the NRHM scam also, anybody who was about to reveal something important, either died a violent death or 'committed suicide' under mysterious circumstances. The CBI is still trying to recreate the whole story of the scam. What is clear, however is that a scam of such huge proportions cannot take place without the knowledge and patronage of the sitting government. Like the 2G scam, where it would be foolish to think that the prime minister and finance minister were unaware of what was going on, it would be equally foolish to think that an authoritarian leader like Mayawati was not aware of such a big scam occurring in her own government.

However, the black money earned via the NRHM scam proved to be jinxed, and a number of those who devoured it at the cost of the millions of suffering people in rural Uttar Pradesh, either died a violent death, lost their jobs or were put behind bars. In the end, this scam proved to be BSP's Waterloo, tainting its image with massive corruption charges, and making it a target of public anger, which finally threw it out of power.

Roots of Insecurity: The Guest House Kaand

People often wonder why Mayawati is so paranoid about her security. The reason perhaps lies in the infamous 'Guest House Kaand' of Lucknow in 1995. After the 1993 assembly elections, in the face of a hung house (BJP 177, SP 109, BSP 67 seats) a coalition government of SP and BSP came to power with Mulayam Singh Yadav as the chief minister, enjoying the support of the Congress, Independents and other smaller parties.

Kanshi Ram entrusted Mayawati with the task of ensuring that the government followed BSP's agenda and Mayawati earned the title of 'super chief minister' for her consistent interruptions in Mulayam's work. Fed up with this uncomfortable situation, Mulayam Singh discreetly started wooing BSP MLAs, in the hope of getting more than a third of them to defect, in order to gain the numbers required for a majority of his own. Other than the Mulayam-Maya personality clash, the clash of the social bases of both the parties was also the reason for their bitter relationship. Reports of Dalit atrocities by Yadavs and other OBC castes that supported SP were flooding Lucknow by then, including a number of incidents, like Sher

Garhi, where the government had used unnecessary force to deal with Dalit agitations.

A cunning Kanshi Ram anticipated SP's grand plan and in response, started his own exercise to outmanoeuvre Mulayam's efforts. By May 1995, he had mustered the required support from the BJP, whose leadership was ready to have a BSP chief minister in order to end its political isolation, by becoming a partner in the coalition government. Since Kanshi Ram fell ill at that crucial time and was hospitalized in Delhi, he asked Mayawati to submit the papers to the governor, withdrawing support from Mulayam and staking a claim for a BSP-BJP government, which she did on 1 June 1995.

The moment Mulayam Singh found out, overcome with rage he allegedly ordered that Mayawati should be taught a lesson. Further, since he refused to step down as the chief minister, he needed to prove a majority in the house, which required sabotaging the Opposition's plan to form a new government. On the night of 1 June, a number of untrustworthy administrative officials were transferred by Mulayam Singh and a loyalist O. P. Singh was brought in as the new Lucknow SSP.

Late in the afternoon of 2 June 1995, Mayawati was talking with her senior party associates in her suites at the Lucknow State Guest House after finishing a meeting with party MLAs, when a crowd of two to three hundred people including SP MLAs, leaders, activists and some women attacked the guest house. Showering caste abuses at the BSP legislators who dared to sabotage Mulayam's government, the Samajwadi Party mob dragged, kicked and beat whoever came before it, forcibly throwing some of the BSP MLAs into cars, to be sent to SP headquarters. There, under pressure, they were forced to sign papers supporting Mulayam Singh.

The mob assembled before Mayawati's suite (which was locked from within by her associates) pounding heavily on the doors, hurling the filthiest abuses and threatening to kill Mayawati after breaking open the doors. The water and electricity supply to the suites was cut off, and while the Samajwadi Party goons made a mockery of law and order by assaulting and humiliating Mayawati and her elected legislators, writing one of the most bizarre and shameful chapters in UP's political history, SSP O. P. Singh watched with indifference while smoking cigarettes.

Any bigger untoward incident was prevented by two SHOs, Vijay Bhushan and Subhash Baghel, who prioritized duty over everything else and prevented the mob from breaking open the doors of Mayawati's suites. The episode continued for more than an hour, and while the SP mob ran amok, beating elected representatives and trying to assault the potential Dalit chief minister, the government machinery and law-and-order mechanism watched silently and did nothing to prevent it. The situation was normalized by the intervention of the Lucknow DM Rajiv Kher, who pushed out the SP mob, ignoring threats of dire consequences from the chief minister's office. He was transferred at 11 p.m. that night.

Though after this episode the Opposition rallied behind Mayawati, who managed to become the chief minister the next day on 3 June, this incident definitely implanted a sense of insecurity in Mayawati's psyche. After this incident she has always been more conscious about her security, prepared to prevent such events from happening in the future.

The PM Dreams

The moment Mayawati won a thumping majority in the UP assembly elections in 2007, people from all quarters, ranging from politicians to media channels started talking about the skilfulness of her social engineering, which had the potential to even help her become prime minister.

Perhaps Mayawati took this media hype too seriously. Not only did Behenji initiate an ambitious project to expand BSP nationwide, but she personally visited different states to ensure success in this venture. Conscious of the strength of her social engineering formula, which was vindicated by successive by-election wins, she changed the rules to put her trusted cabinet secretary, Shashank Shekhar Singh, on par with the chief secretary. She then handed over the administrative responsibilities to him, and marched on to realize her prime ministerial dreams. Within less than a year of assuming the chief minister's office, she had travelled to Chandigarh, Punjab, Maharashtra, Chhattisgarh, Tamil Nadu, Karnataka, Kerala, West Bengal, Uttarakhand and Bihar, apart from Gujarat and Himachal Pradesh with plans to visit Madhya Pradesh next.

In February 2008, an article by Swapan Dasgupta in *Tehelka* talked about the possibility of BSP winning around fifty seats in the Lok Sabha from UP, with a popular vote of around 30 percent, as against nineteen seats and 24.6 percent of the vote share in the 2004 Lok Sabha elections. If she had won so many seats from UP alone, she would surely have been able to call the shots in the future Central government.

The leaders of a non-UPA and non-NDA parties conglomerate, called the Third Front, were also in talks with her prior to the Lok Sabha polls. In March 2009, she hosted a dinner for the Third Front leaders including Janata Dal secular leader H. D. Deve Gowda, K. Chandra Shekhar Rao of the Telangana Rashtra Samiti, N. Chandrababu Naidu of the Telugu Desam Party and the leaders of four big Left parties. Though leadership issues were not discussed, it was assumed that Mayawati would lead this conglomerate.

However, despite all efforts, the party failed to make it nationally; expecting to bag fifty Lok Sabha seats, Mayawati had to contain her PM ambitions for the time being, after winning only twenty seats, just one more than her nineteen seat score of 2004.

Cut off from the People

During her struggling days in BSP in the late 1980s, many people fondly remember Mayawati as an inspiring young lady, full of energy, who would cycle for kilometres to reach out to her electorate and mass-base. The title 'Behenji' or revered sister, which symbolizes her, was given to her during those days, as the Dalits felt that she was one of their own, the one who rose to great heights from the same ground and environment where they still stood. However, once Mayawati made the impossible possible in 2007 by securing a full majority government in UP for the first time after 1991, she perhaps thought it was now time to take a break from her good old struggling days.

Projected as a 'messiah' of not only Dalits but of the Sarvajan (including the majority of Brahmin-Baniyas) who wanted to get rid of SP's 'jungleraj' where might is right, and immortalized in history for being the first Dalit chief minister in India to lead the majority government of a party, she became a prisoner of her own image.

To encourage the deity-like image, she isolated herself, making it hard for not just the common people, but also BSP leaders and officials to approach her. Like Sonia Gandhi, she became inaccessible to her own party leaders. An article in *Open* magazine in March 2012 by Mihir Srivastava reported that out of eighteen BSP district presidents interviewed by him, only two had met her in person in Lucknow in the last two years. This was in stark contrast to her mentor and BSP founder Kanshi Ram's style of functioning, who always used to give directives to district presidents in person.

Shortly after becoming the chief minister of Uttar Pradesh, she discontinued the old practice of the chief minister's Janata

Darbar, where common people could meet the chief minister in person and tell her about their problems. This avenue used to be the last alternative available to people to voice their concerns. In November 2010, she told senior bureaucrats that she would be making 'surprise visits' to various districts of the state from 1 February 2011, meeting common people and reviewing development programmes. But there was nothing 'surprising' about her visits, as the dates were always announced in advance.

However, when she actually made these supposedly-surprise visits (Auchak Nirikshan) there was virtually no way for commoners to actually meet the chief minister. Mayawati would arrive by helicopter at the district headquarters along with Shashank Shekhar Singh and a few more trusted lieutenants. From the helipad itself, security men and district officials would encircle her in such a manner that no commoner could dare reach her. In fact she was not very enthusiastic about meeting the people and when three women broke the security cordon to meet her during the Aligarh visit, not only did Behenji turn a deaf ear to their complaints, but IPC charges were slapped on them with her full knowledge.

On 6 February 2011 when Behenji visited Auraiya, a female schoolteacher approached her with a complaint letter but instead of hearing her, Behenji snubbed her, saying 'Mujhe mat do (Don't give it to me)' and walked past her. The letter was snatched by officers in her entourage and later the teacher was suspended on charges of 'breaking protocol'.

Some students in Allahabad told us that when Mayawati came for a visit, the administration imposed a curfew-like situation on the route she was supposed to follow, making it impossible for anyone to approach her. Content with these arrangements, Behenji too never changed her plan and never embarked upon a new route to meet 'common people', which was supposed to be one of the aims of these visits. Most of the times, these surprise visits were over within an hour, leaving people wondering about Behenji's capabilities, who could review everything from law and order to development and welfare projects in the district within such a short span of time!

Unsung Bahujan Heroes:
The Story of Expendable BSP Leaders

Criss-crossing the by-lanes of the upscale Nirala Nagar in Lucknow, you reach a malin basti (literally, a dirty colony) situated on its edges. In a narrow lane of single room houses, we reach the home of Ram Vilas Valmiki, who was a minister in the 1995 BSP government.

Valmiki was a tax collector in the Lucknow Nagar Nigam and started working for BSP from 1986-87. He was BSP's general secretary and was very close to Kanshi Ram, who appointed him minister even though he was not an MLA. He was a prominent leader of the safai-karmcharis (mostly Harijans) of Lucknow. He also had great influence in other municipal councils and nagar nigams across the state.

After Kanshi Ram's demise, Valmiki lost favour with Behenji over a petty issue and was sidelined. In March 2010, Valmiki suffered a major stroke and went into a coma. His wife has now taken over the role of breadwinner and looks after the family along with a grown-up son who runs a mobile repair shop. Clearly, his income is not sufficient for Valmiki's costly treatment. When we asked if she got any help from the BSP government and Mayawati, she said, 'Kuch bhi nahi. Yeh mantri rahe hain, kahin bade aspataal mein bharti hi karwa diye jaate to ilaaj theek se ho jaata (We got no help. He has been a minister. Had he been admitted to a good hospital, we would at least be relieved that he is receiving good treatment).' No one from the party or the government seemed concerned about this man, who had been a committed cadet and rose to a higher office but was now critically ill. He did not make money or acquire any patta-theka (a licence or contract) as many others in his party did.

When we asked his wife if she and the family held any grudge or if they were thinking of joining hands with a political opponent in the coming elections, she replied, 'Yeh Party ke vafadaar rahe hain, ab hum kahan jayenge? Par jo sarkaar in jaiso ka hi dhyaan nahi rakh sakti, humein nahi lagta ki use log wapas layenge (He has been a party loyalist, so where will we go now? But we don't think that people will bring back such a government that can't take care of its own people).'

On closer scrutiny, a galaxy of such leaders will emerge in the state. One of the first three MPs elected on a BSP ticket in 1989 along with Mayawati, was Ram Krishna Yadav. Now seventy-five years of age, Yadav is a practising advocate in the Azamgarh district court. He claims that Mayawati was very ambitious and had compromised on the basic values of the party and damaged the party and the movement on the altar of her own political ambitions. Ram Krishna is also the cousin of Ram Naresh Yadav, an ex-MP from Congress and now the governor of Madhya Pradesh. He says that he could also have made large sums of money and accumulated property, but because he had internalized the basic philosophy of the movement he could not do that. To this date he doesn't own even a car. An old associate of Kanshi Ram, he fondly remembers Saheb's commitment and hard work to establish and spread the party.

Seeing no hope in Mayawati, Yadav left BSP in 1998 and started practising in the district court. Recently, talking to the *Hindustan Times*, he said, 'BSP is now dominated by three Ms—Money-Mafia-Media.'

Dalit-Bahujan Movement and the Cult of Mayawati

The BSP is an ideological party whose goal is to end caste-based oppression and discrimination. It is a product of the Dalit-Bahujan movement that dates back to the pre-Independence Dalit assertion against the dominance of Brahminical Hinduism. In ancient India, Buddhism and Tantra emerged as two challenges to Brahminical religion, but while the latter was incorporated, Buddhism was destroyed by Brahminical establishments.

Later on, Dr Bhimrao Ambedkar, Jyotiba Phule, Narayan Guru, E.V. Ramaswamy Periyar, Savitribai Phule and others laid down the ideological foundations of a Dalit-Bahujan movement in India, presenting a thorough criticism of the Hindu caste order. They dubbed the backward-lower castes as Dalit-Bahujans, who made up the majority of India's deprived population, while the minority comprised the higher castes that favoured the Brahminical order. An end to this caste discrimination was the objective, and education was seen as the most significant way of achieving it.

A number of political groups emerged from these ideas ranging from Ambedkar's Republican Party of India (RPI) to the Dalit Panthers and many more, but they failed to make much difference. The BSP, which was established in 1984 by Kanshi

Ram, after successful experiments of the BAMCEF (Backward and Minority Classes Employees Federation) and DS-4 (Dalit Shoshit Samaj Sangharsh Samiti), considered political success to be of primary importance in achieving its objectives, and thus their main focus was on electoral victories. Educating common people about ideological content has always been difficult in a backward society like India. It became more difficult for BSP, as its primary mass-base, the Dalits, belonged to the most uneducated and backward sections of society. Individuals become the symbol of ideological movements in such contexts and the same happened with the BSP, which gave Ambedkar (Babasaheb), Kanshi Ram (Saheb) and Mayawati (Behenji) a deity-like stature. For BSP's mass-base, the trio symbolized the ideology, vision, hope, leadership, agenda and strategy of the party.

These were the constraints that shaped the BSP-led Dalit assertion, a phenomenon that emerged in the 1980s. Since the party could hardly afford infighting, which could have arrested its growth, leadership and power; BSP always remained centred in the hands of one authority, which was Kanshi Ram in the beginning. In the initial phases, a popular slogan– 'BSP is Kanshi Ram and Kanshi Ram is BSP'—underlined this characteristic. Till 1997, no internal elections were held within the organization and all office-bearers were nominated. Kanshi Ram was the dictatorial authority in BSP and in an interview to the *Sunday Mail* in April 1989 he said, 'I will never allow anyone to challenge me . . . I must be allowed to concentrate on the final objective.'

Mayawati, the political heir to Kanshi Ram's legacy, continued the tradition, never allowing anyone to rise above herself, and surprisingly, these traits earned her many admirers. In Ferozabad District Court, we heard a Dalit and a Brahmin lawyer praising her for her dictatorial style, saying, 'Jabardast neta hai, kisiki sunti nahin hai (She is a strong leader, never cares about what others say).' A number of BSP activists we spoke to praised Mayawati's strong-arm tactics, 'Behenji ne jo kah diya, woh kah diya (Behenji always has the final word).'

Though this style led to conflicts, with many leaders leaving the party many times, Mayawati's command over the Dalit mass-base prevented BSP from being affected by them, thus rendering the rebels obsolete. The ultimate proof of her control over Dalit votes was displayed in the 2007 elections, when BSP secured about 80 percent of SC votes polled in the state. With this victory came not just vindication for her style of functioning but also brazen arrogance and narcissism.

Considering herself to be the biggest Dalit leader alive, Mayawati started immortalizing herself, acquiring all sorts of luxuries and comforts for herself. Like all dictators, she denied access to herself to all but a select few, hiding herself behind unbreachable walls, leaving the people wondering about the 'Iron Lady' with mystic capabilities. The state machinery became a medium to boost her image and from Noida near Delhi to the Nepal border at Nautanwa, from the forests of Sonbhadra near Chhattisgarh to the foothills of the Himalayas in Saharanpur, roadside poles were adorned with Mayawati's flexes and cutouts.

Senior party leader Ram Prasad Mehra, who was ousted from the party in 2012 says that just after the death of Kanshi Ram, Mayawati stopped the publication of the journal *Bahujan Sangathak* (Bahujan Organizer) and started a fresh one *Maya Yug* (Maya Era). Other than allegations of forgetting Kanshi Ram's legacy, many people have also accused Mayawati of sabotaging BSP's original agenda of Dalit emancipation and turning the party into an ATM machine, printing notes for herself.

Noted Dalit scholar Mudrarakshas, who contested elections

against BSP in the 2012 assembly elections, accuses Mayawati of suppressing the emergence of a new Dalit leadership to strengthen her dominance. 'If any new leadership from the Dalit community attempts to emerge, she will be the first one to strike it down,' said Mudrarakshas. His allegations have a basis infacts. Unlike Kanshi Ram, she has not groomed any leader in BSP to continue the legacy.

Once at a rally in 2008, she declared that she had chosen her successor, a Dalit not from her family, but whose name would only be revealed after her death. However, when people started speculating that the heir was the BSP vice president Raja Ram, Mayawati removed him from his position and later sent him out of the state by making him a Rajya Sabha member and entrusting him with the responsibility of Rajasthan, and then Madhya Pradesh. The treatment meted out to Raja Ram shows that Mayawati cannot tolerate anybody in BSP getting any attention as a future leader. The condition of BSP MLAs from her own Jatav sub-caste is also not very good, as out of the thirty-nine Jatav MLAs, about two-thirds were denied a ticket this time.

The BSP leadership has also started questioning Mayawati's ideological committment. Ambedkar Nagar District BSP coordinator Ram Samhar told *Open* magazine in an interview, 'Behenji has got caught up in parliamentary deviation. She wants to remain in power but has done almost nothing to accomplish the tasks set for the BSP by Saheb (Kanshi Ram).' The March 2012 issue of the magazine raised three points on which Mayawati was criticized by hardcore BSP activists charging her with forgetting Saheb's legacy: considering political power as an end in itself, weakening the ideological sharpness of the BSP and neglecting basic issues like land reforms for the betterment of the Dalits.

Everyone will agree that the ideological essence of BSP has

surely been diluted and Mayawati has replaced the culture of cadre camps with a self-centric cult based on her own persona and fostering sycophancy. However, with regard to the other two objections, one must not take BSP's old slogans like 'Jo jamin sarkari hai, woh jamin hamari hai (the government land belongs to us)' at face value. For BSP is not and has never been a revolutionary party but a statist one, with the sole aim of capturing state power and using it for the betterment of its mass-base, much like a trade union.

To this date, BSP lacks an economic programme, and unlike parties like CPI (ML) in Bihar, which openly confronted the upper castes, BSP has always avoided such confrontations. In fact, in its desperation to capture power, BSP has allied with the same Brahminical forces (like the BJP) that it had pledged to oppose, even during the height of Saheb's power in 1995 and 1997. Though Mayawati has led the BSP to its decay and weakened its ideological edge, she did not transform it from a revolutionary to a statist party, as BSP never was a revolutionary party to begin with.

Mayawati and Kanshi Ram both share many similarities. Both had renounced their families for the greater cause of the Bahujan Samaj, though Mayawati was braver in this respect, for unlike Kanshi Ram who left his family much later in life, Mayawati renounced her family in her late twenties. Further, from working at the grassroots to establish the party to braving threats to her life at the Lucknow Guest House, before forming the first BSP-led government, Mayawati had gone through a number of 'agni-parikshas' (trials by fire) as Kanshi Ram fondly called them.

However, unlike Kanshi Ram who was fond of interacting with people and trusted his team, Mayawati seems insecure, self-centred and could never get along well with others. As her power and influence increased, her arrogance increased in direct proportion, and after Kanshi Ram's demise (he suffered a cerebral stroke in 2003), she became the matriarch of the party.

Unlike Kanshi Ram who never cared for his family which still lives in poverty, Mayawati started showering benefits upon her family once she came to power. While her brother Anand became a significant political personality in Uttar Pradesh during her regime, Mayawati kept amassing wealth, buying palatial houses in her home district, in Delhi and in Lucknow. In contrast to Kanshi Ram who was habituated to an inexpensive lifestyle with no concern for a personal bank balance, Mayawati's assets increased every time she gained power and according to her declaration of assets for the Rajya Sabha elections in 2012, she has property worth Rs 111 crores, including one kg of gold, two shops in Connaught Place (Delhi) and a Rs 62 crore house on Delhi's Sardar Patel Marg.

Like most founding fathers of significant movements, Kanshi Ram was more of a public than a private person, and his concerns had little to do with himself. Mayawati has proven to be very different from her mentor in this regard. Her belief that the Dalit vote was her birthright also proved wrong this time as according to the CSDS (Centre for Sudy of Developing Societies) data BSP's Dalit vote share decreased from approximately 80 percent in 2007 to about 60 percent in 2012, ringing a warning bell for the party.

One may question whether it is fair to blame Mayawati for all the wrongs of the BSP and its government. Yes, if she is credited for all the achievements of the party, she cannot escape the responsibility for its failures. Operating as the central authoritative figure of BSP, she was the leader, the messiah and the chief minister all rolled into one, sharing very little power with others because of her insecurities.

The 2007 victory gave her a historic opportunity to implement the ideology of the founders of the Dalit-Bahujan movement.

Not only did she fail in this regard, but her regime also could not maintain the basic standards of governance provided by other state governments in India. BSP's 'alternative' politics failed to provide any alternatives. Surrounded by sycophants and cut off from people, she wasted these precious five years, possessed by mythical dreams of prime minister-ship and of immortalizing herself. And when she woke up, the situation had changed at the grassroots level.

PART FOUR

POLITICS OF SOCIAL ENGINEERING

WHEN TRAVELLING WESTWARDS FROM THE DISTRICT OF LAKHIMPUR Kheri in Uttar Pradesh, you will find the name of one village constantly appearing on milestones, Panwari. Unaware of what this place was famous for, we wondered why its name recurred so frequently. When finally we enquired about Panwari's history, it became clear that this place is a political landmark in the state's history.

Panwari is a village in Agra district, situated a couple of kilometres from one of the seven wonders of the world, the Taj Mahal. On 1 June 1990 when Dalits belonging to the Jatav (Chamar) sub-caste were walking through Panwari in a marriage procession, the Jat inhabitants of the village felt offended by the fact that the Dalit bridegroom was riding a horse, which was deemed to be a privilege of the upper and middle castes. They tried to stop the Jatavs from proceeding. They cited a custom in the village that no marriage procession or baraat ever follows the route taken by another baraat earlier, and since the baraat of a Jat had recently gone through that very route, the Jatavs must change their route. The Jatavs refused to bow down and the administration too stated that no objection could be raised.

Angry over the Dalits refusing to accept the dictates of the Jats, a panchayat was called immediately, which decided to teach the Jatavs a lesson. The Jats attacked the Dalits' baraat and the latter also resorted to using force, leading to full-scale Jat-Jatav riots that continued for a few days.

When the police intervened to control the rioting, it also favoured the Jats, opening fire on the Dalits. Seven Dalits were killed in the incident and around 210 were injured, catapulting

Panwari into the headlines, with national leaders like Rajiv Gandhi coming to visit the affected families.

This is UP and the caste politics of UP, where sentiments run high and caste pride is considered more important than life, development and governance are of low importance.

In terms of caste and communal politics, Uttar Pradesh has witnessed two of the most significant phenomena—the Mandal (based on the Mandal Commission's recommendation of 33 percent reservations for OBCs) and Mandir (based on the Ram Janmabhoomi agitation) movements. And surprisingly, the most significant political forces championing these two causes (the BJP and the Janata Dal, later precipitating into the Samajwadi Party) who were also hostile towards each other, took up these causes and excelled in the same state.

The success story of a third kind of assertion—that of the Dalits—was also written here, as it is the only state in India where a Dalit-oriented party succeeded in forming a majority government on its own.

UP is the state of all sorts of caste assertions, communal experiments and combinations. It is also the state where erstwhile rivals comprising the upper castes and the lower castes allied together to form the BJP-BSP alliance, where combinations from MY (Muslim-Yadav) to AJGAR (Ahir, Jat, Gurjar) have come into existence. We will talk about a select few of these, focusing on how castes and communities have voted in UP elections 2012.

Dacoits of Chambal: Mirror Image of Caste Politics

Dacoits or bandits are generally perceived to be hard-core criminals, but the ravines of Chambal celebrate them by conferring upon them the title of baaghi or rebel, equating them to people who had participated in the freedom struggle. Since the colonial days, people like Man Singh, who belonged to the local royal family, had taken to arms against oppression or injustices of the establishment and challenged it, giving meaning to the baaghi title.

Till the 1960s, this domain was reserved for the upper castes, such as the Thakurs and Brahmins. The period after the 1960s is said to be the beginning of the caste assertion of the OBCs, which was reflected in the dacoits of Chambal as well. Fed up of being oppressed by the upper-caste elite or government functionaries, people from the Yadav and Kurmi (Patel) communities picked up guns to settle scores, forming OBC gangs in the region for the first time.

One of the first such baaghis was Chaviram Yadav, a dacoit who operated from Shahjahanpur to Chambal and whose acts became a part of folklore in the state. As children, we often heard stories of his bravery, daredevilry and just conduct from the elders of all castes. Patels or Kurmis, the second most dominant OBC community of central and eastern Uttar Pradesh, soon followed suit.

By the 1970s and 1980s, Chambal was full of dacoits of all castes and whenever dominant castes committed any atrocity on the backward or extremely backward castes, the members of that community would either pick up guns to form a new caste gang or approach an existing gang of their own caste for justice. Caste rivalries between Thakur, Yadav, Patel, Gujjar, Pal and Mallah gangs became a regular feature in Chambal during that time. In fact, it was Babu Gujjar's attempt to molest a Mallah girl (Phoolan Devi) that led to a vertical split in the gang, with all extremely backward members following Vikram Mallah who rescued her by killing Gujjar.

Dacoits like Nirbhay Gujjar, Dadua, Thokia were not only dreaded criminals but also heroes of their respective castes and acted as courts of appeal to seek justice. Their own caste people not only provided them logistic support, food and shelter, but also acted as local intelligence units.

The dacoits of Uttar Pradesh were not aloof from the political arena and most of them supported parties that favoured their caste and community. For example, while upper-caste gangs acted as strongmen of parties like BJP and Congress in some cases, the OBC dacoits favoured the Janata Dal and Samajwadi Party. The parties too returned favours in various ways, the most common being refraining from police action against the 'friendly' gang.

With time, political parties also started fielding ex-dacoits as their candidates. When the SP-BSP government of Dalits and other backward classes came to power in UP in 1993, it declared that it would suspend all cases against Phoolan Devi, the infamous 'Bandit Queen', including the one involving the killing of twenty Thakurs at Behmai (Kanpur Dehat) in 1981. Not only did they dismiss all the cases, but SP also fielded her as a candidate for the Lok Sabha elections from Mirzapur in 1996, which Phoolan won.

Since most of the dacoit gangs favoured SP, Mayawati got almost all the remaining gangs eliminated in encounters in her last tenure, with Dadua and Thokia being the most recent hits. However, continuing with its tradition of supporting OBC dacoits, SP fielded the late Dadua's son (a Kurmi by caste), Veer Singh Patel as the party's candidate from Chitrakoot in 2012, which he managed to win.

Nishad Politics in Eastern UP

Nishad, Mallah or Bind is an extremely or Most Backward Caste (MBC) that lives near the rivers in the state and is associated with boating, fishing and other such occupations. Despite living in conditions similar to Dalits, they do not get any preferential treatment.

The SP was the first party to attract the Nishads by fielding Phoolan Devi, who belonged to the same caste, as its Lok Sabha candidate from Mirzapur in 1996. Around the same time, another Nishad politician in the Gorakhpur region was working hard to organize people from his caste. Jamuna Prasad Nishad, an ex-village pradhan in Gorakhpur, envisioned uniting his fellow caste people and organized the Nishad Chetna Yatras in the early 1990s for this purpose, developing a cadre of activists committed to the cause of the Nishad caste in the countryside. His name fast emerged as an influential caste leader, and the Samajwadi Party fielded him as its Lok Sabha candidate from Gorakhpur against Yogi Adityanath of BJP in 1998, 1999 and 2004. However, Nishad could not make much difference in electoral terms.

A clever politician, he kept changing parties and managed to win in the 2007 assembly elections (on a BSP ticket) from Pipraich (Gorakhpur) over an independent candidate and arch rival Jitendra Jaiswal alias Pappu, who was infamous in the region for distributing money and liquor to buy votes. Jamuna Prasad was made the fisheries minister in the new government and he tried hard to give fishing the status of a cottage industry. However, when his name appeared in a case related to attacking the Maharajganj police station in the district in June 2008, where a police constable was killed, Mayawati suspended him from the ministry. Later in November 2010 he died in a road accident.

When we reached Gorakhpur for the first time in April 2011 on our motorbikes, we stopped by a roadside dhaba to have tea. A framed and garlanded photo of a man with a moustache and glasses, who looked like an old-time trade union leader was on the counter. The words 'Sathiyon girte huye jhande ko thaam lena (Comrades, hold tight the falling flag)' were emblazoned on it. When we asked the dhaba owner whose photo it was, he told us that he was Jamuna ji who 'had done a lot for the community'. It turned out that the owner was a Nishad himself and that Nishads in the region used to consider Jamuna Prasad a messiah.

A by-election was scheduled in Pipraich on 8 May 2011 after Jamuna Prasad's fatal road accident. Though Jamuna Prasad was a BSP MLA, the party was not ready to field his wife citing a new directive from the high command that BSP would not contest the by-elections. An angry Nishad supporter (who used to be a rural medical practitioner) told us at a village in Pipraich that Mayawati was not happy with the assertion of extremely backward Mallahs and that was the reason why she got rid of Jamuna Prasad at the first opportunity she got. He also alleged that she was planning to get rid of his widow Rajmati by not fielding her as BSP's official candidate in the by-election and indirectly supporting Jitendra Jaiswal. The allegation proved to be true when after Rajmati's revolt, BSP supported Jaiswal in the 2011 by-election and later fielded him as the party's official candidate in the 2012 elections as well.

While going through villages in Pipraich, we saw the same photo at numerous small shops. A number of people we talked to were sympathetic to Jamuna Prasad asserting that he hadn't been involved in the killing of the police constable at Maharajganj. We were also told on numerous occasions about how the Maharajganj police station officers had refused to register an FIR on the rape of a Nishad girl and Jamuna Prasad had only gone there to ensure that the FIR was registered. All these reasons made people sympathize with Jamuna Prasad.

Even in faraway constituencies like Chauri-Chaura, we came across a number of people who spoke of him with high esteem. When we reached Jamuna Prasad's ancestral home in mid-April, his wife and supporters had joined SP just a night earlier. While interacting with his son and other relatives and supporters, it was revealed that Rajmati was only the symbol for Jamuna Prasad's legacy, as the real political work was still being carried out by his old team of trusted comrades, with an old associate, Daya Shankar Nishad leading the charge. Daya Shankar told us that Nishad voters influenced six assembly constituencies in Gorakhpur region alone and the support of his fellow caste men would now go to the SP. In the by-election, Rajmati emerged victorious and Akhilesh Yadav termed it as a gift to Mayawati on her completion of four years in government. In 2012 again, Rajmati defeated BSP's Jitendra Jaiswal by more than 35,000 votes. Still, Nishad politics in UP is in a very nascent phase as the community is politically scattered and less politicized. The community which is influential in a number of assembly elections in regions from Unnao to Bundelkhand to Poorvanchal is still to identify a state-level leader, who could mobilize and unite it, enhancing its capacity of political bargain.

New Variants of Minority Politics

According to the 2011 census, Muslims constitute 18.49 percent of Uttar Pradesh's total population. UP has always been a big centre of Muslim culture and politics. After Partition, a large section of Muslims acted as a vote bank for the Congress till 1992, when the Babri Masjid demolition by a RSS and BJP-led mob caused disillusionment with the Congress. Mulayam Singh Yadav became the new favourite of Muslims in Uttar Pradesh, so much so that he was called 'Maulana Mulayam'. The fiery SP leader Azam Khan was one of the first politicians in UP to demand the reconstruction of the Babri Masjid at the same site and together with the MY (Muslim-Yadav) combination, SP continued to remain one of the main players in UP politics.

The demolition also created a unique phenomenon—BJP fear psychosis. With this event, the Muslims had witnessed what BJP could do if in power and all they wanted now was to keep it under check so that it could not cause further harm to the community. The fear of BJP scoring a win became so big in the minority circles that they were ready to align with any other formation and vote *en bloc* for it to defeat BJP. This fear psychosis became a very useful instrument in the hands of non-NDA (National Democratic Alliance, an alliance of parties led by BJP at the national level) parties who exploited this fear to secure chunks of minority votes in elections, across the nation.

Gradually, BSP too emerged as a key player in attracting

minority votes and in the 2007 assembly elections, it attracted a sizeable percentage of the total Muslim votes. The Congress had been making many attempts as well to win back the electoral support of the Muslims, while the BJP had been claiming that all parties wanted to appease the minorities to gain votes, in the hope of polarizing Hindu votes. However, in this routine hullabaloo, newer and more radical voices emerged this time, claiming to be the new champions of minority cause.

In September 2008, the Delhi police shot dead two teenagers, Atif and Sazid, in an alleged encounter at Batla House in the Jamia Nagar area, where a police inspector, Mohan Chand Sharma, was also killed. Police alleged that the youngsters were terrorists belonging to the Indian Mujahideen organization that was responsible for many bomb blasts across the nation. This was the time when a number of bomb blasts had shaken the nation from Mecca Masjid in Hyderabad to Malegaon in Maharashtra, and Ajmer Dargah and Jaipur in Rajasthan to the Sarojini Nagar market blast in Delhi.

Under pressure, police arrested a number of people, most of whom were from Azamgarh, christening the district 'Atankgarh' (terror citadel). However, a number of people alleged that the youth from Azamgarh arrested or killed in connection with these blasts were innocent. This theory started gaining currency when, despite many attempts, the police could not provide enough evidence to implicate them. Bizarre situations emerged when anti-terrorism squads (ATS) of different states paraded different individuals arrested by them before the media as masterminds for the same bomb blasts. Investigations carried out by the Maharashtra ATS later revealed that most of the terror acts, like the Ajmer blast and the Malegaon blast, were conducted by some ex-RSS functionaries who had confessed to the bombings. This produced a sense of betrayal and victimization in the minds of the Muslims in the state and the clerics of Azamgarh called the Ulema, built an umbrella formation in September 2008 to resist this injustice. The formation was named Rashtriya Ulema Council.

Claiming to draw inspiration from the freedom struggle, when a number of Ulemas countered colonial power, the Ulema Council pledged to seek justice for the minority community, which was being targeted by the police machinery of different governments, be it the UP ATS of Mayawati's regime or the Delhi Police and other national agencies under the Congress's rule. Accusing the ATS of extorting money from Muslims in the name of terror investigations, the council led a series of rallies in Azamgarh, Lucknow and Delhi including the one in Delhi in January 2009, demanding a judicial probe into the Batla House encounter.

A combination of energies of educated Muslim professionals and students, with the traditional authority of clerics gave it a unique character and unlike other minority groups, it talked of Hindu-Muslim unity, asserting the legacy of the 1857 revolt. The Ulema Council also refused to bow down before the fear psychosis of the BJP scoring a win, that always succeded in uniting minority votes behind parties like SP-BSP or Congress who could defeat BJP and discouraged people to vote for smaller Muslim formations, who would act as 'spoilers' (vote-katwa in local language) in terms of dividing the anti-BJP vote, making it win. It claimed that governments of other parties, like Congress and BSP had been equally bad in terms of neglecting the minorities. Hence it asserted that the Muslims need to come out of the tag of anti-BJP vote bank. They need to vote for a party that takes up their issues more pro-actively unlike Congress and SP, and must support it with all their might, leaving behind the fear that this could help BJP in coming to power, for the SP and Congress were no better than BJP. Thus it called the Muslims to raise a genuine political alternative of theirs, from within their own ranks. For these reasons, political parties who claimed to command minority support were jittery, as the Ulema Council defined democratic rights of minorities in a more modern and nuanced manner. We attended one of their rallies in Delhi where a number of students and teachers from different central universities of the city echoed their support for the cause of the Ulema Council, questioning the government on why it could not guarantee the protection of the rights of its Muslim citizens. The Ulema Council's rallies pulled huge crowds and a number of burqa-clad women were seen partipating, a phenomenon that was quite rare until then.

The party fielded five candidates in the 2009 Lok Sabha elections, including two Hindus. Its Azamgarh candidate, Dr Javed Akhtar polled 59,270 votes, while BSP's Akbar Ahmad (Dumpy) was defeated by BJP's Ramakant Yadav by an almost equal number of votes. Though the party could not win any seats, its performance was not to be ignored. However, the victory of BJP in Azamgarh (due to Ulema Council acting as spoiler) demoralized a number of council supporters and as the momentum around the anti-victimization drive weakened due to a decline in such cases, the Ulema Council started losing ground.

In the 2012 assembly elections, the party failed to win any seat, not even coming second for any of the ten seats at its headquarters in Azamgarh. While the Ulema Council was becoming obsolete, another minority group was raising its head. But unlike the council which had tried to unite the Muslims, this group highlighted its differences, sabotaging the very conception of the Umma (brotherhood).

In February 2008, Dr Ayub, a senior surgeon from Badhalganj, Gorakhpur, floated the Peace Party of India (PPI) which targeted a unique factor of Islam in India—caste among Muslims. Islam denies any kind of discrimination between the faithful, but when it entered India, it could not remain untouched by the caste system which entered Islamic ranks as well; the main groups being forward Muslims or Ashraf and the backward Muslims or Pasmanda.

Ansaris, who are mainly associated with weaving, constitute the most vocal and radical section of the Pasmanda Muslim community in eastern UP. This community became the flag-bearer of the Peace Party. A local journalist in Balrampur told us, 'Ansaris are the main force of Muslim politics in the region, but are least represented in leadership and their socio-economic condition is not very good either. That's why they are attracted to Dr Ayub's Peace Party as it seems to be their own party and promises them a bigger share in the pie.' At a number of places in eastern UP, we encountered upper-caste minority leaders who waxed eloquent against the Peace Party and its crazy Ansari supporters who were so jahil (illiterate) that they could sabotage the interest of the entire Muslim community while supporting 'their own leader'.

The PPI fielded twenty-one candidates in UP in the 2009 Lok Sabha elections, but failed to make any noticeable impact on most of the seats, not winning even one though it polled approximately five lakh votes in total. However, it devised a unique campaign line and election strategy during the 2012 elections. Using its strong hold over the Ansari and other backward caste Muslims, it also fielded candidates from Hindu castes dominant in the constituency to create a winning combination. The party's slogan Ekta ka raj chalega, Hindu-Muslim saath chalega (Hindu-Muslim will march together and their unity will rule) symbolized this arrangement. Its unique approach attracted many unlikely elements; from ex-bureaucrats like former Uttar Pradesh DGP Yashpal Singh to Jitendra Singh Babloo, the suspended BSP MLA from Bikapur who was accused of burning UP Congress president Rita Bahuguna Joshi's house.

Furthermore, PPI urged Muslims to break free of BJP's fear tactics. Party president Dr Ayub targeted all parties, be it Congress, BSP (to a lesser extent) or SP for neglecting the development of Muslims, acting not very differently from the BJP and declining to implement recommendations of the Sachhar Committee, which had advised separate reservation and other affirmative actions for Muslims.

His extensive tours to different areas of UP helped the party create an environment for itself and develop an efficient organizational structure. Dr Ayub asked Muslims to look beyond the Babri Masjid demolition issue, a subject sub-judice in the court. The Peace Party made the progress of Muslims a central concern and speeches by its leaders virtually lacked any inflammatory content.

The party decided to cut into the minority vote base of the Samajwadi Party as Dr Ayub told *India Today* in an interview, 'We are looking at building ourselves by taking away the SP votes.' Promising to strive to have a Muslim chief minister in the state, the party gained a lot of attention in the run-up to the elections, with allegations of working for BJP hurled against it by other parties. In fact BJP leaders were very excited about PPI's good performance as this would have caused a split in the minority votes, giving BJP an opportunity to improve its chances in Poorvanchal. A BJP leader in Barabanki said, 'Peace Party musalmano ka vote khayegi, aur hindu vote ka dhruvikaran karke hum is bar Poorvanchal main pachas se jyada seat jitenge (Peace Party will divide Muslim votes and by polarization of Hindu votes we will manage to win fifty seats in Poorvanchal alone).'

The calculations however did not work.

The Peace Party formed a front known as Ittehad Front or Ekta Manch in alliance with other smaller caste-based parties like Apna Dal, Bundelkhand Congress, and Bharatiya Samaj Party and fielded about 208 candidates of its own in UP.

By the time of the 2012 elections, Peace Party's initial hype started to dwindle, some reasons being infighting among its members, frequent changes in candidates and allegations of taking money to give party tickets. In places like Kapilvastu (SC) in Siddharthanagar district, a last-minute ticket denial brought humiliation to the PPI as there were two candidates from the party there. First, the ticket was given to Moti Lal Vidyarthi and the party's symbol—a ceiling fan—was allotted to him, but on the last day of the nomination, Moti Lal was sidelined and Manju Singh was given the ticket. However, as time was short, the party could not allot her the symbol. Thus, there were two PPI candidates in Kapilvastu—the unofficial candidate Moti Lal Vidyarthi who contested on the official election symbol, and the official candidate Manju Singh who contested on an unofficial symbol. When we spoke to some local Muslim youth about it, they said, 'Dr Ayub ne dukaan khol rakhi hai; jo jyada paisa le ke pahuch jata hai usi ko purane se cheen ke ticket de dete hain (Dr Ayub has opened up a shop; anyone who goes with more money is given a ticket to replace the old candidate)!'

The party's electoral performance fell far short of its expectations. SP had swept much of the minority votes. PPI did manage to win four seats, with one winner, Akhilesh Singh of Rae Bareli, being from the Hindu community. However, Akhilesh Singh's victory cannot be attributed to the Peace Party as he was already a dominant figure in Rae Bareli, winning this seat for a number of years as an independent because of his groundedness and strongman image.

Even so, PPI is the sixth biggest party in the UP assembly in terms of seats, polling 2.35 percent votes in the state, coming second on three seats and third on eight more. BJP's hopes were shattered though, as it could win only eight of those sixty-one seats where PPI won a sizeable number of votes.

Another experiment of creating a Muslim party was carried out by Mukhtar Ansari, the infamous criminal politician of Ghazipur who launched the Quami Ekta Dal (QED) in Ghazipur and nearby districts. As its name implied, the party talked about Hindu-Muslim unity, and refuting media reports claiming that Ansari was only a communal leader, the people of Ghazipur told us that he was supported by Hindus and Muslims alike. A number of educated Ghazipur residents told us with pride that this was the home district of the famous writer Rahi Masum Raza and had never witnessed any communal riots—a fact that frequently appeared in Raza's writings as well. They also said that the riots that had broken out in nearby Mau had been triggered by BJP-RSS functionaries and the alleged killing of BJP MLA Krishnand Rai by Ansari supporters was more because of underworld rivalries than communal targeting. However, the party did not have a distinct agenda or a mass-base and revolved around the personal charisma and influence of Mukhtar Ansari. In the 2012 elections, it fielded forty-three candidates and managed to win two seats, one in Mohammadabad in Ghazipur where Ansari's brother Sibgatullah Ansari won and the other in Mau, where Mukhtar Ansari himself romped home.

Though a couple of these new experiments presented a new brand of Muslim politics, which adopted communal harmony and development as their propaganda, it did not mean that communalism and fanaticism were out of the picture. In the hullabaloo of modern minority parties, a primarily religious outfit of a Barelvi sect known as Ittehad-e-Millat Council (IMC) decided to rely on the time-tested recipe of hatred and fanaticism. What is surprising is that this party, centred only in Bareilly was part of the Ittehad Front led by PPI and was supported by Mukhtar Ansari's QED as well.

Bareilly is a city with a credible history of Hindu-Muslim

unity, though attempts have been made by a number of forces to spread communal hatred and violence. However, the common people of both religions have always tried to prevent this from happening. Some people have tried to change the name of the famous Ayub Khan Chauraha to Patel Chowk, in an attempt to Hindu-ise it by using Sardar Patel's name, but the people of Bareilly refused to communalize spaces in this manner. Ayub Khan Chauraha is still called by that name by the majority of Bareilly's citizens, irrespective of religion.

On 2 March 2010, the day of the Baravafat procession, a riot broke out in Bareilly on a minor issue of brickbatting between Hindus and Muslims. Curfew was imposed, which continued for fifteen days, but when the police arrested IMC president Maulana Tauqeer Raza Khan on charges of inciting riots, his supporters came out in thousands on the roads, breaking curfew to demand his release. Succumbing to the pressure, the BSP government released him and lifted all charges against him, after which fresh riots and arson broke out in the city. Dozens were arrested and many more were injured.

Maulana Tauqeer saw a political opportunity in this incident like his BJP counterparts, and used the moment to rally people behind him. Newspaper reports and statements of a number of people we spoke to alleged that he had incited the riots with hate speeches, while some BJP leaders had allegedly tried to do the same with the Hindus.

In the assembly elections, Maulana Tauqeer's IMC party fielded eighteen candidates and resorted to all sorts of attempts to polarize minority votes, with BJP doing the same. While the IMC managed to win only the Bhojipura seat of Bareilly, the older and more experienced player of such politics, the BJP, proved to be more successful, winning three seats in Bareilly and losing the Baheri seat by a margin of only eighteen votes.

The Smaller Players Fail to Make a Difference

Other than the big parties like SP and BSP that have a mass base in dominant or numerically strong caste groups, some smaller caste-based parties were also trying to make themselves heard by mobilizing less vocal but numerically dominant caste groups in different pockets of the state. One of these was the Apna Dal, founded in 2000 by Sonelal Patel, an ex-BSP leader and associate of Kanshi Ram. The party had once commanded some support of Patel and Kurmi voters in Varanasi and in the eastern UP area. The infamous criminal politician Atique Ahmed of Allahabad had also joined the party and it had won three seats in the 2002 assembly elections. It however, suffered a major blow when Atique Ahmed joined SP in October 2003 along with all three elected MLAs of the party.

Another minor player was Om Prakash Rajbhar's Bharatiya Samaj Party. Bhar or Rajbhar is also a Most Backward Caste and has failed to gain the political, economic or educational benefits of the OBC reservation. Keshav Dev Maurya's Mahan Dal, focusing on Kachi or Maurya voters and Ramavtar Saini's Rashtriya Mahan Dal, which concentrated on Saini, Nai (barber), and Prajapati (kumhar or potters) castes belonging to the MBC community in western UP were some other examples of smaller caste-oriented parties. Most of them came together as allies in the Ittehad Front to contest the 2012 elections together.

Other than Amar Singh's Rashtriya Lok Manch, which did not have a base in any community and was thus expected by all to fail, ex-chief minister Kalyan Singh also launched the Jan Kranti Party (Rashtrawadi) (JKP) (R), confident of spoiling BJP's game and winning a couple of seats because of his hold on the Lodh Rajput voters of western UP and Rohilkhand.

Overall, along with the national and state parties, a total of around 222 parties contested elections in UP, excluding the independents. While Apna Dal fielded seventy-six candidates,

Mahan Dal fielded seventy-four and Kalyan Singh's JKP (R) fielded 208 candidates. Despite securing more than nine lakh votes and 1.24 percent of the total votes polled in the state, JKP (R) failed to win a single seat though it came second on six and third on seven other seats.

The most successful was Apna Dal, as Sonelal's daughter Anupriya won the Rohaniya (Varanasi) seat, with two other party candidates coming in as runners-up. The vote percentage was nearly 0.90 percent of the total votes polled, but it was the lowest in Apna Dal's electoral history. Other parties could not achieve even this, failing to win even a single seat or achieving even 0.5 percent of the total votes polled.

In the absence of a distinct agenda, programme or urge for the betterment of their own caste voters, these opportunistic parties were more like vehicles for individual leaders desperate to shape their own political careers and the voters showed little interest in helping them accomplish this objective.

Targeting Caste Constituencies through Rhetoric: Slogans in UP Politics

Rhetoric is an important part of politics and nothing captures it more aptly than the slogans of political parties. Political commentators have always given due attention to the study of slogans mainly to grasp which sections are being targeted by a party and what strategy it is using to send its message across. For example, in the run up to the 2007 elections, BSP used the slogan 'Haathi Nahin Ganesh Hai, Brahma, Vishnu, Mahesh Hai (the elephant represents Ganesh, and also the trinity, all Brahminical gods)' to signify and justify its coalition of extremes—the Brahmins and Dalits.

The Congress ruled in UP with the same alliance for many years but with a difference. Unlike BSP where Dalits led the alliance, Brahmins were at the helm of affairs in the Congress.

This slogan signified a shift in the politics of BSP as earlier it had always taken a hostile stance towards the Brahmins who they had termed as the upholders of the discriminatory caste system. The initial slogans of BSP were highly derogatory towards upper castes, like 'Tilak, taraju aur talwar, inko maaro joote char (Brahmins, Baniyas and Thakurs represented by the vermillion mark, weighing scale and sword respectively must be given a good beating with shoes)'. The new slogan was a part of the party's exercise to woo the Brahmins by holding a series of

Brahmin Jodo Sammelans (Join Brahmins Meetings) in the state. Sixty such sammelans were held between February and July 2006 in twenty-one districts with many more to come. Reportedly, these were meant only for Brahmins and Dalits were not admitted. In her address at the 9 June state-level Brahmin Mahasammelan at Lucknow, which was attended by around one lakh Brahmins, Mayawati said, 'Ambedkar not only accepted a Brahmin surname given to him by a Brahmin teacher but also married a Brahmin.' She also dubbed them Manavs (Humans) not Manuvadis (followers of the ancient mythological sage Manu, whose social code of ethics or Manu Samhita is considered heavily anti-Dalit and anti-women) and praised them for their role as leaders of social change.

Terrified of BSP's moves aimed at poaching its upper-caste vote base, the BJP resorted to a counter-attack. Playing on the caste ego of the Brahmins, it bounced back with, 'Pandit Nahi Chamar Hai, Haathi par Sawaar Hai (the one who rides an elephant i.e supports BSP is not a Brahmin, but a Chamar)'. The slogan however failed to make much difference to the Brahmins who continued to flock towards the BSP.

Caste is an important factor in UP and depending upon their caste bases, political parties vilify or glorify different castes in the popular language. During our visit to the Farrukhabad district, we heard a BJP Brahmin leader telling a group of Koeris during the campaign, 'Aap ek sau aheeron ko Parliament bhej do, phir dekhna Meera Kumar ghurrati hai ki ghighiyati hain (Send a hundred Yadavs to the Parliament and then see if Meira Kumar shouts or pleads).'

The target was clear: vilify Yadavs and highlight SP's goondaraj to win Dalit votes playing upon the fear psychosis that if SP wins, no one can save them from being thrashed at the hands of the Ahirs or Yadavs.

Earlier the slogans used to be more class-oriented. For example, against Janata Party's anti-Indira slogan of Indira Hatao (Remove Indira) during the 1971 elections, Indira Gandhi shot back with the hugely popular and successful slogan, Garibi Hatao (Remove poverty), which had brought Janata Party to its knees. With time, slogans became more caste-centric, but issues and target constituencies were always kept in mind. In the 2012 elections, SP's Ummeed ki Cycle, signifying new hope triumphed over other opponents.

During elections, every word uttered by the candidates, parties and opponents has significance and an objective. Loosely-made comments prove to be very dangerous for election results. One such example is the defeat of Congress's Koel (Aligarh) candidate, Vivek Bansal. Bansal was said to be a winner by all and the minority voters too favoured him. When we reached Aligarh, we were told by many people how Vivek Bansal lost this election. On the polling day, when he felt that a number of minority voters at a booth were voting for SP candidate Haji Jameer Ullah, he allegedly accused Muslims in the area of doublespeak by promising votes to him but actually voting for SP. Within minutes, this news reached each and every booth of the constituency (courtesy the Opposition parties) and Muslim voters who were angry at being considered mere vote banks, voted *en bloc* against Bansal, who finally lost by 599 votes to SP's Haji Jameer. As we said, every word counts in the electoral contest.

Who Voted for Whom:
Analysis of Electoral Data in UP Assembly Elections 2012

In Uttar Pradesh, upper castes constitute roughly 30 percent of the population, with the biggest segment comprising Brahmins, who are said to be around 9 percent of the population. The Scheduled Castes or Dalits comprise 21 percent, with Jatavs or Chamars being the biggest chunk out of them (around 11 percent), followed by another dominant sub-caste, the Pasis or Rawats. While Muslims constitute around 18.5 percent of the total population, OBCs and MBCs constitute the remaining main chunk with Yadavs making up around 13-14 percent of the total population. It is in this universe of castes and communities that all parties operate and contest to make their way.

The biggest subject of discussion during the last elections was Mayawati's social engineering, which brought Dalits and Brahmins together. In 2012, people said that though Dalits would stay with Mayawati, Brahmins would leave her. Many experts claimed that since Brahmins were leaving Mayawati and going back to BJP or the Congress, the latter would be the dark horse in these elections. However, according to the Centre for the Study of Developing Societies (CSDS) data on the 2012 elections, Brahmin votes for BSP increased this time around.

While in 2007, 16 percent Brahmins voted for BSP, the number increased to 19 percent this time. Congress and BJP both suffered a loss of 6 percent in terms of Brahmin votes received in 2012 and those received in 2007. The party that gained the maximum Brahmin votes was SP, which had succeeded in allaying their fears. While only 10 percent Brahmins voted for SP in 2007, in 2012 it increased by a record 9 percent to become 19 percent.

In terms of Thakur votes, Congress (13 percent in 2012 from 9 percent in 2007) and SP (26 percent in 2012 from 20 percent in 2007) were the biggest gainers, while BJP lost more votes (29 percent in 2012 from 46 percent in 2007) and BSP improved marginally (12 percent in 2007 to 14 percent in 2012).

Congress proved to be the new favourite of the Vaishya community as its vote share in Baniya votes increased from 10 percent in 2007 to 21 percent in 2012, while other parties remained more or less static on this count and the BJP suffered a loss of 10 percent votes among the Vaishya community coming down to 42 percent from 52 percent in 2007.

Despite the common perception and Mayawati's assertion that Dalit voters remained with her, the truth is far from this. According to CSDS data, while BSP received 86 percent of Jatav votes last time, its share of Jatav votes dropped to 62 percent this time. The same was the case with Valmiki voters; in 2007, 71 percent of Valmikis voted for BSP while this time only 42 percent voted for it. Though BSP's share in terms of Pasi voters increased marginally by 4 percent this time (53 percent in 2007 to 57 percent in 2012) in terms of Other Scheduled Castes, its share came down to 45 percent from 58 percent in 2007.

While BJP too suffered a loss in terms of its hold on Dalit votes, SP and Congress proved to be the biggest gainers of Dalit votes in this election. While SP's share in Jatav votes increased from 4 percent to 15 percent, Congress' share increased from 2 percent to 5 percent. Similarly, while SP received 9 percent of Valmiki votes this time as compared to 2 percent in 2007, Congress went from 4 percent in 2007 to 12 percent in 2012.

In terms of Pasi votes, while Congress remained static at 7 percent, the SP's share increased from 16 percent to 24 percent. However, in terms of other SC voters, while SP's tally increased marginally from 16 percent to 18 percent, Congress performed better cornering 17 percent of SC votes in this election as compared to just 4 percent in 2007.

As for OBC voters, the data also holds some surprises. Unlike the common perception that Yadavs voted en masse for SP, the data suggests that the party got only 66 percent of Yadav votes this time as compared to 72 percent in 2007. While Congress's share of Yadav votes remained static at 4 percent, BJP and BSP both increased their share by 4 percent this time making it 9 percent in 2012 from 5 percent in 2007 for the BJP, and 11 percent in 2012 from 7 percent in 2007 for the BSP.

In terms of Jat voters, RLD's hold weakened this time, as compared to its lion's share of 61 percent in Jat votes in the state in 2007, this time it could corner only 45 percent. While BJP and SP's share of Jat votes dropped from 18 percent to 7 percent and 8 percent to 7 percent respectively, the BSP improved marginally from 10 percent in 2007 to 16 percent this time. The Congress emerged as the biggest gainer of Jat votes this time, polling 11 percent as compared to only 2 percent in 2007.

In terms of Kurmi/Koeri voters also, Congress and SP almost doubled their vote share from 6 percent for Congress and 17 percent for the SP to 13 percent and 35 percent respectively, while BJP came down from 42 percent in 2007 to 20 percent in 2012 and the BSP improved marginally from 16 percent to 19 percent in 2012.

In terms of Muslim votes while BSP (17 percent in 2007 to

20 percent in 2012), the BJP (3 percent in 2007 to 7 percent in 2012) and the Congress (18 from 14 percent earlier) improved their performance, SP's share came down from 45 percent in 2007 to 39 percent this time. The share of other parties too increased among Muslim votes from 13 percent in 2007 to 15 percent this time, suggesting better-than-expected performance by new players, such as the Peace Party of India.

The SP not only improved its performance in villages with 29 percent of rural voters favouring it compared to 26 percent in 2007, but also broke the myth that it is a party with a predominantly rural base by cornering 23 percent of urban votes this time as compared to 20 percent in 2007. This is also vindicated by analysis in absolute terms, as SP won 9 out of 35 urban and 32 out of 60 semi-urban seats in the state. BJP remained an urban party as out of its total tally of forty-seven seats, twenty-six were in the urban and semi-urban category while twenty-one were in the rural category. What is more significant in this regard is the fact that out of a total thirty-five urban seats in the state, BJP could corner twenty seats.

In terms of reserved seats, SP's performance was better than the BSP's. While BSP won fifteen out of eighty-five reserved seats securing 27.3 percent of votes polled in them, SP won fifty-eight such seats with 31.6 percent of the total votes polled on these seats.

In terms of Muslim-dominated seats, SP seemed less successful in areas where the Muslim population was more than 30 percent. It won eighty-six out of 139 seats where the Muslim population was between 10.1 to 20 percent and sixty-six out of 121 seats where it was up to 10 percent, while it could win only thirty-five out of seventy-three seats where Muslims were above 30 percent of the total population. One possible explanation for this could be Hindu polarization politics carried out by BJP, which won seventeen out of seventy-three seats in areas where

Muslims were above 30 percent of the population; its best in terms of victory on minority-dominated seats.

The Congress proved to be the fastest emerging choice of poor voters—compared to its vote share of 5 percent poor voters in 2007, it doubled its share this time to 10 percent. While SP improved its performance in this category too (23 percent in 2007 to 28 percent in 2012), the BJP remained static on 12 percent and the BSP lost its hold on poor voters (dropped from 41 percent in 2007 to 33 percent in 2012).

Congress also emerged as the biggest choice of younger voters (18-25 year olds), as its share of this segment increased from 10 percent in 2007 to 15 percent in 2012, the highest in this category. Another significant fact is that SP turned out to be the biggest choice of women voters (31 percent in 2012 from 26 percent in 2007) with Congress emerging as a second choice (12 percent in 2012 from 8 percent in 2007), while the BSP and BJP recorded a decline in the preference of women voters.

The result clearly was a decisive mandate in favour of the SP. Not only did it make significant inroads into all castes and communities, but its hold over the traditional Muslim and Yadav bases was also far above the reach of other parties, despite a few erosions here and there. In terms of the margin also, this mandate was more decisive than the 2007 mandate, as compared to 2007 where 139 seats were won with a victory margin of above 10,000 votes, this time two-thirds of the 222 seats were won by SP.

Apart from this, in overall terms as well, 65 percent of the seats won by SP had a victory margin of 10,000 or above, while BSP had won only 38 percent of such seats in 2007. The BSP could do well only in Bundelkhand and western UP while SP's good performance was distributed among all regions in the state. In terms of total vote share, while BSP suffered a negative vote swing of (-) 4.52 percent, the BJP too suffered a loss of 1.97 percent votes as compared to 2007.

SP's development and hope-oriented campaign proved to be successful in earning the trust of the people of Uttar Pradesh. The party also gained the confidence of all castes including Brahmins and Dalits, with women also seeming to prefer it over others. In this situation, maintaining the current hold over different sections and devising an inclusive development agenda seems to be the logical priority of the party.

The analysis of the 2012 electoral data rings a warning bell for the BJP. The party seems to either remain static or lose on major counts in these elections, making slight improvements among very few sections. It has lost its traditional hold on upper castes and failed to make significant inroads into any new mass-base. Its old appeal as the assertive Hindutva party too has lost currency. New approaches, innovative leadership and fresh issues are the call of the hour for BJP if it is interested in improving its hold in the state.

Despite the current losses suffered by the BSP, it still commands over 60 percent of Dalit votes in the state. Further, its support among the upper castes, especially Brahmins still remains intact. Despite the big difference of 144 seats between BSP and SP, the difference in terms of vote share is merely 3.4 percent (approximately). The party still remains the second-most important player in the state. It has, however, seen that despite immense strength, reach and stability of one's political mechanism and hold over people, nothing can be taken for granted in a state like Uttar Pradesh. Nevertheless, the party is in need of a serious overhaul, without which it cannot stop the decay that had started long ago and has now manifested itself strongly in the current defeat. It also has another factor to worry about—the Congress which is again making inroads into BSP's Dalit mass-base, once commanded by India's Grand Old Party.

Though the Congress has failed to achieve a significant electoral success in this election, it still remains the second biggest gainer on a number of counts. In terms of overall vote percentage, it has experienced a positive swing of (+) 3.2 percent in its favour, the highest after the Samajwadis. Its share of Dalit votes has been constantly increasing in the state since the 2004 Lok Sabha elections, which shows that Rahul Gandhi's trips to Dalit homes may appear as nautanki (acting out) to political rivals but they have managed to make a good impact on the ground level and the Dalits are giving him due weight. In this scenario, it seems to be the only party that can subvert Mayawati's future plans by eating away its base vote, even if very slowly. Congress also remains an emerging choice of the poor, youth below twenty-five, and women.

The same CSDS survey found that in terms of future leadership, 38 percent respondents preferred Rahul Gandhi, while only 20 percent chose Akhilesh Yadav, although it is evident that most of them were keeping national politics in mind. A maximum number of people also chose Congress as the second-best alternative in the same survey. This shows that the party and its chief anchor Rahul Gandhi have succeeded in winning the perception and hearts, if not votes, of the people, as of now. A grounded organization with a vibrant youth and student wing, thrust on pro-poor policies and continuation of the current scale of political intervention may enable the Congress to win back lost ground. But the current state of affairs in UP seems to indicate that Congress leaders and members have little interest in working towards this, planning to sleep for the next one year only to wake up just in time for the run-up to parliamentary elections in 2014.

PART FIVE

IMAGE OF AN AVERAGE UP POLITICIAN

THERE WAS A TIME WHEN THE COLOUR WHITE REPRESENTED PEACE, and khadi represented self-reliance and opposition to the British. Thanks to the hordes of Indian politicians who have monopolized the colour white, it is no longer the case. Lakhs of these elected representatives of the world's biggest democracy, from deep down south to the far north and from the east to the west, have adopted the white khadi kurta as their dress code. It is hard to avoid stereotyping a person dressed all in white as a politician.

It is these stereotypes that we will talk about in this chapter. As discussed earlier, stereotypical profiling does have some basis for branding or labelling a set of people belonging to a particular profession. However, this is not a completely rational exercise; in many cases, numerous exceptions undercut the very logic of this exercise. Politicians in UP do share some common characteristics, nonetheless. Caricatures of some UP politicos will be presented to substantiate this logic, but to make it more interesting, we will also present some characters that challenge this stereotyping exercise—presenting just another aspect of politics in the state.

Different phases of UP politics in contemporary history have been dominated by various political actors with their own theatrical styles. Mayawati in her latest avatar adorned the throne as a Dalit messiah. However, a number of critics alleged that after coming to power, she was more a daulat-ki-beti (money's daughter) than a Dalit-ki-beti (Dalit's daughter); she had purportedly even sent a special aircraft to Mumbai to pick up her new pair of sandals. Social scientist Ashis Nandy puts it in a psycho-analytical perspective: those who have been oppressed in society by a certain section in the past, start emulating the same when they come to power, for despite the hatred of the oppressed for the oppressor, the oppressed holds a sense of veneration and an urge to be like the oppressor.

Another social scientist, M. N. Srinivas, called it Sanskritization—the act of people from lower or middle castes following the traditions and customs of members of a higher caste in order to claim the same high-caste status. Perhaps this emulation of the practices of upper-caste politicians in UP by the ones belonging to middle and lower castes could be termed as Political Sanskritization.

Examples of this phenomenon are numerous. A petty leader who wins an election, even at a zila panchayat level in UP begins to emulate the rituals and gestures of the local landed elite, the Brahmins and Thakurs, or whoever had earlier dominated the political scene in the area. He gives donations to local temples and babas (holy men), is surrounded by a group of yes-men who run to do his bidding. His gestures and body language become similar to the local political elite. Now, the puny creature who had once ridden a cycle for twenty or thirty kilometres a day, develops a pot-belly because he is always driven around in his Bolero or Scorpio. His vehicle's windows are always rolled up and the sun film turns a shade darker. He doesn't meet his electorate as regularly as he used to earlier. He focuses more on 'generating' resources from his share in the local theka-patta (a licence or contract).

Such changes or the lack of them, make or break a newly-emerged leader at the local level. At the higher level, things operate differently.

The average UP politician is not very difficult to recognize, although the characteristics change from region to region and differ from rural to urban areas. We will mostly be talking about men here because there are very few women politicians in UP, although three of the four main parties in the contest were led by women—Mayawati (BSP), Uma Bharti (BJP) and Rita Bahuguna Joshi (Congress).

The usual dress of a UP politician is a white kurta pajama, but those who are older and from the upper castes, are usually found in dhoti-kurtas to set themselves apart from the others. This kurta pajama is mostly made of cotton, but the quality of the cotton differs with respect to the caste and class, as noted by many veteran journalists and political observers.

In Bahraich, a senior journalist told us, 'Aap dekhiyega adhiktar neta jo vaishya jaatiyon se hain unke kurte bade mahin resham ya soot ke hote hain. Aap khoj kar bhi vaise kapda nahi paa sakte hain, pata nahin kahan se laate hain. Aur jo naye aaye hain rajneeti mein—jinme adhikatar pichdi jaatiyon ke log hain, unke kapde Brahmin—baniyon se alag honge (You see, a majority of the leaders who come from Vaishya castes wear kurtas of very fine silk or cotton. You can never find such cloth; who knows where they get it from. And new entrants from OBCs dress differently from Brahmins and Baniyas).'

When we countered that he was stereotyping clothes on the basis of caste, he responded, 'Jab jaati sach hai aur jaati par aadharit sanskritik mulya, rahan sahan sach, to aap kyun "stereotyping" ki angrezi mein ulajhte hain. Yahan ye sach hain, haan jo thode bahar nikal gaye hain, unka aachaar-vyavahar thoda badal zaroor gaya hai? (When caste is a reality and caste-based cultural values and practices are a reality, then why are you getting entangled in the English word like stereotyping? This is true, though those who have been out of the state have changed a bit).'

In Kushinagar, a senior journalist, who was a Brahmin and very reputed in the area, told us, 'Yahan Poorvanchal mein aap neta ki jaati use dekhte hi bata sakte hain. Yahan ke dalit neta door se hi alag dikh jaate hain. In dino baspaiyon mein ek alag hod chali hai—sab safari suit silwane lage hain, safed rang ka. Us par gale mein sone ki moti chain aur haath mein sone ka kada rahega, joota safed sport shoe hoga (Here in Poorvanchal you can tell the caste of a politician just by looking at him. You can easily spot Dalit politicos from a distance. These days the BSP politicians are following a general trend—they all wear safari suits, that too all in white. A thick gold chain around the neck and a gold kada (thick bangle) encircling the wrist are other demarcating features, along with white sports shoes).'

When we begged to differ, he said, 'Shuru-shuru mein hum bhi aisi hi baatein karte the par is ilake mein aapko rehna hai to apni jaat-paat ka samarthan rakhna hoga. Abhi yahan itna parivartan nahi hua hai (When I was younger I also used to speak in a similar fashion, but if you want to live here then you have to support caste and customs, as not many changes have taken place here since a long time).'

But what these two men told us was true to a certain extent in different parts of the state. We witnessed the OBC and Dalit politicians indulging in the same kind of customs and practices as the upper-caste leaders used to in earlier times. In western UP, we met a second generation aspiring MBC leader who had a stable of horses, a kennel filled with half a dozen dogs, including a greyhound, a Great Dane and two Alsatians. He also had a large room-sized cage that held many exotic birds.

At the entrance, you encounter a guard with a double-barrel gun, and the drawing room is tucked away in the far interiors of his home. We found him sitting on an elevated chair among many other people, most of whom were sitting on the ground. He was wearing a white kurta pajama of very fine cloth. A gold chain peeped out from beneath the open buttons of his kurta and his posture and figure reflected that of the 'Thakurs' from old Hindi films.

There were many such people whom we encountered on our journeys. This goes to show that one cannot assume that the empowerment of the middle class in the seventies and eighties, termed by Christopher Jaffrelot as a 'silent revolution', has brought about any substantial change in caste-based oppression and discrimination. Power has changed hands but its character has not changed. The social and political roles that Thakurs or Brahmins had occupied so far, have now been taken over by middle castes, such as Yadavs, Kurmis and Jats. Unfortunately, this 'silent revolution' has not brought about any substantial change in the progress of the poorer and the most downtrodden sections of society. In most places, the OBCs have now become moneylenders and there is a contest to keep a hold on common resources in the village, like grazing lands, ponds, and even panchayati raj institutions, by getting their proxies elected.

Another stereotypical aspect is the Safaris or Scorpios, generally white with fancy numbers and number plates that all politicians move around in. Some have Fortuners and those who have a share in the power sometimes have a Pajero or Prado. Gun-toting, gamcha-clad men accompanying the netajis in their vehicle are a very common spectacle.

SUVs are very popular, not only for their glamour quotient, but also for their utility, as most of the roads in UP are in very bad shape, except for a few national highways. Distinctions also emerge in the politicos' love for SUVs: most aspire to own at least a Toyota Fortuner. The Mahindra Scorpio is now reserved for senior chamchas (yes-men close to the leader) and the Bolero is for the sadharan karaykarta (average worker). When we went to the Darul Shifa, the MLA quarters in the Hazrat Ganj area of Lucknow, we found all the latest SUVs from Toyota, Mitsubishi, Mahindra, and Tata to Lexus parked there.

The professions of the politicians also appear to be determined by their class. Those who belong to families that have been involved in politics for generations possess a distinct confidence and chances are that eight out of ten of them have a gas agency or a petrol station, and if not, then they certainly run a brick-kiln or a cold storage (meant to store potatoes). Many hold multiple petrol stations under the names of various family members. If these stations are within the city or town area then they also double up as political offices and a meeting place for people.

Brick kilns need permission and it is labour-intensive work so those who have a traditional landlord background are found in this trade. They can manage to hire labour easily and environmental and other clearances are not a problem to obtain, as they have enough people in the various departments or ministries to get their work done.

Those who are new or are first-generation netas may own a few trucks, a pharmaceutical agency or an intermediate college (secondary school) because education is big business, although many of them are not even graduates.

Most of the established leaders we met in UP owned an engineering college or a degree college. There are five major roads coming out of Lucknow, and all these roads are lined by private educational institutions, mainly engineering, management, medical, dental and degree colleges. On the Faizabad Road, both sides of the road have huge buildings with impressive façades and most of them are owned by some politician or his family. Educational institutions—mainly engineering and management colleges—have become so rampant that in his last term Mulayam Singh announced a ban on the opening of any new educational institution in Noida and Lucknow till every district in UP had two such colleges. However, Mayawati removed the ban and gave permissions for many new colleges and universities in Noida. About eighteen universities were started in UP in the five years of Mayawati's rule, from

2007 to 2012—many of them owned by politicians from the state, for example: Babu Banarasi Das University owned by Akhilesh Das of the BSP; IFTM University owned by Rajiv Kothiwal, who switched loyalties from the BJP to the BSP; and Noida International University owned by a powerful Thakur BSP leader.

In western UP many politicians also own warehouses, because it is good business and gives them plenty of free time to spend on politics. Warehouses require land, which most of these leaders already own and the permissions needed are easily managed due to their clout in the government.

Our study of UP politicians revealed that there are more strongmen and criminal-politicians, businessmen, caste satraps and contractors than just the run-of-the-mill MLA or elected leader, but there are also a number of characters who do not conform to these stereotypes. A few examples would be discussed here.

The Sadhvi Hat Trick

Sadhus and religious leaders turning to politics in a state like UP are not rare. Because of their hold over the psyche of the people and their ascetic image that projects an apparent disinterest in making money, sadhus and sadhvis often become a good choice for the people over corrupt and money-minded politicians. The Gorakhnath Math of Gorakhpur district is quite an interesting case in this regard; it has kept the Gorakhpur MP seat under its control for more than three decades—first under Mahant Avaiktanand, and now under Yogi Adityanath.

Of all the parties, BJP has given the most number of tickets to religious leaders, and the fairer sex is equally represented in this endeavour. This time around, for the first time ever, the party had succeeded in sending three sadhvis to the UP Vidhan Sabha. And interestingly, all three of them are from the backward-lower castes.

Uma Bharti is a name that needs no introduction. As a girl from the Lodh (OBC) background of Bundelkhand who had taken sanyas (renunciation of worldly ties) as a child, Uma Bharti was soon famous for her brilliance (she is said to have memorized a number of religious texts at a very young age) and oratory skills, while narrating Ram-kathas and the Bhagwad Gita.

Raised under the guardianship of the late Rajmata Vijayaraje Scindia of Gwalior (a prominent BJP leader), she developed a closeness with the BJP and the Ram Mandir agitation brought her into active politics.

After losing her first Lok Sabha elections in 1984, she continued to win consecutively in 1989, 1991, 1996 and 1998 from Khajuraho. After leading the BJP to a clear victory in the 2003 Madhya Pradesh assembly elections, she became the chief minister of the state, but she resigned some time later due to the release of an arrest warrant against her in an old riot case. She was suspended from the BJP twice due to her vocal opposition to the ideological dilution of Hindutva by senior leaders like Lal Krishna Advani, and the prominence given to those who did not have a connection with the people, but were associated with power lobbies.

After her suspension, she formed her own party, the Bharatiya Janshakti Party, which did not make much political impact. In June 2011, she was once again inducted into the BJP and given the task of reviving the party in UP during the 2012 elections. Despite opposition from its own party leaders, BJP did well in the Bundelkhand region where she led the campaign, winning three seats out of nineteen, while earlier it had won none. In terms of reaching out to the people, she left all leaders from all the parties in the entire state far behind, holding a total of 235 meetings during the campaign.

Another sadhvi who made it to Lucknow is also from Bundelkhand. Forty-five year old Sadhvi Niranjan Jyoti of the BJP won from the Hamirpur constituency of Bundelkhand. A Sanskrit undergraduate, Niranjan Jyoti belongs to the Nishad (OBC) caste and like Uma Bharti, she had also embraced sanyas as a child. Her total assets, including house and agricultural land are worth approximately ten lakh rupeess, a pittance compared to her rivals from the Congress and SP, whose fortunes run into crores. Other than being a BJP national executive member, she is also on the directorial board of a number of educational and welfare institutions in the area.

The case of Savitri Phule of Balha SC seat (Bahraich district) is more interesting. Coming from a Dalit background, Savitri's motivation to embrace sanyas was different. As a child, she went to Lucknow with some relatives to attend a rally and witnessed a brutal lathi-charge on the protesters. Moved by their plight, she decided to renounce her family and dedicate her life to the cause of serving the masses. Till date, she does not own a home or any property and lives in an ashram in Nanpara. The affidavit of this thirty-seven-year-old BJP MLA shows total assets worth just two lakh rupees. In the assembly elections, she defeated her nearest rival from BSP by approximately 20,000 votes.

These women politicians present a sharp contrast to the stereotypical image of a UP politician. Coming from low- or backward-caste backgrounds, they have made a place for themselves in the male-dominated world of politics, that too in a state like UP. Unmarried and without a noticeable urge to amass riches, they represent a nobler aspect of politics, where the motivation is still the service of fellow beings.

Dr Uma Shankar Singh Yadav, Varanasi

There exists a whole generation of leaders in Uttar Pradesh who began their careers with student politics in different universities and colleges of UP in the 1980s. The 1980s has its own significance in Indian politics because it saw the emergence of the backward castes in the political arena, which spiralled over time and changed the face of Indian politics.

Dr Uma Shankar Singh Yadav is one such leader, who had stepped into politics around this time from the famous Kashi Vidyapeeth. He was the first OBC president of the Kashi Vidyapeeth in 1989-90. He had been the secretary and vice-president in the preceding years. He was also the president of the Samajwadi Chatra Sabha and had been the secretary of the Samajwadi Party.

He agreed to meet us at a small private hospital on the Varanasi-Jaunpur road. When we reached there and called him, he told us that he would take another hour. Finally, after more than two hours had passed, he arrived on a motorcycle, riding pillion behind someone. He told us that he was held up by a supporter in a village a little further away and that he didn't own a vehicle, so he had to wait for someone to drop him here. We were a little amused that someone who was aspiring for an SP ticket from Shivpur in Varanasi did not even own a vehicle.

When we told him this, Dr Yadav told us that his generation of leaders had been working hard in the field for a long time and had entered politics for the charm of it. His was a generation of leaders that got a taste of politics via student politics and also during the JP (Jayaprakash Narayan) movement in the seventies. They did not have the kind of resources needed for today's politics but they had the advantage of their good work and good image. They did not have any other occupation save politics. Their families were based in semi-urban or rural areas, which provided them with a basis for sustenance.

Dr Singh is one such person who is into politics because he cannot do anything else. The problem is that such candidates are not 'winning' candidates because they do not have the kind of resources that are required to win an election. The average cost of an assembly election campaign in Uttar Pradesh is around one crore rupees. The party cannot take chances on such candidates and this was the case with Dr Uma Shankar Singh Yadav. He had been in politics for a long time and knew all the top SP leaders personally who also admired his work in the area. But when the time for handing out tickets came, they gave it to another person, also a Yadav but one who had good resources because of the hospital he ran in the constituency. Dr Yadav was not happy with this decision and has rebelled against the party. A popular leader not only among the Yadavs but also among the Dalits in the area, he said that he would not go against Mulayam Singh Yadav, but would go against SP. He would contest elections as an independent with Mulayam Singh Yadav's photo on his banner, but not SP's cycle symbol. He finally decided not to contest after getting some assurances from the party leadership.

Some Cases of Criminal Politicians

Hari Shankar Tiwari, Gorakhpur

While roaming around in the narrow lanes of Gorakhpur near Dharamshala area, we chanced upon a huge house with a high boundary wall. Two or three Boleros were parked at the gates, with gun-toting men sitting or standing around them. From the very set-up, it looked like the house of a Bollywood-style mafia boss. And indeed it was; the house belonged to Hari Shankar Tiwari or Baba, the famous criminal-politician of Poorvanchal.

A very soft-spoken, suave man in his early seventies, wearing a dhoti-kurta and a broad smile does not fit the image of a criminal. When you meet him, he greets you appropriately and offers you tea and sweets. He asks you about your work and your whereabouts and speaks with perfect courtesy. People of all ages, castes, and religions attend his baithaks (meetings). He speaks to everyone with the same ease and affection and helps everyone with the same enthusiasm. But when it comes to those who do not comply with his wish, things take on a drastically different hue; as local lore has it, such people soon find themselves 'no longer in this world'. Even so, in his affidavit for the 2012 contest, there are no criminal cases pending against Hari Shankar Tiwari.

In the past, Hari Shankar Tiwari rarely had to reach out to voters in his constituency himself to ask for votes. He had many people to do this on his behalf, but now things have changed.

It was in 1985 when Hari Shankar Tiwari became the first member of the legislative assembly in India to be elected, while being lodged in jail. Then he had clout that many dons would envy. Means of communication and transport were not as developed then and just an image of Hari Shankar Tiwari behind the bars in jail got him a record number of votes, mainly from the Brahmins in the region. This was when V. P. Singh's party was the ruling party in the state and the Brahmin-Thakur conflict helped Tiwari win the election. Brahmins in these areas are not coy and timid but bahubalis (strongmen), owning good land and have control over most of the resources that come with state patronage.

Tiwari has represented the Chillupar seat in the Gorakhpur region six times in a row, from 1985 to 2007; first as an independent, then on a Congress ticket for the next three times and then twice on some little known parties' tickets.

Journalists from his caste never tire of praising him for the development work done in the constituency during his tenure, but people from other castes have a different opinion. Hari Shankar Tiwari has changed parties in the past according to his convenience and his son is a BSP MP from Sant Kabir Nagar. Many of his relatives are into politics in the region, and not only his relatives, but many others with his patronage have also won in the past.

As age catches up with him, however, Hari Shankar Tiwari's clout is on the wane. In 2007 and 2012 he lost to Rajesh Tripathi of BSP. This year his loss was deeper, as he polled in third. Apart from his loss, another casualty included the defeat of his son from the Bansi constituency of Siddharthnagar in the 2012 elections.

Amarmani Tripathi, Maharajganj

Amarmani's story makes a perfect script for a Bollywood film— a heady cocktail of crime, sex and politics. Amarmani is said to have started his career as Hari Shankar Tiwari's driver and sharp-shooter in the eighties. He joined politics and developed his own clout in the state. He had been with Congress, BJP, BSP and SP. When he was arrested for the murder of his paramour, the poet Madhumita Shukla in 2003, he was a minister in the then Mulayam Singh government. He had been instrumental in extricating his political masters from a number of crisis and the 2004 government of SP was orchestrated through the brute force, threat and strong-arm tactics employed by Tripathi, a contribution which is acknowledged by the Mulayam Singh family till date. His wife was also arrested and convicted for the murder, but Amarmani has been out on bail several times.

In the recent election, his son contested from Nautanwa in Maharajganj on an SP ticket. Amarmani Tripathi recorded his voice on a CD, appealing to voters to elect his son, from within the jail. His recorded message went like this, 'Mulayam Singh ki sarkar banwayen. Samajwadi Party ko vote dein, hum jail mein band hain. Mujhpar hue atyachar ka jawab aapko dena hoga. Aapka ek vote mujhe salakhon se mukti mein sahayta karega (Vote for Samajwadi Party to help Mulayam Singh Yadav form the government. I am in jail and you have to avenge the atrocities committed on me. Your vote will help me get out of jail).'

Amarmani has more than thirty-three cases lodged against him, including five charges of murder. He became very popular among the Brahmins of the region who were feeling threatened with the increasing influence and political clout of Yogi Adityanath, who is a Thakur. Many Brahmins in the area do not look at him as a criminal; they believe that he is a product of this system, which pays a premium to your strength—money, muscle and caste. A young Brahmin of around twenty-five years in a village near Nautanwa told us, 'Jab se Bhaiyya jail mein hain, Yogi ki takat badh gayi hai. Ab saare theke-patte thakuron ko jaate hain ya phir brahmano ko thakur ki paa-laagi karni padti hai to kuch milta hai. Amar bhiayya jeet gaye to phir se kuch halat theek hogi (Since Amarmani is in jail, Yogi's strength has increased and all tenders are now going to Thakurs. If Brahmins do not bow to him, they do not get anything. If Amar Bhaiyya wins, things will improve for Brahmins once again).'

Everything is reduced to the access and privileges a caste enjoys because of its hold on power in this region. Differences exist at many levels—between religions, between different castes of the same religion, and even between different sub-castes of the same caste! Your access to power depends on the collective power of your caste and group. This is why people like Amarmani keep coming up from time to time.

Someone like Amarmani who has a chequered personal history, a category 'A' history-sheeter, a criminal who should have been a social outcast for allegedly having an affair with a young Brahmin girl and then killing her brutally, enjoys social acceptance and respect. This is because the politics in the region causes the public to tolerate such people for the sake of their own safety and privileges. When your land is grabbed by strongmen in the village and the police cannot help, you immediately go to the rival strongman. If he is from your own caste, chances of receiving help are better.

A journalist in the area told us that people like Tripathi are born out of the government machinery and bureaucracy. He said, 'Jab aapka kaam koi adhikari baar baar chakkar kaatne par bhi naa kare, aapka apmaan kare aur app tripathi ji jaison se baat karo, to woh use khuleaam gali denge aur chaar jute lagayenge. Tab aapka kaam ho ya na ho, aapko ye zarur lagega ki aapka nyay ho gaya (When an official refuses to do your work, insults you despite repeated appeals and then you approach someone like Tripathiji, he will openly insult the official and give him a good beating. Then, irrespective of your work getting done or not, you feel that justice has been done).'

Such everyday complications of life in these regions give space and legitimacy to people like Amarmani.

Rajas of Democracy: Kunwar Sarvesh Singh of Thakurdwara and Raja Bhaiya of Kunda

Since democracy came to our country over the ruins of feudalism, the feudal lords and princes of earlier times had a natural advantage in terms of influence and resources, to manifest themselves in new avatars as political leaders; the same tradition continues till date at a number of places.

Meet Kunwar Sarvesh alias Rakesh Kumar Singh, five times MLA from Thakurdwara seat of Moradabad district. A 12th pass, Sarvesh Singh belongs to the royal family of Garhwal estate. The Thakurdwara seat was carved out in 1957 and has been under the dominance of the royal family since then. Sarvesh's father Raja Rampal Singh too was four-times MLA and one-time MP from this seat. A typical 'dabang Thakur', Sarvesh has only four cases registered against him, most of which are under sections related to fraud. But ask anyone in Thakurdwara and he will tell you that Raja Saheb's actual record in terms of crimes is something enviable for even category A history-sheeters. His cavalcade of SUVs with guns popping out of the windows of accompanying vehicles are still a source of terror for his adversaries. And the BJP MLAs image too confirms to the stereotypical 'Thakur' of Bollywood films—fair and well-built, short hair, big tilak on the forehead, cruelty on the face, paan-red lips and a thick gold chain popping out of a shirt unbuttoned at chest. A self-styled politician, Singh fielded his wife Sadhna Singh from Mahan Dal at Barhapur seat of Moradabad to cut Thakur votes and defeat his rival Indra Dev Singh who was contesting from his own party BJP. A number of senior BJP leaders tried to prevent him from doing so, but

Raja Saheb gave a damn. The condition of Thakurdwara is quite poor in terms of development works as Raja Saheb has matters of far greater importance to attend to.

Raja Bhaiya's story is a bit similar, but far bigger in terms of magnitude. The five-times independent MLA from Kunda in Pratapgarh, Raghuraj Pratap Singh alias Raja Bhaiya has become a synonym for criminal-political nexus. The successor of Benti Riyasat, Raja Bhaiya first became an MLA in 1993 and it is alleged that he was below the mandated twenty-five year age limit at that time. He was made a minister by the BJP first in 1996, when he helped the party in forming the government by winning over MLAs through intimidation and threats. When he was arrested during the terms of Mayawati in 2002, there were 44 cases registered against him and a huge cache of arms and ammunition was recovered from the raid at his home including AK-56 rifles and hundreds of swords. The raid also recovered a human skeleton from his pond, vindicating the rumours that those who dared oppose him went straight to his infamous pond which had crocodiles in it. The officer R. S. Pandey, who led the raid on his home died in a road accident, shortly after Raja Bhaiya was released from jail by the 2004 SP government; he later became food supplies minister in the same government. An April 2012 expose by *Tehelka* shows how a multi-crore scam was orchestrated by Raja Bhaiya and his aides, and the money and PDS grains meant for the poor were sold to build personal fortunes.

Despite all these glaring revelations, the SP government continued to let him enjoy the ministerial benefits and dared to take action against him only when a far bigger controversy engulfed him in 2013, on the murder of young DSP Zia-ul-Haq. It was at this moment that the SP government asked for his resignation, after realizing that letting him continue would cause an adverse reaction in some sections of the Muslim votaries of SP.

Politicians of a Different Kind

Faisal Hasan Tabrej, Jaunpur

Faisal Hasan Tabrej is a thirty-year-old leader in Jaunpur. He is a postgraduate in political science and Hindi. He has been a student leader and was involved with the National Students Union of India (NSUI) since 1991. He became the NSUI president in Jaunpur in 2001 and remained its president for seven years. In 2004 he was given the award for the best NSUI president in the Indian National Congress.

Another significant fact about Faisal is that he is differently abled. One of his hands has a deformity that makes it a little difficult for him to ride a bike, but it has not deterred him from politics in this dangerous region. We got his number from a common friend and when we called him, he was away in a village working on a Youth Congress campaign in the area. When he reached the designated place after an hour, we were amazed to see a simple young man with a stubble and a very ordinary appearance. It is not very often that young leaders from parties like Congress appear so ordinary.

Faisal told us that politics was his passion and he could not live without interacting with people. He is usually accompanied by a few trusted friends. He has been working with the youth in Jaunpur for many years now. When we spoke to people in Jaunpur and surrounding areas, we found that his claim that every youth in Jaunpur knew him was true. Not only in the city but in the villages and towns, political people knew about Faisal.

It seemed appropriate to describe Faisal as a young leader who was passionate about politics but did not inherit politics. He had done his own groundwork for many years only to have his efforts scuttled. Faisal told us that he had been eyeing the assembly ticket from the Congress party but was apprehensive of the fact that Nadeem Javed, another young Muslim leader based in Delhi had also been trying for the Congress ticket for Jaunpur. His apprehensions came true when the tickets were announced. The ticket went to Nadeem Javed. Javed won the closely-contested elections by a margin of some three thousand votes, after using all the popular tactics, including bringing cine-stars like Ameesha Patel and Mahima Chowdhary to campaign. This highlighted once again that most of the time, simple people like Faisal fail to succeed in today's politics

Ramayan Ram at Sagri, Azambarh

Meet Ramayan Ram, a PhD student from Allahabad University with a UGC NET-JRF scholarship and an exceptional educational record. Even though he is a Dalit, and is from the Chamar sub-caste which Mayawati belongs to, Ramayan was never attracted to the BSP; he considers BSP to be just another statist party, devoid of Dr Ambedkar's ideals, and more concerned with the welfare of its own political leaders than that of the Dalits.

As an alternative, he cites the example of the Communist Party of India, Marxist-Leninist, Liberation (CPI-ML), which raised the issues of Dalits in a more radical fashion in Bihar, fighting armed battles against landlord armies, such as the Ranveer Sena. Ram believes that without an understanding of the property relations and the nature of the economic forces that force Dalits to remain construction workers or unskilled labourers, identity politics alone cannot do any good. Citing the case of Ram Naresh Ram of Bhojpur, a CPI (ML) MLA and one of the founding fathers of the party in Bihar who did not even own a house, Ramayan said that it was politics upheld by people like Ram Naresh that attracted him.

Educated and brought up in the industrial town of Durgapur in West Bengal, he was exposed to Leftist politics at a very early age. However, unlike his father who is a CPI (M) supporter, Ramayan was attracted to the radical flare of CPI (ML), joining its student organization AISA (All India Students' Association) during his university days; he is currently the UP state secretary of the same organization. When a Dalit girl from his village was raped by some upper-caste men and the police refused to register an FIR, it was the persistent pressure and activism of Ramayan Ram which ensured that an FIR was filed and the culprits arrested.

With thirteen thousand rupees in his bank account, Ramayan contested the assembly elections from Sagri in Azamgarh on a CPI (ML) ticket, polling about only 600 votes. Yet he didn't lose his morale.

When asked why he was trying to fight from a far lesser-known party in this area, Ramayan told us about the history of this district, which had a glorious legacy of Left party activism and leadership. He said he was just trying to revive that chapter of history, for in reality, a choice between SP, BSP, Congress and BJP is actually no choice for the people. Critical of the Singur and Nandigram displacements at the hands of the former CPI (M) ruled West Bengal government, he asserted that these parties had lost the essence of Leftist ideology, which needed to be rejuvenated, a task which he believed the CPI (ML) was doing.

Taking a dig at the comments of the Opposition parties that

called him 'vote-katwa' (spoiler who eats into the votes of the main contestants), Ramayan used to say in his speeches, 'Hum vote katwa nahin, jad katwa hain, in logon ki jaden kaatne aaye hain (We are not here to cut the votes of Opposition parties, but to cut their roots).'

Despite the poor electoral show of his party (the highest votes polled by any CPI (ML) candidate was not more than 5,000), Ramayan is hopeful that in the coming years, people will understand the value of his party's politics and embrace them.

In the routine hullabaloo of politics in UP, people like Ramayan Ram represent a fast-disappearing breed of honest and committed politicians, who chose politics as a mode of service over the convenient life of a university teacher. Above all, they represent hope even if it comes from a lesser-known political party.

Sketch of a Minority Leader: Azam Khan

Azam Khan is the biggest Muslim face of SP, a party which is said to command the greatest influence over minority votes. His face appears on almost all of SP's flex boards and posters, along with Akhilesh Yadav and Mulayam Singh Yadav. Considered a firebrand Muslim leader, Azam first hit national headlines during the Babri Masjid demolition in 1992, when he demanded that the Babri Masjid be rebuilt.

Coming from a non-political family background, Azam was educated at Aligarh Muslim University and was politically active right from his student days. Adhering to the socialist principles of SP, till date he is known for not spending extravagantly on election campaigns, and fighting elections by taking chanda (contributions) from people. He is one of the founding fathers of the SP, and one of the most trusted lieutenants of Mulayam Singh Yadav.

Donning the traditional Muslim attire of sherwani or kurta-pajama with a topi (cap), Khan is known for his polished Urdu and fiery oration. People compare the sharpness of his comments with the edge of a Rampuri knife (switch-blade). Not known for holding back his temper, he fired a number of salvoes at even Mulayam Singh Yadav, when he was suspended from SP because of his opposition to Jaya Prada and alliance with Kalyan Singh during the 2009 parliamentary elections. Criticizing Mulayam for joining hands with ex-BJP leader Kalyan Singh, Azam Khan once said, 'Mulayam ki dhoti ke niche sangh ka khaki nikkar hai (Mulayam wears the Sangh's shorts under his dhoti)!' Moving a step further, attacking Mulayam for taking credit for his developmental work in Rampur, he said in a public meeting, 'Mulayam Rampur main huye saare kaam ka sabab khud ko dete hain, lekin phir saara kaam Rampur main hi kyunkar hua? Aur jagahon par woh kyun hijde saabit huye (Mulayam claims to take the credit for all developmental work in Rampur, but why has all this work happened only in Rampur? Why has he proved to be impotent at other places)?' He is also notorious for making sexist remarks during his war of words against cine star Jaya Prada, allegedly asking her not to deprive the people of Rampur of her dancing skills, and that she should perform before them at some point of time.

Despite these shortcomings, Khan is highly popular with his minority brethren, and this can also be assessed from the fact that he has been a Rampur MLA seven times. In the 2012 elections, he defeated his nearest rival by a margin of some 58,000 votes.

Once Amar Singh left the party, Khan was respectfully taken back in the party, with Mulayam personally apologizing to him for past mistakes amid a huge gathering. A teary-eyed Azam Khan rejoined SP at the rally and accompanied Mulayam to a number of places during his election meetings. His clout in the party was displayed by the fact that a helicopter was sent to personally pick him up and bring him from Rampur to Lucknow, to discuss the issue of having Akhilesh Yadav as the new chief minister. In a place like Rampur, known for things as diverse as Islamic learning, knives and minority politics with Tehreer-style speeches, Azam Khan is definitely an uncrowned champion.

*

To conclude, we must say that while some of the cases that we have discussed above confirmed the stereotypical image of UP politicians, most of them do not fit into such profiling and show the nobler side of politics. It is not surprising that politicians of both types continue to thrive in UP. The reason perhaps is the sheer size of the state. UP has 403 MLAs in the lower house, 100 MLCs in the upper house, eighty Lok Sabha seats and a good number of Rajya Sabha seats along with several thousand panchayati raj and municipality representatives. The sheer size of this representation in a state with a population of more than 199,581,477 people enables different kinds of politicians to emerge and flourish. And despite the monotonous majority, it is perhaps the diversity of such 'different' politicians that adds to the beauty of the political landscape of Uttar Pradesh.

The Private Lives of Netajis

UP has always had a rich tradition of politicians carrying on illicit affairs—the great ex-CM Narayan Dutt Tiwari and ex-PM Atal Bihari Vajpayee being the pioneers of this tradition. But gone are the days when illicit affairs, extra-marital relations and pleasure-seeking were hush-hush. Nowadays this phenomena has gripped all parties equally, and is part of common gossip. Talk to any lower- or middle-level politician or journalist in the state capital of Lucknow and you will accumulate a number of stories about the private lives of netajis of almost every party.

From local degree colleges and female hostels to the suave hotels of Lucknow, and from the bars and discos of Delhi and Mumbai to the cheaper foreign destinations of Thailand and Hong Kong—the pleasure hubs of politicians have really expanded. UP politicians are of course no exception to this change. A number of them could be seen catching evening flights to Delhi or Mumbai on weekends, reportedly for business, but a deeper investigation would easily reveal the real motive behind these excursions.

While the charm of Nepal for UP politicians has reduced over the years, Delhi-NCR has become a major centre for all these activities since the late 1990s. Refined escort services, the availability of foreign girls, anonymity and a number of luxury hotels and farmhouses make it a very attractive destination. Furthermore, frequent visits to Delhi raise less suspicion as it is the capital city. Though such destinations lead to the 'fulfilment of needs' without any controversy, 'honey trapping' by political adversaries through spy-cameras and CDs has recently emerged as a dangerous trend. But no significant political leader from UP has been hit by it so far. (Mahipal Maderna of Rajasthan and Sanjay Joshi of BJP were not so lucky.)

Despite this phenomenon, the intimate affairs of politicians that create headlines and furore in state politics are still rooted primarily in the local. Be it the Amarmani Tripathi-Madhumita Shukla affair, the Anand Sen-Shashi affair or the Guddu Pandit-Shital Birla affair, all of them were rooted in the same or neighbouring districts. In all three cases, educated young women fell for influential political strongmen, knowing full well that they were married. All three expected that they would legalize their relations with the strength of their love. And except for the last one (where reason reigned over emotion and Shital Birla decided to put Pandit in jeopardy to save herself), the other two finally ended in extremely tragic situations. While Madhumita and Shashi were brutally murdered, their lovers landed in jail along with their wives.

The Madhumita case seems like a typical, dark Bollywood movie. A smart, budding poetess is attracted to an influential political leader with a strongman's image and, after some favours from the latter, comes to the conclusion that she has met her rescuer. In her diary, she says that after Amarmani arranged a job for her younger brother, she felt that her family now had a 'guardian'. As the diary says (translated from the original): 'I started believing that from now on we would not have to bow to anyone; that we would not have to make compromises anymore. You became not only my but my entire family's guardian.' The immature, raw love of this young woman can be understood when she writes: 'He might have married M (Amarmani's wife Madhumani) but I'm more close to him.' Like a typical young woman deeply in love, she tried searching for happiness in small things, as is evident from the following entry: 'Today, something new has been born. He said we would brush with the same toothbrush. After brushing with the same brush I felt that no one in the world could be as close as we are. Now I feel that all distance between us has vanished.' However, when she insisted that their child be given a legitimate name after a formal divorce from Madhumani and marriage to her, Amarmani sensed trouble for his political career and backed off.

Madhumita reached a dead end, where she had to write in her diary: 'Hum to barbad ho hi gaye hain (I am finally devastated).' The tragic story of Madhumita finally ended with a five-month foetus in her womb and two bullets through her heart. Her lover, Amarmani, is serving a life sentence, along with his wife Madhumani.

PART SIX

OF GANDHIS AND
SIGNIFICANT OTHERS

AS INDIANS, WE ARE EASILY CHARMED WITH A LITTLE GENEROSITY and by anyone with a bit of charisma and a polished manner. Different types of people—religious leaders, sadhus, pirs, maulvis, singers, cricketers, film actors, political leaders—have charmed and captivated us for a long time. M. K. Karunanidhi, Jayalalitha, Chiranjeevi, Amitabh Bachchan, Dharmendra and a whole array of cinematic personalities in politics, both in south as well as north India, are proof of our obsession with filmdom. Examples of temples dedicated to film stars are not a novelty in India—it happens every now and then in almost all parts of the country. And charisma is not only limited to the film stars.

Then there are political families at national, regional and local levels, who command a huge following among the people. Other than the all-time favourite Gandhis, others like the Reddys (Andhra), Badals (Punjab), Madernas and Mirdhas (Rajasthan), Abdullahs (Jammu and Kashmir), Scindias (Madhya Pradesh and Rajasthan), Thackerays and Pawars (Maharashtra) are not just surnames, but symbols of great power, influence and clout in various regions of the country. Though engaged in politics in a democratic set-up, most of them represent dynastic authority and power, handing over the reins of power to the next generation, and commanding authority in states for decades. Such is the scale of this phenomenon that according to a study by writer and historian Patrick French, more than two-thirds of the young MPs in the 15th Lok Sabha belonged to political families. The elaborate arrangement around those belonging to political families, for example, the security teams, cavalcade of vehicles and media hype further adds to their charisma.

There are still others—people who look like any ordinary citizen walking down the road—who command great respect and honour in their respective constituencies. They do not live differently and could easily be ignored by those who do not know them. However, their work, their commitment and their passion for the people make them venerable figures in their areas, elevating them to the standard of a respected elder for many.

This section describes the lives of many such people across Uttar Pradesh and it also looks into the constituencies of India's most popular political family, the Gandhis. We will also talk about some lesser known but equally or sometimes more venerable figures from the hinterlands of UP.

Bankrupt in Pocket Boroughs:
Congress in Rae Bareli and Amethi

In the 2012 elections, Congress failed to win a single assembly seat in Rae Bareli, and only two out of five in Rahul Gandhi's parliamentry constituency, Amethi. News stories have appeared in national dailies that Congress has begun reviewing the performance of the party in the recent assembly elections in UP from Sonia Gandhi's parliamentary constituency, Rae Bareli. It has taken the right step by beginning from Rae Bareli, but not very surprisingly as it happens in Congress, the people who were instrumental in the party's debacle are leading the review exercise.

The *Indian Express* reports that this exercise was started in Rae Bareli by Kishori Lal Sharma, Sonia and Rahul Gandhi's constituency representative. The report mentions that this group considers the following to be some of the real reasons for the party's defeat: the diminishing appeal of Priyanka, and popular announcements of the Samajwadi Party such as unemployment allowance and distribution of tablets and laptops. Mr Sharma also claims that many party leaders and workers felt that the party failed to attract youngsters. When we visited the Rae Bareli district in June-July 2011, we found it hard to believe that when outsiders like us were able to clearly read the writing on the wall that Congress was going to lose badly in these elections, this fact apparently evaded the top Congress leadership. Raghavendra Pratap Singh, the Rae Bareli District Congress Committee president said that the party workers had complained that they could not approach Sonia or Rahul Gandhi directly. It meant that the Gandhis did not care for their own party people and left them at the mercy of people like Kishori Lal Sharma and other intermediaries. It was our first ever visit to Rae Bareli and we had a certain image of the place in mind, given its star status as it has been represented by prime ministers of India in the past; and now, by the most powerful woman in India, the UPA chairperson Mrs Sonia Gandhi. We thought proximity to power would have bestowed many benefits on the district, but the situation here was no better than that of most other districts in the state.

Let's begin with the situation of the party organization and the party MLAs in the Rae Bareli parliamentary constituency. There are five assembly constituencies in Rae Bareli and in 2007 Congress won four of these five. In 2012, Congress could not win even one of these five, translating into the fact that the Congress chairperson, Mrs Sonia Gandhi, is unable to look after her constituency and therefore, the people have rejected her and the Congress party. This proves that the janta (general public) cannot be taken for granted in a democracy like India, which is full of surprises.

Rae Bareli and Amethi, long since known as the pocket boroughs of the Gandhi family, revolted against them this time. This is not the first time that the Congress was uprooted in these constituencies; in 1977, Raj Narain had won from Rae Bareli, defeating Indira Gandhi. As Indira Gandhi was the prime minister of the country, she did not have enough time to visit Rae Bareli herself, and had dispatched Yashpal Kapoor from Delhi to look after her constituency. The local leaders were sidelined and the 'imported' leaders given the command.

This alienated the local leaders and Congress workers and proved dear to Mrs Gandhi, even though her son, Sanjay Gandhi, was present in the constituency to look after the elections.

History repeats itself and those who learn its lessons do not repeat the mistakes, but it looks as though the UPA chairperson and the Congress president for the longest time ever, Mrs Sonia Gandhi, did not learn any lessons from her mother-in-law. She repeated exactly the same flawed pattern. She deputed Kishori Lal Sharma as her constituency representative or political agent, to look after all political and official affairs for the Rae Bareli MP. He also acts as Rahul Gandhi's political representative in the Amethi constituency. In these elections, Kishori Lal Sharma created a lot of discontent that was open and overt. But neither Rahul nor Sonia Gandhi made any effort to find out if their intermediary was bringing them the correct information, thus the party suffered and so did both of them individually.

The second part of Sonia Gandhi's mistake was to assign the task of looking after the campaign to Priyanka Gandhi. Priyanka had not visited the constituency for almost two and a half years after the 2009 elections. Thus, when she came to campaign in 2012, she had to suffer stiff protest from local Congress workers and sympathizers. Priyanka is liked and trusted by the people of Rae Bareli, but she is inaccessible to the common people, as other than elections, it is impossible to reach her; the two and a half year gap that came after her 2009 election visits underlined this in the minds of people. This was not the first time that the party and the Gandhis suffered due to their representative, Mr Sharma. In 2010, almost 70 percent of the candidates selected by Mr Sharma lost in the panchayat elections; 145 out of the 180 zila panchayat members belonged to Akhilesh Singh's opposing camp. If the Gandhis truly believe in the significance of panchayats as tools of de-centralized governance, how did they miss this signal when they were routed out in these elections in 2010? Even then the media reported the discontent among the locals against Mr Sharma's gatekeepership and the disconnect between the Gandhis and the common people of Rae Bareli. It is clear that the responsibility of losing badly in two consecutive elections (panchayat and assembly) rests with the Gandhis, because they could not keep their promises to the people. They could not fulfil their responsibility of representing their people at the highest house, rather breaching their confidence by appointing a political representative. It is astonishing that even seasoned political players, such as the Gandhis, believe that people would take their intermediaries seriously or that their intermediaries would take their jobs seriously. If the people of Rae Bareli have elected Sonia Gandhi as their representative, why should they have to deal with Kishori Lal Sharma? Why should they wait for Priyanka Gandhi to visit so that they can divulge their problems to her? If Kishori Lal Sharma or Priyanka Gandhi are sufficient to represent the people of Rae Bareli, then may be they should contest the elections; what is the need for Sonia Gandhi to contest?

Kishori Lal Sharma is originally from Punjab and there is a network of people around him that does not allow a commoner to come anywhere close to him. When people elect a representative in the belief that they would be heard at the highest house of this country through this leader, they become unhappy and dissatisfied if they realize that they need to go through an intermediary in order to be represented at the leader's house. This is what happened with the people of Rae Bareli. They were never able to meet their MP and a vicious net of middlemen in Rae Bareli, who claimed access to 10 Janpath, exploited the people.

The Case of Parshadepur on Behta Bridge

Sonia Gandhi had built a house or you could say, a camp office-cum-home, on the outskirts of Rae Bareli on Parshadepur Road in a village called Bhuve Mau. Just four kilometres away from this house is a small village called Raghunathpur Kateli, which is primarily populated by Yadavs. This village also has an engineering wonder called the Behta Bridge where the Sharda Canal crosses the Sai River through an aqueduct. It's been listed as a darshaniya sthal (tourist spot) in Rae Bareli.

We met two young men of this village on the Behta Bridge. One of them told us that he worked in a factory near Ahmedabad in Gujarat and the other boy, around twenty years of age, said that he was planning to go to Gujarat with the other boy when he returned. We asked them how much land they or their families owned in the village and they said that they owned about 8-10 bighas (one bigha is equivalent to approximately 0.33 acres). We asked them why they wanted to leave their village when their families had enough land and the village was situated on the banks of the river and the canal. What they told us was a revelation: They said that the Sai River was dry for most of the year because a small dam and some anicuts had been made in the upper stream. They were not authorized to take water from the Sharda Canal even though it has water and passes through their village.

They said that when the Sharda Canal was being built, the Sai River had enough water, and the village did not require an outlet from the canal. Now that the river had run dry, they had been trying for many years to get irrigation water for at least one crop from the Sharda Canal, but their appeals had fallen on deaf ears. They had submitted many applications to Sonia Gandhi's office, but they were sure they had never reached her. They complained that they weren't even allowed to enter the premises of Mrs Gandhi's house when she was around.

These young men told us, 'Bhaiyya hum abhi to Gujarat jayenge par jab bhi chunav ayega, Fervary ya Mai mein, hum zaroor avenge vote dene aur Congress ko harane (We will have to go to Gujarat as of now, but whenever the elections take place, in February or May, we will come to vote to defeat the Congress).'

These boys and some others in different parts of Rae Bareli told us in July 2011 that they did not think that Congress would win even one seat in the upcoming assembly elections and also that Sonia Gandhi's winning margin would shrink in 2014, although people would not vote her out in the hope of a miracle and also for their mad love for the family. A young man in his twenties sitting at a tea-stall on the Parshadepur Road, told us, 'Inke haraye na, par logbaag khush nahi hai. Ee baar jeete ka antar zaroor kum hoga par (People don't want to defeat them, but are not happy also; though this time the victory margin will come down for sure).'

What the Gandhis have given to Rae Bareli

Let's see what the Gandhis have given to the people of Rae Bareli and Amethi and how it has benefited them. Some industries including the Indian Telephone Industries Ltd (ITI) and Bharat Heavy Electricals Ltd (BHEL) were established in the seventies and eighties. ITI is in bad shape and BHEL does not provide employment to locals. The new rail coach factory that is currently being built does not employ locals either and both Rahul and Sonia Gandhi have openly said that they will not recommend anyone for jobs in these institutions. At an interaction with the press and locals, when people asked Rahul Gandhi to recommend locals for jobs in the rail coach factory, he said he did not want to shut down these factories by employing locals there. The indication was towards the general trend of discouraging local recruitment in industries as it is felt that locals could create problems if shunted out which the outsiders can't as they are not rooted alike the locals. Another instance of political immaturity on Rahul Gandhi's part was reflected in Nihalgarh. The Varanasi–Jammu Tawi Summer Express used to stop at Nihalgarh railway station till 2008-09, making the life of the migrant labourers travelling to Jammu and Punjab a little easier. In the UPA-II regime when Mamata Banerjee was the railway minister this train started bypassing Nihalgarh. When people asked Rahul Gandhi to renew the train service, he told them, 'Rail to mujhse abhi naraaz chal rahi hai (Railway ministry is a bit hostile towards us these days)', indicating the rift between Mamata Banerjee and the Congress. People were disappointed and many of them openly told us, 'He is my MP, his mother runs the country and he cannot get a train to stop at a station inspite of that. Then what use is he to us?'

Next in line are: Indira Gandhi Udaan Academy, National Shoe and Apparel Designing Institute and National Institute of Fashion Design (NIFD). If you ask a local who lives close to these institutes or in other places in the district about these institutes and what they teach, they do not have any answers. They do not know what their children would do if they were to go to NIFD or the National Shoe and Apparel Designing Institute. These institutes are of no use to the locals except that they might get the job of a peon or at the most a clerk in these institutes. Their children cannot study there because it doesn't fit into their socio-cultural milieu. Even if they do get admission in NIFD, where would they go? People from rural Rae Bareli and Amethi would probably not waste their time and resources on designing clothes and shoes. Before bringing these institutes here, the Gandhis should have understood the socio-cultural milieu. The people here need basic education and skill training to enable them to get government jobs and other such opportunities. In place of NIFD and shoe and apparel designing, if the Gandhis had brought in two more Navodaya Vidyalayas or Kendriya Vidyalayas or Jan Shiksha Sansthan, it would have benefited the people, thus helping them win over the electorate.

Missing the Essence of Folk Wisdom

This lack of common sense or folk wisdom about the sort of institutes and jobs required in rural areas has caused the Gandhis to make bad policy decisions. Neither they nor their advisers seem to realize that a farmer or even the rural elite do not want their children to become shoes or clothes designers as they don't see these professions as any better than the local cobbler or tailor. Adding more fuel to this sort of thinking, a local SP leader told us that they were telling the local villagers, mainly the OBC communities and lower castes, that the Gandhis think of them as being no better than cobblers and tailors and that is why they have brought these institutions to the district.

The rail coach factory is another blot on their performance sheet. Many years have passed and it has not started working fully as yet. The wall that is being made to secure the factory area is causing a lot of water-logging in the nearby fields and roads, but no one cares enough to listen. The state government says that they cannot interfere in the Centre's project and the villagers cannot access anyone from the Central government. These are just a few examples of what the common people have to go through.

When it comes to political people, the situation is more serious. Kishori Lal Sharma, who controls access to the Centre, is a Brahmin and an outsider. He has developed his own coterie, which primarily consists of Brahmins. Local Brahmin leaders do not consider him to be a Brahmin, given his Punjabi decadence, but they have to abide by what he says. This angers them and even though the Brahmins are for the Congress in the district, they are not very happy.

The Brahmins' closeness to the Gandhis and their access to the Centre has irked the Thakurs who are divided between two camps, niether of which is for the Congress. Along with the Yadavs and Brahmins, the Thakurs are numerically dominant in the district. Most of the Thakurs are behind Akhilesh Singh, Rae Bareli's independent (currently Peace Party) MLA and so are the Muslims and Dalits in the city. In other parts of the district too, Muslims and Dalits largely support the Yadavs and Thakurs.

Akhilesh Singh is a challenge for the Gandhis, but they have failed to meet it because they cannot give the time to the district that Akhilesh Singh gives. People say that Akhilesh Singh has maintained the power balance between different communities in Rae Bareli, mainly the Muslims and Hindus, and so they vote for him. He is seen as a Robin Hood by the poor Muslims and Dalits, and at the same time he is also perceived as a strongman, whose presence is reassuring to the people in city, mainly the business community.

Akhilesh Singh suffered a setback at the hands of Dinesh Singh, MLC, when his representative lost the zila panchayat polls to Dinesh Singh's brother's wife. Later all the tenders for the panchayat's work went to the Dinesh Singh lobby. Akhilesh Singh then tried to join the Congress, but the Brahmin lobby and Dinesh Singh did not want that. Had he joined the Congress, it would have overturned the situation in Rae Bareli.

Media and the Gandhis

In the English language press and electronic media, Rahul and Priyanka Gandhi are the words for hope. As a reporter if you have their beat, you are in for a mixed bag of pleasant surprises and unexpected shocks. You know that you have an important assignment; you also hope that you do not miss a single development, but you also know that there is no definitive source of information about their movements. They never give any exclusive bytes and you know your colleagues in rival channels are in the same situation as you are. Thus, you share many leads because you never know which ones are authentic.

On the ground, among the regional language journalists and stringers of local news channels, things are totally different. They hardly get a chance to cover the Gandhis because most of the time, their channel or newspaper will send someone from Delhi or Lucknow, as if the Gandhis have come here for a highly secretive scientific experiment! A stringer for a local channel in Robertsganj told us, 'Bhaiyya, jab kabhi Rahul Gandhi aate hain, hamari to dihadi maari jaati hai. Waise hi mahine mein do-ek khabarein lagti hain par inke aane par to channel wale wahin se kisi ko saath bhej dete hain, jaise hum kuch jaante hi na ho (Whenever Rahul Gandhi comes to this area, we suffer losses because seniors in the channel send someone along with him from Delhi and Lucknow, as if we do not know anything)!'

Another interesting opinion about Rahul Gandhi was expressed by a senior journalist in Poorvanchal's Kushinagar who had been heading the political bureau for quite a long time. He had this to say: 'Rahul Gandhi admi achche hain. Imaandar hain, mehnat karte hain par neta nahi hain. Yahan bhondu panchayat pradhan bhi paanch saal mein rajneeti ke gur seekh jaata hai aur inhe parliament mein dusra term hai. Ya to woh poor student hain jahan sudhar ki gunjaish bahut nahi hai ya phir bahut shatir hain aur kisi mauke ke intzar mein hai (Rahul Gandhi is an honest, hard-working gentleman, but he is not a leader. Even a dumb panchayat head learns the tricks in five years—and it is Rahul's second term in the Lok Sabha. Either he is a poor student, in which case there isn't much scope, or he is very shrewd and is waiting for the right moment).'

While he cannot write this in his newspaper, he keeps expressing such opinions wherever he gets the chance—and this is how opinion and image is made or broken in distant places, where people in Delhi think it doesn't matter.

The Gandhis carry such weight that no one in the media industry, from the top to the bottom, wants to take any risks with them. In a channel, the best producer will cut the bytes that will get the best voice-over, and the output head will look at the news story himself or herself before it goes on air. There is an unsaid note of caution in most media organizations about the Gandhi stories—there should not be any goof-ups. And all this is 'unpaid', meaning that the Congress party does not dole out any favours to media organizations for better coverage.

Rahul Gandhi has his own news value and in most organizations, the reporter handling the beat holds a special status. Most of his colleagues view him with some degree of jealousy, but in reality his job is tough and he never gets any of the so-called favours from the party or Rahul Gandhi's office. But they still need to run their errands to get the news, which actually does not exist, except when the Gandhis allow it to happen.

When Rahul Gandhi went to Bhatta village, riding a motorcycle in May 2011, the media went crazy. They started following him from the very next hour till late evening when he was arrested briefly and released on bail. Later, his padyatra (journey on foot) from Jewar to Aligarh was an extended media picnic, where the reporters followed him in the dust and heat of the villages along the Yamuna Expressway. During the elections, almost all of Rahul Gandhi's rallies and all of Priyanka Gandhi's visits were covered by almost all the channels in Delhi and in the state.

But despite all this, in the end RG (as he is fondly called in close circles) fails to impress anyone for a long time. Other than praising his sincerity, people find nothing else significant to talk about him, like our Kushinagar journalist. Every Gandhi had some unique virtue—Nehru had intelligence, Indira had will, Sonia Gandhi has managerial abilities but RG is yet to show his USP.

A Case of Reverse Popularity:
The Fall of the 'Vikas Purush'

Till 2009, when he joined the Congress, Beni Prasad Verma was one of the biggest Other-OBC leaders of the Samajwadi Party in UP, representing the Kurmis. He won the 2009 election on a Congress ticket and the Congress believed that it had won over a bigger section of the OBCs in the state and that would help it in Mission 2012. However in 2012, Congress did not win even a single seat in Beni Prasad's Parliamentary constituency. Even his son, Rakesh Verma polled third on his seat in Barabanki. Now, Beni Prasad Verma has supposedly lost favour with the Rahul Gandhi camp and has earned a permanent foe in Mulayam Singh Yadav. But equations were not so earlier.

Beni Prasad Verma was once a pre-eminent Socialist leader of UP and very influential among the OBCs, mainly Kurmis. He has worked under both Ram Manohar Lohia and Chaudhary Charan Singh and has been a six-term MLA and five-term MP. He began as a grounded peasant's leader and first became an MLA in 1974 with Charan Singh's Bharatiya Lok Dal (BLD). Later with the changing structure of the Janata Party he became one of the founding members of the Samajwadi Party, in October 1992. He always stood firmly by Mulayam's side and did not leave him even when the BJP tried to split SP into two parts in 1993 and offered him chief ministership in return.

But with Amar Singh's rise, not only Beni Prasad, but other Socialist stalwarts like Janeshwar Mishra (Chote Lohia) were sidelined in the SP.

Beni Babu left Mulayam Singh just before the 2007 assembly elections. Beni was demanding that the then labour minister and SP MLA from Bahraich, Dr Waqar Ahmed Shah, be denied a party ticket, as Shah and his son were allegedly involved in the murder conspiracy of Ram Bhulan Verma, a staunch Beni supporter in the area. Mulayam Singh Yadav, under Amar Singh's influence shrugged away Beni Babu's demand. Beni Babu revolted and he and his supporters floated the Samajwadi Kranti Dal (SKD) with Beni Babu as its president. It attracted a lot of attention as many significant OBC and Muslims leaders approached it to contest elections under its banner.

However, with age, the magic of the once 'Vikas Purush' diminished; his SKD did not get a single seat in the 2007 elections though it spoiled SP's chances at a few places. Beni thought of himself as a Kurmi messiah, but a lot of things had changed between the 1980s when he had emerged as a Kurmi leader and 2007 when he launched his own party. Now he was not the only Kurmi leader, as people like Om Prakash Singh of Chunar, R.K. Chaudhary of Basti and many other leaders in different parts of Poorvanchal, like Vinay Katiyar of BJP, had emerged as new Kurmi leaders.

Later Beni Prasad merged the Samajwadi Kranti Dal with the Congress before the 2009 Lok Sabha elections. Congress thought of Beni Prasad as a big shot in its arm that would help it to make inroads into the lost grounds of UP. It accepted Beni's many precarious conditions before the 2009 Lok Sabha elections, because it needed some important faces from different castes in the rainbow coalition of partners in 2009. Beni Babu won the election and Congress did perform well in 2009 but this was mainly on the plank of the farmer's loan waiver and the National

Rural Employment Guarantee Act (NREGA). Beni Babu, like the Congressmen who are hardly in touch with the people at the grassroots level, did presume that this success was due to his charisma, at least in Kurmi-dominated areas, which actually was not the case.

In the run-up to the 2012 elections, Congress was desperate to improve its score. It planned to make inroads into the OBCs section to create a new social base. To lure them, mainly Kurmis, Beni Prasad's status was elevated from minister of state to Union cabinet minister in July 2011. Beni once had been a Union minister of the same status but the Congress did not give him the berth when the UPA-II came to power in 2009. They elevated him in July 2011 because they thought it would help the Congress' chances with the Kurmis in 2012, as they hold the key to more than three dozen constituencies in the state, mainly in Poorvanchal and Awadh. The central leadership did not realize that Beni's charisma had waned and he was more of a liability than a performing asset. Such flawed assessment of individuals has always been a problem with the Congress in the state.

What happened on the ground after this was actually the opposite of what the Congress leadership believed would occur. Beni Prasad had been backing his cronies for tickets and was adamant on certain seats in the Tarai and Awadh regions in districts like Bahraich, Gonda, Balrampur, Sitapur, Barabanki, Ambedkar Nagar and Faizabad. Media reports claim that Rahul Gandhi had given him a freehand in more than twenty-five of the fifty-five seats, which went to poll in the first phase. Though he had his say in the ticket distribution, his candidates nose-dived in the electoral contest.

Many Congress insiders or old loyalists in the Tarai region were not happy with the party for giving such a freehand to Beni Prasad Verma. Many of them had genuine grudges. Their prime contention was that their tickets, or fates so to speak, had been left in the hands of a leader who they had opposed all their lives. They had fought against SP and Beni in the same region and now Beni was deciding on who would get tickets. Many of these leaders alleged that Beni was obliging his old loyalists by giving them Congress tickets, as these tickets come with a huge sum of money to the tune of twenty to fifty lakh rupees per constituency. They even alleged that Beni was also making money by taking a share of the money from each candidate who was given a ticket.

Further, people of different assembly segments in Gonda expressed their anger at Beni Prasad Verma, who they alleged had visited Gonda only three to four times after becoming an MP. Because of this combined unrest against him, at many places Beni was not allowed to speak from the dais even in the presence of Sonia and Rahul Gandhi. In Gonda, Sonia Gandhi had to intervene when locals started hooting at Beni Babu when he rose to speak in her public meeting. They could not be pacified and only Sonia Gandhi spoke and Beni could not.

With the election results of 2012, Beni Prasad has been reduced to an old man with his own whims and fancies. The nature of politics has not changed much—it has remained a 'patron-client' relation, but the claimants for political largesse have increased in number. This has made leaders like Beni Prasad redundant for the new generation of voters and leaders.

The Significant Others

Shyamdev Roy Chaudhury of Varanasi

Shyamdev Roy Chaudhury has won for the sixth time in Varanasi. In December when we were sitting in a sweet shop at Assi, a friend told us the following anecdote. He was sitting outside a printing press and checking some proofs. A few minutes later the owner came out and asked,

Dada kahan gaye (Where has Dada gone)?

Kaun dada (Dada who)? our friend replied.

The owner said, *Yahin tumhaare samne jo baithe the* (The one who was sitting right in front of you).

Woh ek ladka aya tha cycle par aur unse bola ki kuch kaam hai kachhari mein aur vho uske peeche baith kar chale gaye (A boy on a cycle came and told him that there is some work in the court and he went with him on his cycle), our friend replied.

He was then told that the middle-aged man in a long kurta, who had been sitting on the stone slab opposite him, was their MLA, Shyamdev Roy Chaudhury! He doesn't move around in a car or an SUV but in rickshaws or on foot. It is difficult to believe that such leaders exists in UP today and they are winning elections, when the average cost of MLA elections in UP is, some insiders say, 1.5 to 2.5 crore rupees!

Bhulahi of Naurangia, Kushinagar

When we talked to Maulvi Samiullah at the Darul-Uloom-Mohammadeen in Kaptanganj in May 2011, he told us passionately that if we had come so far, we should venture a little further and meet Bhulahi, the BJP ex-MLA of Naurangia. He lived in Pagaar Chapra village, post office Laxmiganj, district Kushinagar. It was a little off our planned route but we decided it was worth listening to the appeal of a Maulvi of a madarsa for a Sanghi MLA!

Pagaar Chapra was a small village and locating Bhulahi's home was not very difficult. We actually found his son outside the village, who took us home. This was a simple structure of two pucca rooms and a lot of open space in front. There was another pucca structure on the other side, which was used as a kitchen. A lean, old man was crouching on the ground in the shadow of a neem tree, making envelopes out of old newspapers. He was Bhulahi. We did not have any words to greet him upon seeing him—an ex-MLA in UP, crouching on the ground in this kuchcha-pucca house! He gestured towards one of the only two wooden chairs to sit on and asked if we had had water. When we said no, he asked his son to bring us some water. The boy brought water in two clean steel glasses. Later, he brought tea in the same glasses with some Parle-G biscuits.

We were astonished by the simplicity and the limited resources of this man. He had been elected twice as an MLA of Naurangia—once in 1974 on a Jan Sangh ticket and another time in 1977 on a Janata Party ticket. However, possessed only a small piece of land and in his free time, he made envelopes for a living.

Bhulahi was born in 1924 and has a BA degree from St Andrews College, Gorakhpur (1955), an MA degree from Agra University (1957) and an MEd from Gorakhpur (1962). He had also participated in the freedom struggle but has never taken the benefits of a freedom-fighter.

Bhaurao Devras and Nanaji Deshmukh inducted him into the RSS in 1944. He was inspector of schools in Deoria from 1962-64. On Nanaji's advice, he left his job in 1964 to contest a by-election that he lost by only 250 votes. He was a dedicated RSS worker and had also handled some responsibilities in RSS's newspaper, *Tarun Bharat*.

The last election he contested was the 2002 assembly election from Nuarangia, which he lost.

He told us that the party respected him for his work in the area and for his glorious past, but times had changed. Politics was more about money and power these days and he could not match others in these areas. He was content and satisfied with what he had achieved in his life and the fact that the people of his area still respected him for his honesty.

Pramod Tiwari of Rampur Khas, Pratapgarh

Pramod Tiwari was a Congress Legislative Party leader for the last six terms in the Uttar Pradesh assembly. In the 2012 assembly elections, he won for the record ninth time from Rampur Khas. If one goes to the Rampur Khas area, one would find roads in very good condition and the area doesn't look as if it is in UP! We met several people in his constituency and most were content with Pramod Tiwari as their representative. The reason is simple—he is approachable and he never fails to help his people in times of need.

Pramod Tiwari was a practising criminal lawyer at the Allahabad High Court before he ventured into politics in 1980. His father was a social worker in the area. Tiwari runs a chain of educational institutions in the area where he has employed a few hundred people. These people double as his political functionaries. His daughter Mona told us that she has been her father's constituency representative since 1996. She is now married but pays regular visits to the area and looks after the constituency in his absence.

Tiwari is a seasoned leader and fits perfectly into the realpolitik of UP. When Rahul Gandhi was accosted with black flags in Allahabad when he launched his campaign, Pramod Tiwari was one of the two Congress leaders to kick the SP boys in full view of the media, along with Jitin Prasad. This was a spontaneous reaction, as Tiwari thought it not just a breach of security, but also an insult to the Gandhi scion. He still does not agree that this kicking episode was a low in the democratic tradition of the country where showing black flags is a standard way of registering protest.

However, such loyalty and considerations were not always praised in party circles, especially in Rahul Gandhi's entourage, as the episode kicked off a controversy and the party had to face uncomfortable allegations from the Opposition, which termed it 'fascist' and 'undemocratic'. In many of Rahul Gandhi's rallies Pramod Tiwari was seen standing behind him on the dais. Despite its discomfort with him, Rahul Gandhi's entourage could not stop him, at least in the areas around Allahabad. At a rally in the Lucknow DAV College in February, where Rahul Gandhi had torn the SP 'false promises' into pieces, Pramod Tiwari was standing behind him. As Rahul Gandhi was agitating over the false promises and expressing his 'anger' by tearing the piece of paper, Pramod Tiwari was seen laughing. This sent a very bad message to the public and many people pointed it out to the senior leaders and Gandhi managers, who later asked for him to be kept out of frame when the leader was speaking.

However, as a local leader and Rampur Khas MLA, he has a definite command over the pulse of the people. For the last three terms at least, Pramod Tiwari never spent time within the constituency during the elections, as being a senior Congress leader, he has responsibilities in other parts of the state. Still he wins every time because he spends his weekends during non-election periods in his constituency.

Another secret of his success is that he never gets involved in the local politics of the panchayats. In Lucknow, anybody from his constituency is welcome to visit his home and he tries to help his people in whatever way he can. He is a benevolent man and has friends in all the parties. His opponents allege that he wins by having 'setting' (adjustment) with other party people in terms of keeping the party weak in the state, in return of personal victory and works getting done. A number of political analysts will agree to this allegation but as famous Chinese leader Deng has said: the colour of a cat does not matter, what matters is its capability to catch mice. Pramod Tiwari is a many terms MLA who keeps his electorate contented, and this is what matters in the realpolitik in the end.

Manoj Kumar Singh

In Uttar Pradesh, Chandauli district is better known for its coal-related crime and violence and also for alleged Naxalism in some parts. Saiyad Raja is the last town in Uttar Pradesh on the Grand Trunk Road before you reach Bihar. The place wears a battered look, with weathered roads, and there is always a line of trucks stuck in a traffic jam on the road. A little away from this town is the village of Manoj Kumar Singh 'W'.

A friend in Varanasi had asked a Samajwadi leader in Chandauli for Manoj Singh's number so we could fix a time and place to meet him. This friend accompanied us to Saiyad Raja that day. In the two hours it took us to get there, he must have received at least thirty calls from people across the district— young and old, men and women. They all had one request: that the Samajwadi Party must give Manoj Singh a ticket if it wanted to win the Saiyad Raja seat. We were confused about why people were calling us for an SP ticket. We then realized that when our friend had called someone in Saiyad Raja to ask for Manoj Singh's number, his people found out that someone 'important' was coming to the area. As we had experienced earlier, there was a popular feeling among the candidates and their supporters that the party was conducting a survey and we were a part of it. Our friend told them that we did not have anything to do with any party, but no one was ready to listen to us! We admired Manoj Singh's network, which immediately got to know what was happening in his area and provided him with the information.

Later, Angad Yadav called up and said that he was one of Manoj Singh's main supporters and wanted to meet us. We were also looking for more information in Saiyad Raja on Manoj Singh, so we fixed up a meeting on the way.

A few kilometres before the designated place, we found a jeep blocking our way. A tall man wearing a kurta pajama came out and introduced himself as Angad Yadav. We asked him to sit in our jeep and had a long conversation where he described all that Manoj Kumar Singh had done in the area and how he was the most eligible candidate from the party. We were again amazed at Manoj Singh's capacity to tap information in the field. After the conversation Angad gave us directions to Manoj Singh's village.

The village has a pucca road but is faraway from any main road. Whenever we stopped to ask for directions to the house of Manoj Kumar Singh, we were directed towards the village of 'W' Singh. As we neared the village, we saw a very big building surrounded by a large compound whose walls were almost ten feet high. As we entered the compound, two tall men appeared from both sides of the gate. They stopped us and asked who we wanted to meet. By then, a man of medium height dressed in a kurta pajama appeared and told them to let us enter.

As we entered the compound, we saw two Pajeros, one Outlander, other SUVs, tractors and a few horses. In the middle of the court, a few men were sitting on takhats (wooden beds) and chairs. When we asked if we could meet Manoj Singh, a thin man directed us towards a room inside the compound. A little later, Manoj Singh entered the room and asked the thin man to bring water and tea. Singh told us about the work that he was doing in the area, including a three-day Ganga Kataan Yatra in the nearby villages, which was attended by more than 10,000 people.

Later other people in the area told us that only Manoj Singh could win from this seat and no one else from any other party stood a chance. This was the first week of June 2011 and they told us that if SP did not give him a ticket, he could win as an independent, which was what eventually happened.

Manoj had been organizing mahapanchayats of villagers of all castes in the region and had been promising to develop the area. He had already spent a lot of resources—money and time—on the area. He had prepared an agenda for Saiyad Raja's development and people were impressed with him.

It was not his work alone, people also knew that he was rich and powerful and could stand against criminals like Brijesh Singh, whom he eventually defeated by a margin of more than two thousand votes. People wanted someone with a clean image but who was also a strongman and could stand by them in their need. Manoj Singh had already proven that through his many yatras and panchayats and also by having the courage to stand for election against Brijesh Singh. His charisma is renowned in the constituency and even small children know his name. Finally in the elections, he contested as an independent candidate from Saiyad Raja assembly seat of Chandoli and won.

There are many more such figures in UP, spread over distant towns and villages, who command the respect and regard of the people they work for even when they are not in power. We have talked of only a few representative figures above. However, while some have earned their popularity through their actions, others like the Gandhis are born with it. Be it earned or inherited, charisma continues to play an important part in UP politics.

EPILOGUE

ON THE MORNING OF 6 MARCH 2012, POLITICAL EXPERTS AND NEWS channel anchors expected day-long, and later week-long deliberations as the UP election verdict was about to be announced. The reason was simple: everybody expected SP to get the maximum number of seats, but absolute majority was out of the question. In this scenario, the main questions being asked were: Who would be SP's alliance partner—RLD or the Congress? And what sort of bargain would be struck between the two parties?

As the initial results started pouring in, BJP appeared to be leading at a number of urban centres in UP (along with Goa and Punjab, which they finally managed to clinch). In live chatshows members of the BJP began predicting the demise of the Congress and the emergence of BJP on the national scene, with a number of anchors across news channels concurring with them.

However, the initial leads soon nosedived and BJP stalwarts, who were hogging the air space, not allowing anyone else to speak, also disappeared from the scene. SP, which had maintained its lead, appeared to cross 170-180 seats around afternoon. The debate in the newsrooms shifted to 'the pound of flesh' (to quote Arnab Goswami of Times Now) that RLD was likely to demand of SP in return for supporting SP as a junior partner to clear the road to form the government.

Within an hour this issue became irrelevant as the SP continued its march, finally winning 224 out of 403 seats, making it the most decisive victory in the political history of UP since 1991. Giving an insider's account on SP expectations about this election, Neeraj Shekhar, son of ex-PM Chandrashekhar and party MP from Ballia said, 'Hum 180-90 seeton ki umeed kar rahe they, lekin ye 224 ka jo nateeja aaya hai, ye to samajhiye Janata ne apna ashirwad humain diya hai (We were expecting about 180-190 seats, but the 224 seats victory seems as though the people of UP have blessed us with their support).'

The people of UP gave a historic mandate this time around, and in return, had a lot of expectations from the government. To paraphrase SP's TVC Umeed Ki Cycle (cycle of hope), they expected an umeed ki barish (shower of expectations) to pour down on their homes, as promised by the Samajwadis. What happened in reality was quite different.

On the very same day that the results were declared, twelve-year-old Danish was killed in Sambhal (Badaun district) in the celebratory gun-fire indulged in by SP workers. The same day, SP party members engaged in violent clashes with the Opposition and some media persons at Firozabad and Jhansi over some issues. When the supporters of SP's Amroha MLA, Mehboob Ali, resorted to heavy celebratory firing to welcome him back, such was the scale of the bullets fired that the police had to suo motu register a case against them.

Less than a week after the results were announced, supporters of SP's Bah (Agra district) MLA, Aridaman Singh killed Munna Lal Jatav, husband of the Dalit pradhan of Parvati Purva village by beating him to death. His crime was refusing to vote for the Samajwadi Party candidate during the elections. Within a few days, hutments of Dalits in Auraiya district were burned by SP workers, to settle political scores, as the former were BSP supporters. The height of this phenomenon was witnessed at the La Martiniere College grounds during the swearing-in of Chief Minister Akhilesh Yadav, when disorderly SP cadres ran amok, vandalizing the venue immediately after the swearing-in ceremony in full view of the media and SP leaders.

All of this fed the people's fear that SP's return would lead to the worsening of the law and order situation. To allay these fears, control the damage and maintain the momentum of the party for the upcoming Lok Sabha elections, party supremo Mulayam Singh Yadav pledged strong action against the culprits in the media, and suspended some functionaries for the violence in March itself. Orders to prevent the misuse of the party flag on the vehicles of non-authorized functionaries, and common SP workers, worsening the law and order situation were also released by him during the same time. A lot of water has flown down the Gomti since then; the law and order situation is still in stark contrast to what the SP had promised in its election manifesto and speeches.

On the Law and Order Front

In the 7 March 2012 edition of *The Economic Times*, Sruthijith KK wrote an article about the jubilation at the SP headquarters in Lucknow that he had witnessed on 6 March. Talking about the celebratory mood of the party cadres after this victory, he reported a minor incident. When an SP supporter Rajiv Kumar Yadav was pushed by a guard during a celebratory dance, he retorted, 'Paanch saal dhakka khaaya, ab kya dhakka doge (For five years we have been pushed around, now, who will dare to push us)?'

This small incident perhaps characterized the general mood of most of the SP supporters after the victory. For five years they had faced the rage of the government machinery run by a rival party in the form of blows, frame-ups and strict police actions. The absence of government contracts, licences and quotas dried up their sources of income and the apathy of the government officials in acting upon their complaints made them the laughing stock of the people, who used to pay homage to them earlier to get their work done.

After five painful years this was the time to reclaim their right on everything they had lost earlier. And now, they had no patience to get it all back in instalments; they wanted everything to be restored immediately. The hue and cry raised to corner government contracts immediately after the government's formation, is an example that illustrates this impatience. Such was the thirst and desperation to get government contracts that a number of inter-party feuds emerged across the state. For example, in Basti, the SP cadres alleged that minister Raj Kishore Singh was cornering all the contracts in the district, leaving nothing for other SP members.

Other than the contracts, the SP cadres also wanted government officials to respect them as the representatives of the new government. They wanted the restoration of all benefits that they had lost earlier. And above all, they wanted their adversaries to learn a lesson and face the consequence of their wrong-doings. The immediate acts of violence committed against BSP supporters were the physical embodiment of this sentiment. But it is just a part of the whole law and order story that includes a number of other aspects.

Before writing this epilogue we travelled across more than fifty districts of UP from June to August 2012 and everywhere we heard the same stories. In Mathura, during the Nagar Palika elections some SP cadres created a ruckus when their candidate had lost to a BSP candidate and they alleged that there were some irregularities behind this loss. When they refused to be pacified and tried to stop the highway traffic in protest, the local administration ordered a lathi-charge to control the situation.

One SP leader suffered a fracture and some others received minor injuries, but the incident immediately enraged SP workers, who asked for the blood of the administration and the police personnel 'guilty' of this 'atrocity'. Bowing before the heavy cadre pressure, the government ordered criminal cases to be registered against a Sub-Divisional Magistrate (SDM) and more than half a dozen police officers, under section 307 IPC, charging them for attempt to murder. This would have led to the immediate suspension and arrest of all the police personnel involved. Sensing trouble, the PCS (Provincial Civil Services) Officers Association of UP jumped into action, threatening to protest strongly if the SDM was penalized for doing his duty.

Ultimately, a compromise was reached, but the incident lowered the morale of the police and administrative machinery in the area: 'Is ghatna ke bad ab mandal bhar main koi bhi police ya prashashan ka admi sapa ke admiyon ke khilaf koi karyawahi karne ki himmat nahin karega (After this incident, no police or administrative officer would dare to take action against the SP people in the whole zone),' a police officer told us in Agra. And he was quite correct in the observation, for the state government's message was clear—be prepared to face the fire if you to dare penalize party workers, as the government considers them to be dearer than anybody else. After all, it was because of these karyakartas (party workers) that SP came to power and it hopes that it is their strength that will enable it to achieve Lakshya 2014, their target of clinching sixty out of eighty Lok Sabha seats in UP.

Other than the violence resorted to by the SP workers, the actions of the SP MLAs and ministers are also quite remarkable. During a district board meeting in Bulandhshahr, SP MLA and history-sheeter, Guddu Pandit abused the district magistrate in full view of the media, while the minister in-charge, Raja Bhaiya watched the incident passively, doing nothing to stop Pandit.

When we talked about the incident the day after reaching Bulandhshahr with some locals, a prominent political person said, 'Ye to kuch nahin hai, Guddu Pandit to kal ko DM ko gira kar marega, sapa bus loksabha chunav ka intezar kar rahi hai, uske bad sapaiyon ko taandav karne ki puri chut de di jayegi (This is nothing, Guddu Pandit will soon beat the DM. SP is only waiting for the Lok Sabha elections; after it the SP people will be allowed to do whatever they wish).' The same sentiment and fear echoed in the statements of a number of people across the state.

Another incident is also quite revealing. In Ballia, BJP MLA Upendra Tiwari told media persons in April that revenue minister Ambika Chowdhary ordered a number of houses in Kapuri village to be bulldozed as he wanted to protect his illegal occupancy over this land, and when Tiwari opposed it, he was threatened by the minister's supporters. Asking the government to intervene, Tiwari demanded security from the Akhilesh Yadav government as he feared for his life. When an MLA in UP does not feel safe, how can one expect ordinary citizens to feel secure?

In addition to this, activities of 'rogue' ministers are creating bigger problems. In October 2012, UP minister for revenue and rehabilitation Vinod Kumar alias Pandit Singh was charged of kidnapping Gonda's CMO Dr S.P. Singh; Pandit Singh had criminal cases registered against him earlier as well. Dr Singh, who reportedly gave a slip to his kidnappers registered a complaint against the minister, accusing him of kidnapping and criminal intimidation. The reason—Dr Singh refused to accomodate the minister's nominees in the department's list of doctors to be appointed by the health department under contract for the National Rural Health Mission. Though the government machinery initially tried to push this issue under carpet, the hue and cry raised by media forced the minister to offer his resignation 'on moral grounds'. However, once the issue got old, Pandit Singh was taken back in the cabinet in a re-scheduling held in February 2013. The case of Raja Bhaiya is however more severe, as always.

This independent MLA from Kunda assembly seat (Pratapgarh

district) got two ministry portfolios in the Akhilesh cabinet—Prisons and Food and Civil Supplies, despite the fact that he is alleged in a multi-crore PDS scam done during his earlier tenure. The known history-sheeter and strongman MLA faced bad days during the succesive Mayawati governments who dared police raids on his palacious house, got him arrested and brought him to book for his crimes. Once back in power, the minister started enjoying his earlier stature and such was his clout that he got six SP's transferred in Pratapgarh in last 12 months. However, his wings were trimmed in the February re-scheduling of cabinet when Prisons portfolio was taken from him and given to the SP spokesperson Rajendra Chowdhry. The reason allegedly being Akhilesh Yadav, who is said to have a bad impression about such 'rogue' SP MLAs who are detrimental to the image of current government which he is trying to build. Perhaps the young CM was more than accurate for a new trouble was in the making.

32-year-old DSP Zia-ul-Haq, the circle officer of Kunda expressed his unwillingness to bow down before the minister from the very day he was posted there. Not only did he refuse to go and meet Raja Bhaiya as per the custom, he also started investigations in the communal riots that happened last year in Pratapgarh, allegedly with the involvements of some close aides of the minister. On 2 March, Nanhe Yadav, pradhan of Ballipur village and a local SP leader, was gunned down by a rival group which led to enraged protests and attack on a police station by his supporters. When Haq rushed to the scene and tried to control the situation, the angry mob allegedly retaliated which led to cross-firing and resulted in the death of Nanhe's brother Suresh. In the later mayhem, the mob caught hold of Haq as eight policemen escorting him reportedly fled the scene and Haq was thrashed badly before being shot repeatedly in the back. Though the first FIR filed in the case did not mention

Raja Bhaiya, the later one filed by slain DSP's wife Parveen Azad names Raja Bhaiya and his driver as accused. The murder raised a furore as everybody from Opposition to media to political commentators lambasted the Jungle Raj in UP. Succumbing to pressure, the UP government asked for the resignation of Raja Bhaiya (which he gave on March 4) and ordered a CBI enquiry in the case. Cornered, the ex-minister got unexpected support from Gorakhpur BJP MP Mahant Adityanath (who belongs to same Thakur caste and is a known Muslim hater) who warned of a state wide agitation if 'innocent' Raja Bhaiya was penalized to 'appease the Muslims'. While some people consider naming of Raja Bhaiya in the FIR something done on the behest of CM Akhilesh to get rid of him, others allege that the increasing closeness between Raja Bhaiya and newly-appointed BJP chief Rajnath Singh (also a Thakur) led to bitterness in SP-Raja Bhaiya relations. Whatever be the case, the incident shows that even the top police brass is not secure in the state and in such conditions, the tall claims of SP on law and order remain exposed. As of now, the CBI team enquiring the case is finding it impossible to find eye-witness accounts as nobody dares speaks against Raja Bhaiya, despite assurance of anonymity and security by the CBI.

Apart from these kind of incidents, one very disturbing feature is the rise of instances of communal violence in UP. Till the time of writing, around forty small or big cases of communal violence have been reported in Uttar Pradesh, with almost all big cities like Allahabad, Bareilly, Lucknow and Mathura witnessing arson and stone-pelting. At Bareilly, the government machinery could not stop communal tensions from escalating, which resulted in the death of four people, while curfew in the city continued for more than half a month. In Lucknow, violent protests and stone-pelting led to the imposition of curfew after people from the Muslim community took to the streets, at the end of Ramzan. Similarly in Allahabad, curfew had to be imposed after increased communal tension in the Allahabad west area. At Kosi Kalan in Mathura, communal clashes erupted in June this year, resulting in the death of four people and widespread arson.

The most recent incident took place in the Masuri area of Ghaziabad, where an angry mob belonging to a minority community attacked the local police station and the police resorted to heavy firing, killing six people. The reason was the discovery of torn pages from a Quran at the nearby railway track. While people started gathering to protest this desecration, the police did nothing to prevent the situation from getting out of hand by pacifying the angry protesters. When the mob resorted to attacking the police station, reportedly at the instigation of some outside miscreants, the police resorted to fire. Locals allege that all six killed in the firing were not protesters as one of the deceased, Wasim, a final year BCom student is said to have died of a head injury brought on by a policeman's rifle butt. Wasim's family alleged that he was only coming back from the gym when he was caught in the police-protesters clash and was killed by police officials.

While the government failed to effectively control these incidents, its ministers' statements indicated that they were trying to use the situation for electoral gain. Talking to a media person about the Bareilly violence, PWD minister Shivpal Yadav alleged that there were 'some communal forces working for electoral benefits' behind the scene. This statement invited strong opposition from the BJP, which rightfully pointed out that the work of the government was not to make allegations, but to initiate probes and take action if it felt that way. The BJP leadership alleged that SP was letting these incidents snowball into bigger riots so as to exploit the fear-psychosis of the minority in the upcoming Lok Sabha elections.

Along with this, the 'routine' crime situation in UP is continuing unabated. Murders, rapes, looting continue to take place just as they did earlier, and the police is trying to underplay them by not registering the FIRs. In June, the chief minister himself agreed that since the swearing-in ceremony in March uptill 15 April, on an average, fifteen incidents of murder and six of rape had been reported everyday in the state. In September, he again accepted before the media that the police department in the state was not functioning properly.

To further worsen the situation, reports of an increase in the activities of dacoit gangs in the bandit lands of Chitrakoot have started pouring in. Breaking the peace established after the encounter of dreaded bandits Dadua and Thokiya in the BSP regime, a new dacoit, Swadesh Patel alias Balkhariya, has emerged on the scene.

In August this year, thirteen members of the erstwhile Dadua and Thokiya gangs escaped police custody, and the very next day, five people were brutally murdered, allegedly by the Balkhariya gang in Chitrakoot's Dodamafi village. While the incident brought back fears of the renewal of dacoit-raj in the region, the police could only arrest one out of the thirteen bandits who had run away.

A senior crime reporter at Orai, Jalaun, told us, 'BSP ke shasankaal main dakaiton ka safaya hua, phir bhi hathiyar aur sampark to bache hi rahe. Sarkar yadi thodi bhi dheel degi to yahan dakait phir uth khade honge, par lagta hai is sarkar ne to rajnitik labh ke liye unhain dheel ki jagah aparoksh samarthan de rakha hai. Pahle bhi sapa ke log isiliye badnam the (Weapons and networks remained intact even after the crackdown on bandit gangs in BSP's regime, which erased dacoits from the region. If the government relaxes even for a minute, it will immediately result in the rise of bandits once again. But this government seems to have extended indirect support to them in lieu of political benefits. SP was infamous for the same earlier too).'

A number of people alleged that this new beginning of dacoity is a direct result of SP's patronage to the bandit gangs here, since these gangs help by dumping booths and terrorizing opponents during elections. Whatever be the truth, it is beyond doubt that BSP's record of dealing with the bandit menace was far better than that of SP's.

During the election campaign, Akhilesh Yadav had identified the SP government's bad record on law and order as the biggest roadblock in winning the confidence and support of the people. Due to this, extreme efforts were made to allay these fears and ensure that this time, SP would not tolerate any nuisance, even by its own cadres. Though this exercise was successful and people of UP had trusted SP's assurances, they now feel cheated. And many of them feel that the worst is yet to come, as after the Lok Sabha elections, the SP will unleash greater terror, since there will not be any big electoral contests for the next three years. In the current situation, if the Akhilesh government fails to overcome this handicap, SP's dreams of winning more than half the Lok Sabha seats in UP will never turn into reality.

Electricity Problems: Crisis Like Never Before

Electricity shortage has always been a problem in the state. Due to the shortage of power production, rampant line-faults, transformer failures and heavy power theft, electricity has always remained scarce and all sections of the society have suffered due to it. While the peasants don't get electricity for irrigation, the industrial sector has suffered from a heavy power crunch for long and cities remain submerged in darkness for hours across the state.

The BSP government had tried to deal systematically with this issue by formulating the New Energy Policy in 2009, which aimed at increasing the electricity production in UP by 10,000 megawatts by 2012. It succeeded in making significant progress on this count; efficient distribution, timely service and fewer failures made electricity problems more bearable in BSP's time.

SP promised to give twenty-hour supply to rural and twenty-four-hour supply to urban areas within two months of coming into power, but its track record on this count in the last six months has lessened people's hope. Other than some VIP districts like Mainpuri, Kannauj, Rampur, Etawah, Rae Bareli and Amethi, even sixteen to eighteen hours' supply is not available in other districts.

At Azamgarh, SP had won nine out of the ten assembly seats, but the actual electricity supply in the city was far below fifteen hours a day when we visited the district. People were very angry, as they used to receive electricity for longer hours during the BSP government, and now when they had given such a huge electoral boost to SP, they were getting a far lesser supply of electricity in return.

In Hardoi, where SP won six out of the eight seats, such was the scale of the electricity problems that people had resorted to angry protests in two Vidhan Sabha seats of the district. The police had resorted to firing bullets and tear-gas shells at the protesters to control them, and a curfew was imposed later on.

While travelling through Mau district, we were caught in a violent protest led by the local villagers, who had blocked the road to demand better electricity supply. Angry protests, roadblocks and stone-pelting by people demanding more electricity became a regular feature in the newspapers across all districts of the state.

Ambedkar Nagar district was considered a BSP bastion, as BSP MLAs had won all five assembly seats in the district, and the district MP also belonged to BSP. In the 2012 elections, SP emerged victorious, winning all five seats. People hoped that since they had supported the party so strongly, they would be rewarded with more development projects and better electricity. What they received was quite the opposite. Ambedkar Nagar was receiving a little more than twelve hours of electricity when we were there in August and its residents were abusing SP leaders. 'Pura zila inke naam kar diya magar bijli pahle se bhi kum milti hai (We gave them the whole district and yet we are receiving less electricity than before),' said a villager at a tea shop in a nearby village. 'Isse to Mayawati ka time behtar tha, kumse kum jitna bola jata tha utni to milti thi, yahan to 16 ghante ki ghoshna hoti hai aur 12 ghante bhi bijli nahin milti (Things were better during Mayawati's government, at least we got the amount of electricity that was declared. Nowadays declarations are made for sixteen hours of electricity supply, but what we actually get is lesser than twelve hours)!' said another. Once he said that things were better during Mayawati's government, a number of heads started nodding in agreement. Mayawati had said at the time the results were declared in March that within less than six months people would start saying that her regime was far better than the present one. What we observed during our visit confirmed this.

The Carrot Called Unemployment Allowance and Other Promises

In the eyes of analysts and political experts, one of the biggest game changers in these elections was SP's promise of giving an unemployment allowance to the educated youth in UP, which brought in support from a large chunk of young voters. Long queues of unemployed youth, waiting to register at employment exchanges were showcased as proof of this promise's wide impact. The youth who had supported SP in the elections hoped that the party would give allowances to them as it had done the last time it was in power.

Things were however different this time. Fearing that giving unemployment allowances to large chunks of the youth would dry up the state resources, the new government made terms of eligibility stricter this time. Conditions such as making a number of documents mandatory in order to apply, a stricter age limit, limitation of only one beneficiary between a husband and wife, mandatory ten-day work in return of the allowance were imposed, which resulted in a sharp decline in the expected number of applications. The youth had to spend a lot of time and money to complete all these formalities and many could not apply due to lack of the relevant documents. To control this damage, terms and conditions were relaxed again, with the last date of application being extended again and again. More than nine official orders were made by the government to amend the requirements for applying under this scheme. This exercise decreased the magic of the unemployment allowance.

'Sarkar ki ummid thi ki is bar wah 8 lakh logon ko bhatta degi, jinke liye is bar budget main dhan aavantit kar diya gaya tha, par August tak 1 lakh se jyada lawarthi chinhit hi nahin kiye ja sake (The government hoped to give the allowance to eight lakh applicants and money was provided in the budget for the same, but till August it could not identify more than one lakh beneficiaries),' says Manoj Singh, a senior journalist at Gorakhpur. Stressing that stricter conditions for submitting the applications decreased the excitement of the unemployment allowance among a number of youth and debarred many others from applying, leading to fewer applications. He further said, 'Jab sapa ke sabse bade wade ka ye hal hai, to baakiyon ke bare main soch hi sakte hain (When such is the state of SP's biggest promise, then one can imagine the status of the other promises).'

Though it would be wrong to say that there were no people at the employment exchanges five months after the government was formed, the numbers had decreased significantly with as few as three to four thousand applicants in some districts.

Whatever the case may be, Chief Minister Akhilesh Yadav had flagged off the scheme by giving unemployment allowances to more than 10,000 young people in Lucknow on 9 September, but all poll promises did not meet the same fate.

Most of the students who have passed their 10th and 12th class examinations are yet to get the tablets and laptops they were promised in SP's poll manifesto. Farmers are still to get free irrigation facilities as promised by SP leadership during the elections. However, the TET (Teaching Eligibility Test) candidates who had expected a lot from the new government have already received their dues. Less than a week after the new government had formed, TET candidates demanding that the new chief minister should not cancel the results of the TET exams that they had already passed were severely lathi-charged by the UP police in Lucknow, despite the fact that they were just trying to march peacefully to the Vidhan Bhavan. Later on, Akhilesh Yadav cancelled the TET exam held during BSP's regime, with which the hopes of thousands of candidates who had cleared the exam were crushed.

But everything is not so gloomy and there is some good news too. Cases against the agitating farmers of Bhatta-Parsaul and Tappal were lifted by the government as promised, giving huge relief to some of the friends we had made at Jehangarh.

The Mahakumbh 2013 arrangements are also a feather in the cap for the Akhilesh government. Arrangements for world's biggest religious congregation, which saw more than approximately thirty million visitors this time, is an uphill task and the UP government was praised by all, including overseas observers for the hygiene, transportation, accomodation and general arrangements. The tragic incidence of stampede that claimed more than a dozen lives at Allahabad Railway Station was blamed on the railways, which is a central service and the UP government was rightly excused of sharing the blame.

The UP government also fulfilled its much-talked promise of distributing laptops to class 12th students of UP board. On 11 March 2013 UP Chief Minister Akhilesh Yadav distributed 10,000 HP laptops to students at a function in Lucknow. Though it got praises from a number of quarters, an unexpected problem did crop in. The laptops had a built-in tamper proof wallpaper with photos of Akhilesh and Mulayam and when some students tried to do away with it, their laptops crashed immediately.

The attempts to keep a good impression on farmers were also continued. On the issue of giving greater autonomy to private sugar mills, the government replied in the negative, saying it would further crush sugarcane farmers and hence was absolutely out of the question. Still, the government has not proven itself to be farmer-friendly in terms of deeds. Despite the big promises made, it has made a meagre allocation of around 500 crore rupees in the budget for farmers' loan waivers, which does not even come close to meeting the requirement. Out of it, the farmers have not received anything up till now (March 2013). In the hope of getting their loans waived, most of them have not deposited their dues even after the last date, for it had passed. If the government does not come to their rescue soon, many of them will be ruined by the repayment of loans and fines.

Sensing this sentiment, Akhilesh Yadav declared in his Independence Day speech that the government would soon launch the loan waiver as promised. Any further development on this count has not been reported yet.

In July this year, senior minister Azam Khan declared that all contract workers working in UP municipalities and nagar panchayats without the sanction of the present government would be removed from their jobs. The BSP alleged that this would result in the loss of about 34,000 jobs in a state that already suffers from high unemployment rates, bringing distress to thousands of families.

Overall, if we talk about the general sentiment across the state, people feel that the government has failed them, that it has failed to fulfil what they expected from it, despite the fact that it has made a few achievements. Probably the reason lies in Samajwadi Party's thumping victory. Since the people had voted in the party with an absolute majority, like the SP cadres they too were desperate to see the changes immediately. Or may be SP is losing because the reality of its government is far inferior to the dream it had created during the poll campaign.

Which CM Do You Want to Meet?

The SP government has repeatedly been criticized for its indecisiveness and change of positions, be it the issue of giving the Vidhan Parishad seat to Ahmed Bukhari's relatives, of ordering malls to close by 8 p.m., or of the infighting between Azam Khan and Akhilesh Yadav camps.

The main reason behind this is said to be the heavy clash of interests within the SP leadership. In political circles in Lucknow, it is a common saying that there are five chief ministers in the UP government: Mulayam Singh Yadav, Shivpal Singh, Prof Ramgopal Yadav, Azam Khan and Akhilesh Yadav, who is said to be the weakest of all. The Bachcha CM as some people call him is in the most uncomfortable situation because even though the party came to power keeping him in the forefront, it has now taken control out of his hands and the old troika of the three big Yadavs is running all the affairs in the old manner, with senior lieutenant Azam Khan too conveying his displeasure at being neglected time and again.

The Missing Messiah and Congress Restructuring

During the elections, Rahul Gandhi had announced that he is in UP to change it, and will remain active in the state irrespective of the poll results. When the Congress nosedived in terms of expectations and seats won, he again reiterated this statement and a number of people were assured that this would be good for the state as it would check and balance the SP government.

More than twelve months have passed since then, but the messiah has not been seen in UP, other than a few short visits to Amethi. And forget UP, the Gandhi scion was not visible on the national scene either, with just a few visits to Assam, Karnataka, etc. On Rajiv Gandhi's birth anniversary, the media reported that Rahul Gandhi was not seen at the official programmes held at his samadhi, and a number of Congress people spoke to us about this. In fact the whole state unit of the party seemed to be under a lull, till August, with nothing to do.

The lull was broken with the declaration of Nirmal Khatri as the new PCC president and division of the UP party organization in eight zones, each with a separate president. An MP from Faizabad, Khatri was probably chosen as PCC president for his clean image and less assertive nature, as firebrand leaders have been made zonal presidents and an equally assertive PCC president would have led to constant clashes among state and zonal presidents. The eight zones include ten Lok Sabha seats per zone, and P.L. Puniya, Jitin Prasad, R.P.N. Singh, Anugrah Narayan Singh, Chaudhry Virendra Singh, Kazi Rashid Masood, Vivek Singh and Rajaram Pal have been made zonal presidents, reportedly on Rahul Gandhi's behest. The party has said that this decentralization will help it in effectively handling the state and preparing for the upcoming elections in a better manner. Social engineering is also kept in mind while doing it as the new presidents include one Brahmin, one Muslim, three OBCs (one Jat, one Kurmi, one Pal), one Dalit, and two Thakurs. Further, all of them are reputed to be very active and grounded leaders of the Congress. Still, what comes out of this manoeuvring is yet to unfold as the party is increasingly becoming unpopular at a national level due to charges of corruption, inflation and subsequent hikes in fuel prices.

Lakshya 2014 and the Lok Sabha Scenario

Within a few weeks of SP's victory in the March 2012 elections, the party came out with a new sticker to show its sincerity towards the Lok Sabha elections in 2014. The sticker had Vijay 2012 written on one end with Akhilesh Yadav's photo, and Lakshya 2014 written on the other end with Mulayam Singh's photo. The sticker tried to signify that while the party has fulfilled its victory 2012 goal, by making Akhilesh Yadav the UP chief minister, it has yet to clinch the more significant goal of victory in the 2014 elections to make Mulayam Singh the prime minister of India. If you happen to go to UP right now, you will find this sticker on three out of every five four-wheelers belonging to SP supporters. And when we were there, we happened to pass through cavalcades of SP observers in at least a dozen districts, who had come there to meet the ticket applicants for the Lok Sabha elections.

The party completed its first-hand information-gathering sessions for the Lok Sabha elections by August 2012 and in detailed meetings with party district functionaries and functionaries of SP's frontal organizations, the Samajwadi leadership has chalked out plans to record a win in the upcoming elections.

About its Lok Sabha target, the party leadership began by saying that it is targeting to win fifty seats in UP (currently it has twenty-two), but now they claim that they will win at least sixty out of the eighty seats in UP. Mulayam Singh is hoping that in case of a weak performance by BJP and Congress, which is not unlikely, SP will emerge as the third biggest party with around sixty seats, thus leading a loosely-formed group of regional parties and the Left, termed the Third Front, and he would emerge as the strongest contender for the prime minister's post, as the Congress too would have to support it to prevent BJP from coming to power.

Though CPI (M) general secretary Prakash Karat has mocked these ambitions and dreams of Mulayam Singh in an interview, the SP supremo is continuing to make prophecies of the emergence of a Third Front in the upcoming Lok Sabha elections, which he says will be held earlier than the scheduled period. For a recent meeting of SP's national leadership in September, the party chose Kolkata as the location to convey that its orientation is now becoming national.

However, despite all the statements and claims made by the SP leadership, everyone else is quite apprehensive about its performance for two reasons. One, till now SP's best performance in Lok Sabha elections was in 2004 when it won thirty-five seats and nobody expects it to improve the score this time. Secondly, the alarming law-and-order situation and electricity problems are continuing to worsen and if they persist, they could prove to be the Waterloo of SP's aspirations.

In the current situation, it would be in SP's greater interest if the elections were held as early as possible, before the party's image worsens further, and it still has the advantage of being ahead of the others in poll preparations.

After the initial set-back in March, the BJP too has managed to collect its political wits. In the June local body elections, BJP won ten out of twelve mayoral seats in UP, giving the impression that it is going to be a power to reckon with in the 2014 elections. The national scenario of rampant corruption cases against UPA II, sky-rocketing inflation and BJP's stance where it appears to be countering it, may also help the party in increasing its Lok Sabha tally from the current ten seats.

However, some experts are questioning these possibilities. In the 9 July edition of *The Times of India*, Rajiv Srivastava wrote:

'Political analysts believe that unavailability of options on mayors' seats in terms of party candidates as the SP and the BSP didn't contest and the Congress' failure to make a mark in the last two decades in the state, gave advantage to the BJP. But there was no saffron wave at the level of wards where the candidates' personal connect mattered the most.' He highlights that two-thirds of the wards in BJP's mayor seats were won by independents, which weakens the theory that BJP is going to be a champion in the 2014 contest as well. Whatever the case may be, surveys conducted by some channels clearly give a significant advantage to BJP over the Congress in the upcoming Lok Sabha elections, and it now depends on how the party succeeds in capturing the advantages of this general mood of the people in its favour.

The BSP is a silent player as always. Its moves however, are well calculated and confident. To win back the OBC confidence in UP, it promoted Swami Prasad Maurya to the post of national general secretary, while Ram Achal Rajbhar was made state BSP president; both of them belong to the OBC community and both are from Poorvanchal, where the party suffered heavily in the 2012 elections. The move is aimed at plugging all loopholes and weak points. BSP has declared candidates for almost all eighty Lok Sabha seats, and its new state president is busy running from pillar to post to conduct activist conventions across the state, so as to orient and prepare the cadres for the upcoming elections. While travelling across Poorvanchal, we saw a number of such hoardings at many districts. The manner in which the whole BSP machinery erupted in protests across the state against the breaking of Mayawati's statue shows that the organization is still capable of working wonders.

With the legitimacy of the Akhilesh Yadav government failing, people have started saying, 'Isse to basapa ka raj achcha tha (BSP's rule was better than this)'. In this situation, it would not be wrong to say that the party could make it to one of the two top positions in the state, in the upcoming Lok Sabha elections.

In the End

Antony: She is cunning past man's thought.
Domitius Enobarbus: Alack, sir, no;
her passions are made of nothing but the finest part of pure love:
we cannot call her winds and waters, sighs and tears;
they are greater storms and tempests than almanacs can report:
this cannot be cunning in her; if it be,
she makes a shower of rain as well as Jove.

We tried very hard to come up with words that could express our feelings about UP and its politics. In the end, we thought these lines from Shakespeare's *Antony and Cleopatra* conveyed it the best. For despite all the shortcomings, treacheries, violence, backwardness and insecurity, we found UP to be a manifestation of pure beauty and nobility in essence.

While narrating the political stories of UP, we travelled through its most beautiful and difficult parts, from the foothills of the Shivaliks in Saharanpur to the wastelands of Chambal and the mountainous forests of Chandauli-Sonbhadra. From experiencing the silent beauty of the Nilkantha temple at Kalinjar to feeling the invisible presence of Princess Chandrakanta at Sonbhadra's Vijaygarh fort at night, there were innumerable attractions that kept pumping adrenaline into our veins and motivating us to continue. And it is after all these experiences that we dare say that UP may appear to be selfish, cunning and ruthless, but in actuality it is beauty, peace and love, nothing else. Innumerable tempests play in the lap of its politics on the one hand, but on the other it still possesses the capability of changing the face of the nation, that too for the good of all.

Complexity and simplicity, love and hate, in other words, extremes, are so neatly intertwined in it that it always destabilizes the narratives of all those who dare to write about it, including us. Many political storms have come out of it till now, and many will emerge in the future, but the perpetual motion of innumerable factors causing and destroying them will never cease and will continue to attract adventurers and journalists, sages and political experts, travellers and settlers alike.

Package